SAMUEL HOPKINS
AND THE
NEW DIVINITY MOVEMENT

SAMUEL HOPKINS
AND THE
NEW DIVINITY MOVEMENT

*Calvinism, the Congregational Ministry,
and Reform in New England
Between the Great Awakenings*

Joseph A. Conforti

CHRISTIAN
UNIVERSITY
PRESS

A Subsidiary of Christian College Consortium
and Wm. B. Eerdmans Publishing Company,
Grand Rapids, Michigan

FOR
DOROTHY AND ANTONIA

Available from Wm. B. Eerdmans Publishing Co.
255 Jefferson Ave. S.E., Grand Rapids, Mich. 49503

Library of Congress Cataloging in Publication Data
Conforti, Joseph A.
Samuel Hopkins and the New Divinity movement.
Bibliography: p. 233
Includes index.
1. Hopkins, Samuel, 1721-1803. 2. Theology, Doctrinal—New England—
History—18th century. 3. Congregationalism—History—18th century.
I. Title. II. Title: New Divinity movement.
BX7260.H6C66   230'.58   80-28268
ISBN 0-8028-3551-1

CONTENTS

PREFACE

SAMUEL HOPKINS was the closest friend and disciple of the man generally considered to be the greatest religious mind America has produced — Jonathan Edwards. Hopkins became the leader of the New Divinity, a major religious movement within New England Congregationalism during the late colonial and early national periods. By explaining and extending Edwards's thought, Hopkins and other advocates of the New Divinity established the first indigenous American school of Calvinism.

The New Divinity men also made significant contributions to the emergence of the religious reform movements that were so important in the late eighteenth and early nineteenth centuries. Hopkins, for example, was one of the leading antislavery reformers in Revolutionary New England. He preached and actively crusaded against slavery and the slave trade while serving as the pastor of a church in a major slave-trading port of eighteenth-century America — Newport, Rhode Island.

This study is not a personal biography of a New England divine. While I have tried to capture the central elements of Hopkins's inner life (what Philip J. Greven, Jr., has termed the evangelical Protestant temperament), this study emphasizes Hopkins's public life and religious thought. Furthermore, I have attempted to use Hopkins's life and work as a point of departure for a reassessment of the standard historical interpretation of the New Divinity movement. Thus more often than not, the analysis extends beyond Hopkins to the New Divinity movement, and through it to the larger context of the social and intellectual history of late eighteenth- and early nineteenth-century New England.

This book originated as a doctoral dissertation at Brown University, where I had the good fortune to work under William G. McLoughlin, who introduced me to the study of American religious history and who was a constant source of encouragement during a difficult period for graduate students in the humanities. He helped me appreciate how Hopkins felt personally and intellectually indebted to Edwards. At Brown University I also benefited from the criticism and support of Gordon S. Wood. William J. Scheick of the University of Texas at Austin, Bruce Tucker of Dalhousie University, and my colleague J. Stanley Lemons of Rhode Island College read drafts of the study and made helpful comments and suggestions. Portions of this book appeared in *The William and Mary Quarterly*, *The Historical Journal of Massachusetts*, and *Rhode Island History*, and I would like to thank the editors of these journals for permission to use previously published material.

Finally, I have dedicated this book to two individuals who have had nothing to do with it but for whom I have the strongest affections of benevolence.

NEW LIGHT AND NEW DIVINITY

IN NEW ENGLAND the Great Awakening of the eighteenth century inaugurated one of the most theologically creative periods in American religious history. Until the revival Puritan theology in New England remained dependent upon and derivative from European Reformed thought. To be sure, the first one hundred years of New England Congregationalism produced important innovations: the requirement, instituted in the 1630's, of a public "relation" of conversion as a prerequisite for church membership; the Half-way Covenant of 1662, which offered baptism to the children of unregenerate worshippers; the Saybrook Platform of 1708, which established a semi-presbyterian church system in Connecticut; and the practice called Stoddardeanism, which opened communion to all moral persons whether or not they were regenerate. These changes, however, were not solely theological; indeed, for the most part they were instituted to deal with problems of church polity rather than theology. Even the widespread development of sacramental piety in the late seventeenth and early eighteenth centuries—of which both the Half-way Covenant and Stoddardeanism were a part—was a clergy-inspired movement designed to promote practical piety, not theological discussion and knowledge.[1]

After the Antinomian controversies of the 1630's, only rarely prior to the Great Awakening did doctrine embroil a minister in a dispute with his congregation. Ecclesiastical practices, salary problems, or incompetence were the usual causes of ministers' dismissals. Even Arminianism failed to make significant inroads in New England's religious establishment until after the Awakening.[2]

The revival itself did not focus on theology; its clerical supporters maintained that the doctrines of Calvinism had not changed, but the behavior and piety of New Englanders had. Jonathan Edwards insisted, for instance, that "an increase in speculative knowledge in divinity is not so much needed by our people as something else. Men may abound in this sort of life and have no heat." Edwards cautioned that "our people do not so much need to have their heads stored, as to have their hearts touched; and they stand in greatest need of that sort of preaching that has the greatest tendency to do this."[3] The Awakening touched the hearts of so many New Englanders because it was essentially an undogmatic, pietistic call for the regeneration of American society. Revivalists attempted to promote a renunciation of the contention, avarice, and materialism that economic and population growth had stimulated in New England.

Ironically, the Awakening not only encouraged another form of the contentious, socially disruptive behavior that it proposed to reform, but it promoted theological divisiveness as well. An unprecedented emphasis on the unconditional and instantaneous nature of rebirth became an unsettling presence within the Congregational establishment as reborn laymen, goaded by radical revivalists, attacked spiritually dead preachers and justified ecclesiastical separations. Across New England both the laity and clergy hotly debated and frequently parted company over such critical issues of the Awakening as the nature of and need for spiritual rebirth, the authenticity of mass conversions, the role of means (prayer, Bible reading, and church attendance) in regeneration, and the coming of the millennium.

These issues fostered divisions within the Congregational church, divisions whose complexity is not conveyed by alleging simply that a single pro-revival New Light faction opposed a unified anti-revival Old Light party. The configuration of the New Light party in Connecticut alone in the aftermath of the Awakening reveals the extent to which this religious upheaval fractured the Congregational establishment. Separate New Lights predominated in Windham and New London counties in the east, where rapid economic expansion had unsettled society and where the Awakening had been particularly intense. These ecclesiastical radicals advocated withdrawal from existing churches and construction of pure churches comprised only of members who had experienced conversion. New Divinity supporters gained a stronghold in western Connecticut, principally in Litchfield County. These followers of Edwards wished to remain within established churches and to concentrate on developing the theological implications of the Awakening. Within the New Divinity school itself two identifiable groups emerged — those who accepted the major innovations that Samuel Hopkins made in Edwards's theology, and those who followed more closely the neo-Edwardsianism of another leading New Divinity theologian, Joseph Bellamy. Finally, between the radical New Light Separates and the theological-minded New Divinity men there stood moderate New Lights, like Rector Thomas Clap of Yale, who rejected what they saw as ecclesiastical and doctrinal excesses and who sought to institutionalize and control "new birth" as a tool for the creation of social order.[4]

As the hyper-Calvinist wing of the New Light movement, the New Divinity represented not only the major theological legacy of the Awakening but also the first indigenous American school of Calvinism. In the years after revival, and particularly during his Stockbridge exile (1751–1757), Edwards assumed the task of refining and systematizing its theological implications. His untimely death, at the height of his intellectual power, in 1758 left his ambitious project far from finished. Edwards's New Divinity followers, or "Consistent" Calvinists as they were also called, who had aided him in his theological efforts continued his work of building a complete and consistent system of evangelical Calvinism.

In addition to mounting a theological defense of the revival, the mission of Edwards and his followers took on a related objective as a result of the growth of Arminianism in the middle of the eighteenth century. Partly under the influence of English rationalists, liberal Calvinists preached this heretical nemesis of Calvinist orthodoxy that legitimized human effort and the operation of the free will in the conversion process. In his *Farewell Address* delivered in 1750, Edwards warned his Northampton congregation of the spread of Arminianism since revival ardor had waned in 1743: "These doctrines at this day are much more prevalent than they were then; the progress they have made in the land, within this seven years, seems to have been vastly greater than at any time in the like space before. . . ." In Edwards's view, the Arminian contagion threatened "the utter ruin of the credit of those doctrines which are the peculiar glory of the gospel, and the interests of vital piety."[5] The evangelicals were alarmed by liberal Calvinist acceptance of Arminianism and also by the failure of the dominant Old Light party to confront and refute this heresy. New Lights began to charge that Old Light Calvinism was tainted with Arminianism and that it had promoted the current outbreak of the heresy. In fact, Samuel Hopkins argued, moderate Calvinism was nothing more than moderate Arminianism.[6] Hopkins and other New Divinity clerics proposed to assert the "consistent" evangelical Calvinism that flowed from the Awakening as the best antidote for New England's Arminian affliction.

The New Divinity was rooted in the broad, experimental religion of the Awakening and was initially dependent upon the thought of Edwards. Both the revival and Edwardsianism marked a break with traditional New England Calvinism and served, Old Light William Hart observed, as "the root of the tree which . . . [the New Divinity] cultivated and adorned with many of its branches."[7] The New Divinity in itself, however, did not develop into an influential movement until well after the Awakening and about a decade after Edwards's death. Moreover, the Consistent Calvinists so radically extended and modified their teacher's ideas that many New Lights, such as Baptist leader Isaac Backus,[8] claimed for themselves the name of Edwardsians and rejected the New Divinity as a bastardizing of Edwards's thought.

The term "New Divinity" was first used as a pejorative in 1765 in reference to Hopkins's argument that an unregenerate but awakened sinner who used the means of grace appeared more guilty in God's eyes than an unawakened sinner who remained unconcerned with his spiritual state. In New England, beginning in the 1760's and extending into the early decades of the nineteenth century, the New Divinity increasingly won the allegiance of young clerics, college and post-graduate students studying for the ministry, and backcountry congregations. In his autobiography written in 1795, Hopkins outlined the growth of the New Divinity movement. It was true, he admitted, that only a handful of ministers embraced Consistent Calvinism in the immediate aftermath of the Awakening. "But these sentiments have so spread since that time among ministers, especially those who have since come on the stage," he claimed, "that there are now more than one hundred in the ministry who espouse the same sentiments in the United States of America." Furthermore, Hopkins reported in 1795, the movement appeared to be "fast increasing."[9] By this time Hopkinsianism had become virtually identical in the popular mind with the New Divinity. Two decades later, in 1813, William Bentley, the liberal Calvinist minister of Salem, Massachusetts, reluctantly concluded that Hopkins's "System of Divinity is the basis of the popular theology of New England."[10]

In its first years the New Divinity movement was both numerically small and geographically confined. Seizing on its apparently provincial sources and appeal, opponents of Consistent Calvinism dismissed it as the "Litchfield" or "Berkshire divinity," in reference to the two westernmost counties of Connecticut and Massachusetts where the New Divinity party first achieved prominence. Between 1760 and 1820 the movement spread across the length and breadth of New England. In the judgment of its first historian, the New Divinity became the dominant theological force in New England Congregationalism by the early nineteenth century and may be justifiably called *the* New England theology.[11]

Yet in spite of its importance in the region's religious history, the New Divinity has not received the scholarly attention it deserves. For one thing accounts of the movement have remained on a theological level, and the social context and significance of Consistent Calvinism have been largely ignored. One reason for this neglect is that, because of its intellectual rigor and commitment to consistency, many historians have argued that the New Divinity became divorced from social reality and the dynamic piety of the Awakening.[12]

Over a decade ago Richard Birdsall questioned the easy acceptance of this view.[13] Since that time a number of books and essays have enlarged our knowledge of both New England Calvinism and Puritan society in the eighteenth century. These works provide a basis for a fresh analysis of the New Divinity movement—an analysis sensitive not only to the nuances of Puritan thought but to the realities of New England society as well. Such an approach suggests that the New Divinity functioned not only as a critique of New England's theological condition, but, like the Awakening itself, as a protest against the evolution of New England society.

Samuel Hopkins's well-known doctrine of disinterested benevolence, for instance, which required complete self-denial (even to the point of being willing to be damned for the glory of God and the good of the universe), was far from simply an abstract theological argument that was unconnected to social reality. Hopkins's doctrine originated in the mid-eighteenth-century debate over the nature of true virtue — a debate that derived from efforts to define authentic spiritual sentiments in light of what many saw as the false piety and emotional excesses of the Awakening. The controversy also had a social dimension; it was in part a response to what the New Divinity men viewed as a crisis in social thought in mid-eighteenth-century New England. Hopkins, for example, was disquieted by the conflict between traditional social values and the behavior of New Englanders in a time of critical change. Like other evangelicals, he inherited a social ethic that stressed corporate obligation, personal restraint, and communal harmony and simplicity. But the economic and demographic expansion of New England during his lifetime promoted acquisitive, egocentric patterns of behavior at odds with those norms.[14]

On one level, the doctrinal "paper war" revolving around the problem of true virtue arose from some theologians' attempts to close the gap between values and experience by formulating new theological legitimations for behavior. With his doctrine of disinterested benevolence Hopkins endeavored to discredit liberal, Old Light, and even New Light compromises of inherited social theory. In the process he gave evangelical Calvinism an activist, social thrust that became particularly evident during the Revolutionary era, when the self-effacing principles of Hopkinsianism merged with the public-spirited anti-luxury tenets of republican political thought. Furthermore, by breathing new meaning and relevance into traditional social ideals, the New Divinity encouraged a continuing conflict between Christ and culture in New England that found an outlet in the revivalism and reforms of the Second Great Awakening. In short, the New Divinity men did not betray their origins in experimental religion by over-intellectualizing the piety of the First Great Awakening; rather they preserved and bequeathed to the next generation of revivalists its creative tension between social theory and social practice.

Samuel Hopkins's clerical career began in the First Great Awakening and ended in the midst of the Second; thus it spanned almost the entire period during which the New Divinity rose from obscurity to dominance over New England Congregationalism.

As a prolific and original neo-Edwardsian theologian and as a committed social reformer, Hopkins's contributions to the success of the New Divinity equaled, if they did not exceed, those of any other individual. Therefore, a study that focuses on Hopkins's career in the ministry can disclose much of the social and intellectual significance of Consistent Calvinism.

chapter one

THE CONNECTICUT BACKGROUND

HISTORIANS of early New England religious history have generally recognized that the New Divinity men were for the most part Connecticut natives and graduates of Yale. Yet little more is known about the backgrounds of the members of this important religious movement. As a result of a preoccupation with clerical theological criticism of the movement, historians have overlooked, or failed to take seriously, a suggestive body of clerical social criticism of the New Divinity men. A common theme runs through much of this social criticism — the New Divinity men were unfit to be clergymen of the Standing Order. To the urbane, cosmopolitan Ezra Stiles, pastor of the Second Church in Newport, Rhode Island, from 1757 to 1777 and later president of Yale, the New Divinity men lacked a sense of professionalism and seemed unable to accept the traditional role of the clergy as peace-seeking shepherds.[1]

Stiles and other ministers complained that a formal education had not refined the manners and conduct of the New Divinity men. In the eyes of liberal Calvinist William Bentley of Salem, Daniel Hopkins, brother of Samuel and pastor of the Third Church in Salem, was not like other Congregational ministers: "His images were uncouth, his language low and his manners were as singular as [one] can well imagine." New Divinity minister Samuel Niles, Jr., of Abington, Massachusetts, was no different in Bentley's view: "He is much known in this part of the country by his inclination for religious controversy, for his zeal for Hopkinsianism, and by his uncouth appearance and manner." "It is the unsocial character of the professors of this [New Divinity] sect," Bentley maintained, "which makes them odious."[2]

9

To moderate Calvinist William Hart, the New Divinity men were parvenu clerics whose theology represented little more than "upstart divinity" and "upstart errors."[3] Bentley came to a similar conclusion. "There has always been a sect to whom uncharitableness, seems particularly to have belonged," he noted in his diary in reference to the New Divinity men. "Once it was the Anabaptists but they have since risen to some importance and can subsist without it. It is now left to others who are struggling to rise." Bentley labeled the New Divinity men "Farmer Metaphysicians," implying that they were country parsons whose bearing and behavior were acceptable to churches in the New England backwoods but undignified in the eyes of many clergymen and church members in more cultured and populous areas.[4]

Joseph Bellamy, the influential New Divinity minister of Bethlehem, Connecticut, recounted an incident in which a congregation agreed with Bentley's assessment. After preaching during a probationary trial to a church in the city of New York in 1754, Bellamy refused a less than unanimous call to serve as its pastor. As he saw it, a sizable minority of church members opposed him partly because of his social shortcomings. "I am not polite enough for them," Bellamy reported. "I may possibly do to be a minister out in the woods but am not fit for the city."[5]

As both the social criticism by other clergymen and Bellamy's self-consciousness suggest, by the middle of the eighteenth century the Congregational clergy were divided not only along doctrinal and ecclesiastical lines but also by an awareness of social differences within the profession. A sense of "social distance,"[6] for example, separated village and small town parsons from ministers in populous towns and cities. Furthermore, prior to the Awakening many Congregational clerics, especially those in urban areas, cultivated an image of themselves as a courtly, professional elite. This self-image was threatened by New Light revivalistic fervor, particularly by the "unprofessional" doctrinal and ecclesiastical disputes that New Divinity and Separate-Congregational ministers encouraged.[7] In the decades after the Awakening the courtly self-image of liberal and moderate Calvinist clergymen was Anglicized. Like other colonial elites in the middle of the eighteenth century, the rational clergy increasingly looked to England for cultural norms and to the London gentry for standards after which they could model their own behavior and judge that of their fellow ministers.[8]

The social criticism leveled at the New Divinity men may be traced to the social perspective of the liberal and Old Light clergy. By and large, the New Divinity men were small town or village parsons who, in the eyes of the rational clergy, were not sufficiently professional, genteel, or Anglicized. Yet there was another source of the antipathy directed toward the New Divinity men — another dimension to their lack of gentility in the eyes of the rationalists. The vast majority of the "Farmer Metaphysicians" of the New Divinity movement were from modest or obscure social backgrounds.

Some recent studies in social history provide a starting point for a comparative collective biography of the New Divinity men. These investigations, based on college and clerical biographies as well as genealogical and town histories, are a rich source of information on the social backgrounds of New England college graduates in general and Congregational ministers in particular. Social historians generally agree that if the occupation of the father of a college graduate cannot be ascertained from existing records, the individual was most likely from a "middling" or ordinary farming or artisan family which was undistinguished by wealth, social and political standing, or education.[9] An analysis of the backgrounds of the nearly 400 students who graduated from Yale between 1702 and 1739 established the occupations of only 52 percent of the graduates' fathers.[10] A similar study of Harvard and Yale graduates who became clergymen between 1700 and 1760 identified the occupations of only 45 percent of these ministers' fathers.[11] These studies suggest that both the Congregational ministry and the Harvard and Yale student bodies from which it drew clerical recruits were comprised of large numbers of individuals from modest backgrounds and not simply of the sons of New England's upper-class families.[12]

Furthermore, the percentage of Congregational ministers from "middling" or ordinary backgrounds increased during the first half of the eighteenth century as the clerical profession became less appealing to young men from the upper class.[13] The college class rankings of Congregational ministers between 1700 and 1760 give a clear indication of this development. Students were ranked on the basis of a complex system which took into account their intellectual ability, the general social status of their families, and the personal standing of their fathers. In the seventeenth century when college classes were small—averaging less than ten students at Harvard—and relatively homogeneous in social composition, intellectual ability counted for more than it did in the eighteenth century. When enrollments expanded at Harvard and Yale in the eighteenth century, and when classes of twenty-five to fifty students representing a significant cross-section of New England society became common, social ranking assumed new importance.[14]

In the ranking system students were usually divided into three groups. The highest rankings went to a small group of students who were the sons of prominent families, governors, lieutenant governors, superior court judges, and members of the upper houses of the colonial assemblies. The next highest rankings went to a larger number of students who were the sons of ministers, other college educated professionals, and alumni. Finally, a third and the largest group of students consisted of the sons of successful, but socially or politically undistinguished, merchants, farmers, and artisans as well as the sons of lesser yeomen, artisans, and seamen. The fathers of the sons in this last group are precisely those "middling" and obscure individuals for whom occupational information is most difficult to find.

During the first half of the eighteenth century, the Congregational ministry became less attractive to students who were highly ranked on the class lists. In 1700, 47 percent of ordained Congregational ministers were in the upper half of their classes. This figure declined to 37 percent in 1740 and to 33 percent by 1760.[15] Moreover, a recent study of the Congregational clergy at the time of the Awakening found that the pro-revival New Light party attracted a high proportion of ministers from modest backgrounds—ministers who had experienced upward mobility. Over 70 percent of the New Lights, as compared to 58 percent of the Old Lights, came from middle- or lower-class families.[16] Nearly 42 percent of the Old Lights were the sons of upper-class families, while only 29 percent of the New Lights came from comparable social backgrounds. Old Lights also had stronger family ties to the ministry than New Lights. Twenty-six percent of the Congregational clergy at the time of the Awakening were the sons of clergymen. Nearly 65 percent of these ministers' sons sided with the Old Light party.[17]

New Light ministers as a group were not only more socially mobile than Old Lights, they were also more geographically mobile. A clear majority (66 percent) of the New Lights were born in the small secondary towns and hamlets of inland New England. By contrast, 60 percent of the Old Lights were natives of the larger towns and cities of New England. Since these populous areas contained a majority of the Congregational churches, Old Lights often settled in the ministry close to home. New Lights, on the other hand, usually had to travel far from their small home towns to secure pastorates.[18] Some moved to the large towns and cities and preached side by side with Old Lights. Others left home to fill pulpits in newly established churches in the developing backcountry of New England. Samuel Hopkins's career in the ministry illustrates these New Light mobility patterns. From his small Connecticut home town, he journeyed to Berkshire County, Massachusetts, to serve a newly organized frontier parish. Then, he moved farther away from his native town and became the pastor of one of the Congregational churches in Newport, Rhode Island. Many other New Divinity men were also geographically mobile, moving from their Connecticut home towns west into Litchfield County or north and northwest into western Massachusetts and Vermont.

Indeed, not just the mobility pattern but the other social characteristics of a clear majority of New Light ministers — modest social origins, birth in a small town or village, and no parental ties to the clergy — were also the most typical characteristics of the New Divinity wing of the party. Of fifty-six New Divinity men identified (comprising at least 50 percent and probably closer to 75 percent of the Consistent Calvinists in New England between the Great Awakening and the Revolution) most came from modest or obscure social backgrounds.[19] The occupations of the fathers of only twenty-one New Divinity men can be established from published sources. Four New Divinity men (only 7 percent) had clergymen fathers. Two fathers were doctors, one was a lawyer, and one was a weaver. The fathers of the remaining thirteen New Divinity men were farmers. Three members of this last group were the only fathers of New Divinity men to be elected or appointed to political office on the provincial level.

In addition to the modest backgrounds of most of the twenty-one New Divinity men whose fathers' occupations can be identified and the thirty-five (nearly 63 percent) for whom such information is lacking, the Yale class rankings of the New Divinity men also indicate that they came from undistinguished and even obscure families. Twenty-six New Divinity ministers graduated from Yale between the Great Awakening and 1768, when social ranking was abolished. Only two New Divinity men were placed in the top quarter of their classes. Seventeen, or 65 percent, were in the bottom half of their classes, with 9, or 35 percent, in the lowest quarter, and often at the very bottom of their class lists.

The remaining New Divinity men who attended Yale graduated after class lists were put in alphabetical order beginning in 1768. From time to time, fathers had expressed dissatisfaction with the system of social ranking both at Harvard and Yale, and its abolition was surely welcomed by many, including the significant number of New Divinity men who had received low placements.[20] A letter written by David Avery in 1767, who was a Yale junior at that time and who later became a Consistent Calvinist minister, probably expresses the sentiments of many other New Divinity men. He wrote to the famed New Light minister and founder of Dartmouth College Eleazar Wheelock, endorsing the abolition of social ranking and describing a new atmosphere at Yale:

> There appears to be a laudable ambition to excel in knowledge. It is not he that has got the finest coat or the largest ruffles that is esteemed here at present. And as the class henceforth are to be placed alphabetically, the students may expect marks of distinction to be put upon the best scholars and speakers.[21]

Avery, the son of a Norwich, Connecticut, farmer, had originally decided to become a carpenter and had apprenticed himself to a local tradesman. Conversion changed his future plans and he enrolled as a "charity student" at Wheelock's Indian missionary school in Lebanon, Connecticut, to prepare for entrance into Yale and a career in the ministry. Had social ranking not been abolished, in all likelihood Avery would have been placed near the bottom of his class.

Avery and four other New Divinity men were natives of Norwich, one of the most populous towns in Connecticut. But a large majority of the New Divinity men from Connecticut were raised in the inland, secondary towns and small farming villages of the colony rather than in its coastal ports and "major county towns."[22] Only two New Divinity men were from New Haven, for example, and only one was from Hartford.

Most fathers of the small-town Connecticut boys who, in the main, comprised the New Divinity movement probably had the means to send their sons to New Haven for four years. Nevertheless, some families undoubtedly had to sacrifice or require their sons to wait on tables at commons to meet the expenses of a Yale education. Other young men most likely received financial help from private benefactors. Sometimes a wealthy parishioner or a local pastor helped provide for the education of a home-town boy of intellectual ability and personal piety who aspired to the ministry but could not afford to pay for preparatory tutoring or college itself. Thus, Eleazar Wheelock took a personal interest in John Smalley of Lebanon, Connecticut, whom he prepared for college without charge to Smalley's father. Once at Yale, Smalley received financial help from tutor Ezra Stiles. Jonathan Edwards took a similar interest in the education of John Searle, a young man of limited means from Simsbury, Connecticut, whose family formerly lived in Northampton.[23] Searle and Smalley were two of the New Divinity ministers who were ranked at the bottom of their classes.

In the notebooks from which he composed class lists, Yale rector Thomas Clap sometimes described the families of low-ranking students like Smalley and Searle as "of middling estate, much impoverished."[24] While ministers from such backgrounds were found on both sides of the revival and among the several factions within the Congregational clergy, there were important social divisions inside the clerical profession. Both clear and subtle differences appear in the recruitment lines of the various clerical parties. In comparison to Old Lights and also — though to a lesser extent — to other New Lights, a high proportion of New Divinity men came from "middling" to obscure farming or artisan families. Only a small group of New Divinity men could claim fathers with some professional or social-political standing. Samuel Hopkins was one of these fortunate New Divinity men. He was the eldest son of a successful farmer and political leader in the small western Connecticut town of Waterbury.

The history of the planting of Hopkins's family roots in Waterbury is a familiar story of migration from England, settlement along coastal New England, and resettlement in the interior, a process that carried the Puritans from their "city upon a hill" and scattered them in numerous towns and villages across the breadth of New England in about one hundred years. The patriarch of the family, John Hopkins, emigrated from England and settled in Cambridge in 1634. Two years later he moved his family to Hartford, most likely as part of the contingent of Puritans that Thomas Hooker led into the Connecticut River Valley.[25] The descendants of the elder Hopkins remained in Hartford until 1680, when his grandson and namesake, John, moved west to Waterbury. The settlement of Waterbury, then called Mattatuck, had begun in 1677 when a group of young men from Farmington, just to the west of Hartford, cleared the underbrush, erected crude houses, and established themselves at the edge of the Connecticut frontier on the banks of the Naugatuck River.[26] Beyond this settlement lay the uninhabited wilderness of what was to become a seedbed of the New Divinity movement — Litchfield County.

The youthful John Hopkins came to Waterbury with a purpose. In 1679 a committee of town proprietors proposed the construction of a grist mill and provided an inducement for prospective builders: "We grant such persons shall have Thirty Acres of Land Layd out and shall be and remain to them and their heirs and assignes for ever, he or they mayntayning the sayd grist mill as afore sayd forever."[27] Stephen Hopkins of Hartford, son of the partriarch and father of John, saw this as an opportunity to settle his oldest son. He constructed the mill and sent John to operate it and take title to the land. The Hopkins family probably knew the Farmington migrants who settled Waterbury, for Farmington itself had been established by people from Hartford. Thus, although not an original proprietor of Waterbury, John was quickly accepted by the townspeople. He became a proprietor and shared in the divisions of town land. He emerged as one of the leaders of the community, filling various town offices as well as serving several terms in the Connecticut General Assembly as Waterbury's representative.

While John prospered the town as a whole did not. After Waterbury's incorporation in 1686, a series of what many residents would have called "providential afflictions" visited the town.

16

Indian threats and attacks hampered the orderly growth and development of the settlement. Natural catastrophes also struck the town. In 1691 flooding brought about by heavy rains and melting snow in the hills and mountains surrounding the Naugatuck River Valley washed away much of Waterbury's topsoil. In 1712 an epidemic spread through the town killing a number of inhabitants. Consequently, for the first thirty years of Waterbury's history the town's population barely increased at all, and Waterbury remained a small, compact settlement of approximately thirty-five families totaling about two hundred people.[28]

By the time the second generation came of age, beginning around 1700, the poor prospects offered by the town made Waterbury's young men restless. Migration had already started from the settlement, and the proprietors expressed concern for the town's future. In 1697 the proprietors introduced the granting of land to the town's young men under a system of "bachelor proprietorship." A young man who desired to settle in the town could receive thirty acres of marginal land (land in swamps or bogs) and a forty pound allotment in any future divisions of the commons, provided he agreed to build a house and improve the land within four years. For the next twenty years a significant number of Waterbury's future leaders received land under "bachelor accommodations."[29] Among these second generation bachelor proprietors were two sons of John Hopkins — Stephen and Timothy, the father of Samuel. A third son, Samuel, after whom the New Divinity pastor was named, was sent to Yale and graduated in 1718. He entered the Congregational ministry, was installed over the church at West Springfield, Massachusetts, and became a well-known supporter of Indian missions in New England.

While Samuel was upholding the religious ideals and serving as the conscience of the Hopkins family, his older brothers were sharing the rather substantial family patrimony. Timothy, for example, was designated as the heir of the Hopkins house and homestead; and in 1719, when the young man of twenty-seven married the daughter of a deacon in the Waterbury church, his father deeded him half of this property.[30] After his marriage Timothy brought his eighteen-year-old bride to the Hopkins homestead where Samuel, the first of their nine children, was born in 1721. The child was given the name of his uncle, Samuel of West Springfield, with the intention that he too would enter the Congregational ministry. "As soon as I was capable of understanding and attending to it," Samuel later recalled, "I was told that my father, when he was informed that he had a son born to him, said, if the child should live, he would give him a public education, that he might be a minister or Sabbath-day man, alluding to my being born on the Sabbath."[31] Yet throughout his youth the prospect of a career in the ministry remained remote from Samuel's thoughts. He was content to labor on his father's farm and have his waking hours consumed by the typical duties of a farmboy in eighteenth-century New England. Like his parents young Samuel was pious and hardworking. He regularly attended church with his family, and late in life he recollected that as a youth he was "rather of a steady and sober make." He readily submitted to parental authority, avoided the use of profanity, and labored industriously on the family farm, so that, he reflected in his autobiography, "as I advanced in age, I gained the notice, esteem, and respect of the neighborhood."[32]

The Waterbury of Samuel Hopkins's youth was a small, back-country agricultural community similar to many of the other settlements that dotted the landscape of eighteenth-century New England. Numbering about three hundred inhabitants in 1727 when Hopkins was six years old, the town's population soared to nine hundred when he left to enroll at Yale ten years later.[33] Late in life, after having lived in Newport, Rhode Island, for more than twenty-five years and having seen extensive urban and commercial growth in New England during the course of his career in the ministry, Hopkins remembered and described the Waterbury of his youth in idyllic terms. He thanked God that he was "born and educated in a religious family, and among a people in a country town, where a regard to religion and morality was common and prevalent, and the education of children and youth was generally practiced in such a degree that young people were generally orderly in their behavior, and abstained from those open vices which were then too common in seaport and populous places."[34]

During the years in which Hopkins was growing to maturity, Waterbury seemed a simple, usually quiet community, an assessment that is heightened by contrast with the Waterbury of the late eighteenth century, after decades of economic and population growth. But the town in the 1720's and 1730's was hardly as placid as Hopkins's recollection suggests. Waterbury experienced its share of political and ecclesiastical contention which, as in other New England towns in the eighteenth century, stemmed from the growth and dispersal of the population.[35] In 1733 the inhabitants of the northwest section of Waterbury petitioned the General Assembly to set off their community as a separate parish. It was inconvenient for the residents of this outlying district to travel to the meetinghouse in the center of town, and they desired "parish privileges"—the right to construct a meetinghouse, call a minister, and apply their portion of the town's religious taxes to the support of their church. The town opposed the request for parish privileges, and clashes between the "outlivers" and the residents in the center of the town occurred throughout the 1730's. When a town committee finally decided to allow the establishment of the new parish in 1738, disputes arose over boundaries. A year later another section of the town was marked off as a separate society.[36] Clearly, the sense of community that John Hopkins and other first-generation town residents had experienced did not characterize the Waterbury of his sons and grandsons.

The youthful Samuel Hopkins was certainly aware of the controversies which brought about the decentralization of the religious structure of the town. Indeed, he must have heard frequent discussions of these problems in his home, for his father was one of the social and political leaders of Waterbury. Timothy Hopkins, following the example of his father, served the town as a selectman, justice of the peace, and deputy to the General Assembly. As a leader of the community Timothy was burdened with responsibility for solving many town problems. He was repeatedly appointed or elected to committees dealing with boundaries, land divisions, roads, or repairs to the meetinghouse.[37]

Timothy inherited not only his father's social and political prominence but much of his wealth as well. Gradually John Hopkins deeded his property to his sons. The Waterbury tax list of 1730 shows that Timothy and his brother Stephen were among the wealthiest men in the town. When John Hopkins died in 1732, the sons inherited the remainder of his estate, and their tax rate rose even higher.[38] The Hopkins brothers were clearly important and influential men in Waterbury. Still, the agricultural society that deferred to them, sought their views and advice, and made them feel established and prestigious was but a small and obscure corner of the Colony of Connecticut. In 1730, for example, over fifty years after its settlement, Waterbury sent to the General Assembly one of the lowest tax returns in the colony. Out of forty-four towns in Connecticut at this time, Waterbury ranked forty-first in the amount of its tax levies.[39]

As a son of one of the leading families in the community, young Samuel Hopkins felt comfortable and established in Waterbury. Throughout his youth he was constantly reminded by family members that he was to attend college as preparation for a career in the ministry.[40] Yet until the age of fourteen he did not think seriously of leaving Waterbury. Apparently he expected to follow in the footsteps of other Hopkins men and to become a successful farmer and a pillar of the church and town. At the age of fourteen, this obedient, pious, Puritan son paid closer heed to the wishes of his parents and took the first step toward fulfilling his father's dream that he would become a "Sabbath-day man."

During the seventeenth and eighteenth centuries fourteen was a crucial age in a boy's life. At this time most New England youth came to some decision concerning a future occupation. Fourteen was the most opportune age to begin the standard seven-year apprenticeship for a trade, so that by the age of twenty-one a young man would be prepared for economic independence. If a son desired to attend college, fourteen was the appropriate time to begin preparation for entrance into college two years later. When pious young New Englanders turned their thoughts to a future livelihood, spiritual introspection accompanied worldly calculation, for they viewed an occupation as a calling and therefore felt obligated to try to discover God's will.[41] Thus the winter after he turned fourteen, during the quiet interim between the fall harvest and the spring planting, Hopkins spent much time alone, carefully reading the Bible and thinking about his future. Gradually, he reported in his autobiography, he "began to feel more inclination to learning, and less to working on a farm." An important reason for his change of heart, Hopkins recalled, was the fact that "our farming business did not go on so well as it had done, by reason of some particular circumstances which had taken place. When my father perceived this, he told me if I was inclined to go to learning, he would put me to a place where I might be fitted for the college; to which I readily consented."[42]

The circumstances Hopkins alluded to may have accounted

for the fact that several years after his decision to prepare for college, his father abandoned the Hopkins homestead and moved from the center of town. As early as 1732 Timothy had begun to dispose of the family's landholdings, which Samuel's grandfather had accumulated. After the grandfather's death that year, Timothy and his brother Stephen sold the family grist mill and the thirty acres of mill land that John had been granted in 1680. In 1743 Timothy sold the old Hopkins homestead and all its contents for £540.[43] Then shortly after Timothy died in 1749, Samuel, who as the oldest male heir was in charge of his father's estate, sold much of the remaining acreage that the family owned in Waterbury and used the money to finance the Yale education of his three younger brothers. All of these developments suggest the seriousness of the "circumstances" that influenced Samuel's decision to forsake the family farm for a college education.[44]

The boy prepared for Yale under the Reverend John Graham of Woodbury, ten miles to the west of Waterbury. Born in Scotland and educated at the University of Glasgow, Graham, like many other New England ministers, supplemented his salary by preparing boys for college. After two years with Graham, Hopkins was ready to be examined by the Yale tutors for admission to the college. He passed the examination and enrolled at Yale in September, 1737, just as he turned sixteen.[45] Hopkins was ranked sixth in a class of twenty, the third highest placement among the New Divinity men, exceeded only by the two individuals ranked in the top quarter of their classes. Although Samuel's father may have been in straitened economic circumstances at the time Samuel enrolled at Yale, Timothy was still a man of some social and political standing. Yet, as the son's class placement suggests, the father was a man of local prominence and certainly not a member of the provincial elite.

When Hopkins entered Yale in 1737, the college was housed in a single three-story wood-framed building constructed in 1718. The structure provided both classroom and dormitory space. By 1737 the building was in need of extensive repairs. But Yale required more than new shingles on its roof in order to meet the needs of the increasing numbers of Connecticut youth who made their way to New Haven. The old building accommodated only forty-six students, but the enrollment had risen to eighty-five by 1737. The trustees of the college requested both repairs and a new dormitory from the General Assembly. The deputies voted money for new repairs but refused to erect a new building. Consequently, while Hopkins lived in the dormitory, almost half of the Yale undergraduates had to find lodging outside of the college community.[46]

A hierarchical social system prevailed at the college. At the bottom of the social pyramid were the freshmen who were obliged to run errands and function as servants for the seniors who dominated undergraduate life. The rector and the trustees stood at the top of the pyramid, with the tutors and resident graduates between them and the undergraduates.[47] This hierarchy introduced Hopkins to the first society he had known outside of his small home town. Withdrawn and studious, he remained aloof from New Haven social life as well as from his fellow students. "I avoided the intimacy and the company of the openly vicious," he later recalled, "and, indeed, kept but little company, being attentive to my studies."[48]

Two tutors who were recent graduates of Yale instructed the students for the first three years of their education. Freshmen studied Latin, Greek, Hebrew, logic, and mathematics. In their sophomore and junior years, undergraduates added natural philosophy, rhetoric, geography, and oratory. The rector rounded out a Yale education by instructing seniors in metaphysics, ethics, and divinity. The rector's task was to instill in a formal way the orthodox theology that students heard repeatedly at the several weekly religious services they were obliged to attend while enrolled at Yale. Connecticut's future leaders memorized the Westminster Confession and read the important works of Reformed theology.[49]

At Yale Hopkins applied himself to his studies, shunned social intercourse with his classmates, and avoided conflict with his superiors. He accepted orthodox doctrine and spent many hours reading the Bible. Each summer he journeyed back to Waterbury and worked on his father's farm. Sometime in either his sophomore or junior year he made a profession of faith and joined the family church in Waterbury. Hopkins was following a conventional path toward the Congregational ministry. Then, in his senior year, the Great Awakening engulfed Yale and brought a crisis, and ultimately new meaning and direction, into his life.

chapter two

THE GREAT
AWAKENING AND
THE SCHOOLS
OF THE PROPHETS

A S the Great Awakening (1740–1743) roared across New England it attracted individuals from all segments of Puritan society. The wide appeal of the revival stemmed from its message of practical piety, for many New Englanders in the middle of the eighteenth century felt a need to purge their souls by participating in a movement that called for a return to the personal as well as communal values of the past. Within the broad social response to the Awakening's pietistic theme, however, there were different degrees of intensity. Men were more susceptible to revival preaching than women, and young men in particular found the Awakening appealing. Furthermore, in New England the revival appears to have been most intense in areas of Massachusetts and Connecticut where economic problems, land hunger, and limited prospects for young men spurred migration.[1]

The heightened religiosity of young men during the Awakening was not a fad which passed with the decline of the revival but the beginning of a pattern that became more visible in the late eighteenth and early nineteenth centuries as local revivals and the Second Great Awakening burst upon New England's religious scene. The relatively stable agrarian society, in which career choices and opportunities were clearly defined and limited in scope, dissolved more each year, and a dynamic complex society with a rapidly expanding population and a land shortage emerged and transformed the traditional life patterns of young New Englanders.[2] Revivalists made more frequent and increasingly successful appeals directly to the "rising generation," so that by the early nineteenth century the *Christian Spectator* could observe of a local awakening, "as in most other revivals, of which particular accounts have been published, the subjects of this work are principally young people. . . ."[3]

As a result of the First Great Awakening, New Lights came to see grace as the major prerequisite for the ministry. Thus for many pious young men conversion led directly to thoughts of a clerical career, for which they felt well-qualified by the very fact of their conversion. From the First to the Second Great Awakening revivalism was linked with the recruitment of ministers. The young men converted in the First Great Awakening, for example, were urged by Jonathan Edwards to become "captains of the host" in the spiritual war which would bring the kingdom of God to America.[4]

The New Divinity was a movement of a particular group of pious, young New England men, students from small settlements in rural Connecticut who were converted either in the mid-century revival, in subsequent local revivals, or in the Second Great Awakening. Few established or older ministers were won over to Consistent Calvinism; rather the New Divinity movement captured the minds and hearts of young ministerial candidates from modest to obscure social backgrounds. The professional aspirations of such individuals were encouraged by New Light charges that the ranks of the clergy were filled with spiritually corrupt, unconverted men. After 1740 external qualifications for the ministry, including one's social background, were no longer as important to New Lights as a conversion experience and personal piety. Furthermore, the incessant warnings against the danger of an unconverted ministry altered the traditional mode of preparing young men for the profession. Many ministerial candidates felt obliged to study for the ministry under a converted clergyman. It was no longer acceptable to these young men to return home after college and be tutored by a local minister who opposed revivalism. Hence, aspirants to the ministry began to converge on the homes of prominent pro-revival clerics who turned their parsonages into "schools of the prophets." Many of these schools were run by New Divinity men who won over to their movement a significant portion of the next two generations of ministers in New

England. The "schools of the prophets," moreover, stamped their graduates with the clerical values and style that marked the pattern of the New Divinity ministry.

In the fall of 1740 George Whitefield arrived in Newport, commencing his grand tour of New England and carrying beyond local boundaries the regional revival spirit that had waxed and waned in America for several years. Whitefield's mission was twofold: to collect souls for God and money for his orphanage in Georgia. In New England he fulfilled both objectives, as he had in Philadelphia, New York, and countless smaller communities throughout the colonies. From Newport Whitefield journeyed to Boston, where nearly eight thousand people assembled on the common to hear him preach. Harvard provided the only disappointment for the English revivalist. There he found that "Discipline is at a low ebb, [and] Bad books are become fashionable among the tutors and students."[5] From the Boston area he traveled north into New Hampshire and Maine and, returning to Massachusetts, headed west to Worcester and towns along the Connecticut River. At Northampton he stayed with Jonathan Edwards long enough to conclude that "I think I have not seen his fellow in all New England."[6] With New England now ablaze, Whitefield set his sights on New York, and on the way he spent a weekend at Yale where Samuel Hopkins heard him for the first time on October 24, 1740.

Rector Clap welcomed Whitefield and opened the college hall for his use. Within twenty-four hours religious emotions were at a white heat in New Haven. Townspeople as well as undergraduates flocked to hear Whitefield's well-publicized and novel style of preaching. They saw a dramatic young man of twenty-five who freely made gestures to the audience while he methodically and enthusiastically delivered his sermon without ever referring to a written text. "The assemblies were crowded and remarkably attentive," Hopkins remembered, "and people appeared generally to approve, and their conversation turned chiefly about him and his preaching."[7] The undergraduates received the special attention of Whitefield. "I spoke very closely to the students," he noted in his *Journal*, "and shewed them the dreadful ill consequences of an unconverted ministry."[8] The students could not help being impressed with the young evangelist only several years their senior whose preaching cast a spell over all of New Haven, including the Governor and General Assembly then meeting in the town. Hopkins attended Whitefield's public sermons and the private meetings he held with the undergraduates "and highly approved of him. . . ." But not all members of the Yale community accepted the revivalist's work; Hopkins found himself defending Whitefield in the discussions which followed his departure from New Haven.[9]

At Yale, as throughout New England, the revival became uncontrollable after Whitefield excited people's emotions only to withdraw as quickly as he had appeared and hand his captives over to less temperate and less skillful itinerants. A host of exhorters and itinerants converged on Yale to complete Whitefield's work.[10] By the middle of the winter, the revivalists succeeded in overturning the normal activities of the college. Prayer meetings became more important then recitations. The sermons of unordained, uneducated exhorters created more interest than the lessons taught by tutors. Students preferred to make inquiries into the living spiritual reality of their own souls rather than to examine the thoughts of dead scholars. Conversions multiplied and so did emotional excesses. Weeping and shrieking accompanied visions of damnation. Once awakened to a conviction of sin, individuals shouted and screamed for relief. Spiritual agony expressed itself through bodily contortions, while some revivalists gloated over the influence they exerted on their audiences.

In March Gilbert Tennent, the most popular itinerant among Yale students, preached seventeen times at New Haven and raised the extravagances of the revival to new heights. He graphically portrayed the "Rottenness and Hypocrisie"[11] of unconverted ministers and laughed at awakened sinners. The inflammatory effect of Tennent's rhetoric surpassed even that of Whitefield. On the basis of Tennent's performance at New Haven, Hopkins "thought he was the greatest and best man, and the best preacher I had ever seen or heard." As a result, Hopkins later recalled, he decided that after graduation he would live and study with Tennent, "wherever I should find him."[12]

A number of other Yale undergraduates were as deeply impressed with Tennent as Hopkins was. Moved by the itinerant's preaching, a group of zealots led by sophomore David Brainerd defied the college's social rules and visited every dormitory room, probing the occupant's spiritual state and stressing the need for regenerating grace. Hopkins highly approved of the activities of these radical New Lights, until he found himself confronted by the impassioned Brainerd. In spite of his support for the Awakening and his participation in revival meetings at Yale since September, Hopkins still had not experienced conversion. As Brainerd pried into his spiritual life, Hopkins "resolved to keep him in the dark, and if possible prevent his getting any knowledge of my state of religion." But Brainerd did succeed in further awakening Hopkins to a conviction of his sinful state.[13] For the next several weeks Hopkins suffered the spiritual agonies that commonly afflicted awakened sinners. His feelings of vileness and guilt increased each day. He thought that his condition was hopeless and that his life was rooted in pride and evil. The horrors of hell, which he had heard itinerants depicting since September, now passed vividly before him. And all the while he attended private prayer meetings and ashamedly told inquirers that he had not yet been converted. The external pressure and internal agitation mounted until conversion eased the stress:

> At length as I was in my closet one evening, while I was meditating, and in my devotions, a new and wonderful scene opened to my view. I had a sense of the being and presence of God, as I never had before; it being more of a reality, and more affecting and glorious, than I had ever before perceived. . . . I was greatly affected, in the view of my own depravity, the sinfulness, guilt, and odiousness of my character; and tears flowed in great plenty.[14]

Hopkins's agonizing abated, but he did not immediately associate the experience with conversion and continued to assume that saving grace had not touched his heart.

As the September commencement approached, the Great Awakening entered a critical stage. Itinerant meetings had become increasingly disorderly and the invective that flowed from revivalists' lips increasingly scurrilous. Gradually groups coalesced to oppose the revival. A week before commencement James Davenport arrived in New Haven, and Yale authorities braced for his onslaught. Since Davenport was the most radical of all itinerants, stories of his extravagances preceded his coming to Yale, and he did not disappoint the audiences or authorities at New Haven. He carried the attack on the established ministry to a new level of vituperation. He assailed Joseph Noyes, pastor of the First Church, and encouraged his parishioners to separate from him because he was an unconverted Pharisee. As a result, Davenport was driven out of New Haven, and a movement crystallized to protect the town and the college from further evangelical intemperance.[15]

In light of these events and the religious turmoil of the past year, Yale authorities and undergraduates looked forward anxiously to commencement, when Jonathan Edwards, the individual who had done more than anyone else to promote the revival in New England, would address Samuel Hopkins and his fellow seniors. On commencement day, the trustees took their first step to control the New Lights and voted "that if any Student shall directly or indirectly say, that the Rector, either of the Trustees or Tutors are Hypocrites, carnall or unconverted Men, he Shall for the first Offense make a public Confession in the Hall, and for the Second Offense be expelled."[16] Doubtless, both Yale authorities and New Light students looked to Edwards for support and guidance. Most of the Yale audience had probably never heard Edwards preach before, but like Hopkins many had certainly read some of his sermons or at least his famous *Faithful Narrative* describing the conversions during the Northampton revival of 1735.

Edwards's commencement sermon foreshadowed his later important work on the *Religious Affections* and focused on the underlying problem not only of Hopkins's spiritual crisis but also of Davenport's behavior and the excesses of the revival in general: What are the external signs of God's grace at work? "My design therefore at this time," Edwards began his ringing endorsement of the revival, "is to show what are the true, certain, and distinguishing evidences of a work of the Spirit of God, by which we may safely proceed in judging of any operations we find in ourselves, or see in others."[17] The inordinate emotionalism, unrestrained conduct, censorious attitudes, and other objections that critics raised to discredit the revival, Edwards argued, "are no evidence that the work is not of the Spirit of God."[18] What, then, were the positive signs of God's work? A love of Christ, an acceptance of Christian truths, a concern for eternal salvation, a sense of one's odiousness and smallness: "These," Edwards concluded, "are the manifest tokens of the Spirit of God."[19]

Edwards went on to offer his own interpretation of the danger of an unconverted ministry. The major stumbling blocks to the success of the revival and the progress of the millennium were ministers who cited the irregularities of the Awakening to justify their resistance or neutrality to what was truly a work of God. Such action provoked God and would bring a curse upon the land.[20] Edwards closed his important sermon with the practical inference "that the extraordinary influence that has lately appeared causing an uncommon concern and engagedness of mind about the things of religion is undoubtedly in general from the Spirit of God."[21]

The sermon furnished spiritual reassurance for the New Lights at Yale. For Hopkins, about to leave the college and strike out into the world, Edwards's words were spiritual signposts on his journey toward salvation. He still did not believe he was saved, but he undoubtedly saw the resemblance between his own religious experiences and the distinguishing marks the great preacher had delineated. He had no further contact with Edwards at New Haven, but under the sway of his sermon changed his plan to reside with Gilbert Tennent "and concluded to go and live with Mr. Edwards, as soon as I should have opportunity. . . ."[22] As a New Light, Hopkins could not seriously consider a career in the ministry until he became reasonably confident of his own rebirth. Both in his earlier decision to live with Tennent and in his later selection of Edwards, Hopkins's intention was to seek guidance while praying for an outpouring of God's grace. In small prayer meetings that followed the public sermons during the Awakening, itinerants offered guidance to sinners under conviction. Often awakened sinners besieged a prominent revivalist's home in search of spiritual solace. In his *Life of Edwards*, Hopkins described the theologian's Northampton parsonage at the height of the revival as constantly "thronged with persons to lay open their spiritual concerns to him, and seek his advice and direction. . . ." Troubled souls from all over New England made their way to Edwards's doorstep, and he "received and conversed with [them], with great freedom and pleasure, and had the best opportunity to deal in the most particular manner with each one."[23] Once Hopkins revealed his soul to Edwards and the latter consecrated his religious experiences, he was ready to battle the unconverted ministers of New England.

Immediately after commencement, Hopkins returned to Waterbury to make preparations for his trip to Northampton. For nearly three months he isolated himself on his father's farm and fasted and prayed. All the while, itinerants drifted in and out of Waterbury and the revival raged throughout the land.[24] In the middle of December, 1741, he came out of seclusion, mounted his horse, and started his eighty-mile pilgrimage to the new spiritual hub of New England.

He arrived unannounced at Edwards's parsonage, only to discover that the revivalist was not at home but had left on a preaching tour. Nevertheless, Sarah Edwards, by now accustomed to strangers seeking the counsel of her husband, welcomed Hopkins and invited him to stay for the winter.[25] In January, Samuel Buell, Hopkins's classmate at Yale and now an ordained revivalist, came to fill Edwards's vacant pulpit and received an enthusiastic response from the Northampton parishioners. Hopkins traveled with Buell on a preaching tour towards Boston and saw him arouse sinners and inspire conversions. Here was a young man the same age as himself who only several months before had been a college student and who now itinerated as a successful New Light minister. Undoubtedly, Buell's example encouraged Hopkins's clerical aspirations. At this time he began to feel more assured that he had been converted at Yale. When Edwards returned to Northampton in February, Hopkins opened his soul for scrutiny. He revealed his spiritual experiences at college, and the fasting, praying, and Bible reading, which had become a daily routine. He divulged as much of his inner longings and fears as he could put into words and waited for the master's verdict. Of course Edwards did not offer an absolute judgment; only God really knew who were saved and who were damned. But he did leave Hopkins with a strong impression that regenerating grace had visited his soul. "From this time," Hopkins remembered, "I turned my thoughts upon preaching the gospel."[26]

At the end of March, 1742, he left Northampton and returned to Waterbury intent on obtaining a license to preach. Preparation for the licensing examination consumed his time, while the certainty of his salvation increased. "I have late entertained a hope," he recorded in his diary in April, "that I did experience a saving change over a year ago; and I find myself more and more established in it." He prayed that he had not been deceived, "for I have some thoughts (God willing) of being examined, next week, in order to preach the sweet and everlasting gospel of Jesus."[27] On April 29 he passed his examination and was licensed to preach. Almost immediately he joined the ranks of the itinerating New Lights. The First Church of Waterbury opened its pulpit to him, and other preaching opportunities arose in the backcountry of Connecticut.[28] What Hopkins needed now, along with this practical experience, was further grounding in divinity so that he might defend the theological implications of the revival against all detractors. As summer approached Hopkins decided to return to Edwards's school of the prophets to pursue his theological studies.

During his second stay in Northampton Hopkins made extensive use of Edwards's library, which included works ranging from the classics of Reformed theology to the books of famous heretics. He read as much as he could and discussed his impressions with Edwards. Occasionally he preached in his mentor's pulpit or traveled to Suffield, Hampton, or Westfield to fill a vacant pulpit. At times he saw results equal to the success of the famous revivalists he had been observing for a year. "I had a freedom in speaking which I never had before," he noted in his diary on July 3. "I could not be heard all over the meeting house, by reason of the out cries of the people. Oh! wonderful, that the Lord should make me his instrument to feed his lambs."[29]

In the fall of 1742, Hopkins left Northampton and journeyed to Bethlehem, Connecticut, where for several weeks he replaced Joseph Bellamy, who had left on a preaching tour. The twenty-four year old Bellamy had already gained a reputation as a powerful New Light preacher who was both a protege of and a match for Edwards. Thus, upon completing his preaching assignment in Bethlehem, Hopkins had filled the pulpits of two of the most successful and well-known revivalists in New England. The end of his apprenticeship was in sight. He would soon have a pulpit of his own.

Hopkins's first call to settle over a congregation came from Simsbury, Connecticut, a small town a few miles north of Hartford. He served the people from December 1742 to May 1743 but refused to be considered as a candidate for a permanent position, "having no inclination," he told them, "to settle in the ministry at present. . . ."[30] He needed more time to complete his studies under Edwards. He returned to Northampton in June and found a teaching position. But a rheumatic illness interrupted his studies after only two weeks.

While he was still recovering from his sickness, an emissary from Housatonic, Massachusetts, arrived in Northampton with a request that Hopkins preach as a candidate to the inhabitants of this backcountry hamlet in Berkshire County. Hopkins accepted the offer of the Housatonic representative, and at the end of June he began his journey to the raw settlement on the edge of the Massachusetts frontier.[31] For the next twenty-five years he would labor in this obscure corner of his Lord's vineyard.

The career lines of many New Divinity men disclose a pattern of conversion, a ruminative inclination toward the ministry, preparation in a school of the prophets, and ordination in the New England backcountry. Joseph Bellamy, for example, experienced his conversion as a young man fresh out of Yale in 1735 and began to read theology under the minister in his home town. But news of Edwards and the "frontier revival" brought him to Northampton, where he sought the theological understanding that his local minister could not impart.[32] The conversion of Nathanael Emmons, who like Bellamy was a prominent New Divinity theologian and teacher, also followed his graduation from Yale in 1768 and precipitated his decision to enter the Congregational ministry. Emmons did not return to Yale as a postgraduate student of divinity or seek the guidance of his home-town pastor; instead, he traveled to New Britain, Connecticut, and entered the theological school of New Divinity minister John Smalley.[33]

During the First Great Awakening, similar decisions of numbers of young men aspiring to the ministry led to the appearance of schools of the prophets. The New Light attacks on the established clergy encouraged many ministerial candidates to overlook their local pastors as potential tutors and to seek out teachers with proven theological reputations and, above all, evangelical piety. Repeatedly, revivalists issued warnings against the danger of an unconverted ministry composed of "hirelings," "dead Drones," and "Pharisees."[34] In New England, the condition of the clerical profession prior to the Awakening lent substance to such evangelical indictments. By the early decades of the eighteenth century, the Congregational clergy had evolved into a highly self-conscious, and even socially pretentious, professional class. Many ministers viewed themselves and attempted to live and work as members of a social elite.[35] New Lights perceived such worldliness as evidence of an unconverted, spiritually languid ministry; more importantly, the evangelicals' moral critique of the clergy's social and professional ambitions held particular appeal for ministerial aspirants from modest to obscure social backgrounds.

The New Light assault on an unconverted ministry logically led to an attack on the institutions which sustained that ministry. The term "schools of the prophets" had originally applied to Harvard and Yale, whose main function had been to produce clerical leaders for New England. Even as late as 1735 Samuel Willard, in a manual for postgraduate ministerial candidates, referred to the provincial colleges and the "weighty trust committed to them who have the instruction and Government of our Youth in the School of the Prophets. . . ."[36] But the revival convinced many New Lights that the term could no longer be applied to Harvard and Yale, for these two schools seemed as corrupt as their graduates who filled the ministry. In April of 1741 George Whitefield published the installment of his *Journal* that dealt with his New England tour and that condemned Harvard and Yale, where "Light is become Darkness, Darkness that may be felt, and is complained of by the most godly ministers."[37] Earlier Whitefield had heaped praise on William Tennent's Log College, begun in Pennsylvania to educate evangelical clergymen. The crude twenty-foot log house was derisively called a college, but to Whitefield "it seemed to resemble the school of the old prophets."[38] He suggested that only unconverted ministers failed to see God working through the Tennents. Here was an authentic school of the prophets which established a precedent and furnished a rough model for the New Divinity schools.

After Whitefield's attack on New England's colleges, the New Light charges that Yale was an institution of the unconverted clergy and not a school of the prophets appeared to be confirmed by the actions of Rector Clap. In September of 1741 he prohibited itinerants from preaching at the college and forbade students to attend revival meetings. Rebellious New Light students refused to accept Clap's orders and persisted in attending itinerant meetings and neglecting the college's religious services. In turn, Clap meted out stiff discipline to the recalcitrants.[39] One action for which he was never forgiven by many New Lights was the expulsion of David Brainerd from Yale. This pietistic young man had been one of the student leaders of the revival and had been instrumental in a number of conversions at the college. When Clap began his counteroffensive against the Awakening, Brainerd encouraged students to defy his orders. But Brainerd's fatal transgression was to accuse Tutor Chauncy Whittelsey of having no more grace than a chair. In the minds of many New Lights, the departure of Brainerd from Yale extinguished any claim the college had to being a school of the prophets. By the fall of 1742 a group of New Light students had become so disgusted with affairs at New Haven that they attempted to establish their own school in Connecticut. The New Lights left Yale and enrolled at Timothy Allen's "Shepherd's Tent" in New London. Although its existence was short-lived, Allen's seminary reflected the same antagonism toward existing ministerial education that marked the early history of Tennent's Log College and that produced the New Divinity schools of the prophets.[40] When Edwards published his *Thoughts on the Revival* in 1743 he joined the chorus of evangelical critics who were attacking Yale, and in 1749, in his *Life of David Brainerd*, he canonized the young prophet whom Yale authorities had found unfit to graduate.

The claim of the New England colleges that they were schools of the prophets was further undermined as enrollments expanded at mid-century but the percentage of graduates becoming ministers declined. Students of social rank tended increasingly to choose secular professions and to bypass the ministry.[41] Thus the clerical profession became more accessible to persons lacking the traditional social attributes of the clergy. Furthermore, the New Light emphasis on an internal call to the ministry as opposed to external qualifications had social consequences for the recruitment of Congregational clergy.[42] To a pious young man in rural New England of little or no social rank, to enter the Congregational clergy had been a high step up the social ladder. But after the Awakening, as a result of widespread criticism of the unconverted ministry and the new stress on grace as the major qualification for the ministry, socially obscure young men were less inclined to be overawed at the prospect of entering the clerical profession. These new aspirants to the Congregational ministry continued to attend college out of necessity. But the Awakening compelled many ministerial candidates to see the inadequacies of their college educations and to realize the need for training under evangelical theologians in authentic schools of the prophets.

Between the Great Awakening and the establishment of the Yale Divinity School in 1822, theological education in Connecticut was largely in the hands of New Lights — especially New Divinity men. Among the many Consistent Calvinist ministers who transformed their parsonages into schools of the prophets, Joseph Bellamy was by far the most successful in the eighteenth century. Almost from the outset of the Awakening he saw the need for a new approach to ministerial education. Using his experience in Edwards's parsonage as a model, Bellamy opened his home in Bethlehem, Connecticut, to candidates for the ministry. In his backyard he erected his own two-room Log College, which functioned as a classroom and study, while the third floor of his parsonage served as a dormitory. Many of Bellamy's students became Consistent Calvinists.[43] Indeed, between the Awakening and the Revolution Bellamy instructed more New Divinity men than any other theological teacher.

Nathanael Emmons's efforts surpassed even the successes of Bellamy. Beginning his work in the 1780's as Bellamy began to fade from prominence, this thoroughgoing Hopkinsian became the major theological tutor of the second generation of New Divinity men. From his parsonage in Franklin, Massachusetts, Emmons sent ninety men into the ministry and rejected many others who sought his tutelage.[44]

The New Divinity schools of the prophets did more than simply impress a theological mark on many of their graduates. These institutions transmitted a distinct mode of life and set of professional values, which became characteristic of the New Divinity men. Their commitment to theological speculation, their deemphasis of the pastoral duties of the ministry, and their lack of concern with personal secular affairs can all be traced to the Consistent Calvinists' experiences in the schools of the prophets.

The traditional clerical apprenticeship consisted of a single student studying under a local pastor. The minister aided the apprentice in his study of theology and exposed him to the routine pastoral duties of a clergyman — visiting parishioners, calling on the sick, as well as performing baptisms and marriages. Prior to the Awakening and the emergence of theological parties, the preparation of a candidate for licensure involved the mastering of an accepted body of divinity.[45] Once a student demonstrated a sound grasp of orthodoxy, and assuming he avoided any taint of heresy, the local association granted him a license to preach.

After the Awakening, doctrinal preparation for the ministry became more rigorous, particularly in New Divinity schools of the prophets where grounding in systematic divinity was stressed at the expense of training in the practical tasks of the ministry. The Awakening split New England Calvinism into contending theological factions and generated a continuing controversy revolving around the doctrinal implications of spiritual rebirth. Even with the waning of the revival, doctrinal concerns did not diminish, for with its passing the New Divinity men began to explore and debate the theological meaning of the Great Awakening. The issues aroused by the Awakening, Joseph Bellamy reflected long after the event, "have engaged me . . . to devote my whole time for above twenty years to inquire into the nature of Christianity."[46] Bellamy and other New Divinity men continued to fulfill the pastoral duties of their office, but they emphasized the role of the minister as a theologian—a role for which Jonathan Edwards furnished a model. Edwards, Hopkins reported in his biography of the famous theologian, did not usually visit his parishioners, "unless he was sent for by the sick, or he heard they were under some special affliction." Hopkins agreed with Edwards that the latter "could spend the time in his study to much more valuable purposes, and so as much to promote the great ends of his ministry."[47] Nor did Edwards concern himself with the management of his parsonage farm land. His parishioners were more involved with his worldly affairs than he was, Hopkins observed, and Edwards seldom knew "when and by whom his forage for winter was gathered in, or how many milk herd he had; whence his table was furnished, etc."[48]

Few New Divinity men allowed personal secular matters to interfere with their theological studies. Most would have agreed with Nathanael Emmons, who upon entering the ministry resolved "not to begin to do the least manual labor, nor ever superintend my secular concerns; but to make my study my home. . . ." A former farm boy, Emmons boasted that as a minister he did not perform "so much as an hour's labor in the garden or in the field."[49] Students saw their theological mentors spend from thirteen to eighteen hours a day reading, speculating, and writing

upon post-Awakening theological problems. The doctrinal preoc-
cupations of the teachers provided not only a curriculum but a
clerical role model for the students.

The New Divinity men believed that along with conversion
a solid understanding of systematic divinity constituted the best
preparation for the ministry. Instructors viewed students as future
theologians defending the Awakening against Old Light and liberal Calvinists. To be sure, Hopkins and other ministerial candidates found opportunities to preach and received advice on sermon
composition and techniques of evangelical preaching while completing their theological studies. However, practical experience
was clearly ancillary to theological preparation. Each teacher placed
in the hands of his students an extensive list of questions covering
a complete system of divinity; the topics ranged from proof of the
existence of God to the nature of regeneration to the coming of
the millennium. The questions supplied the outline of a complete
course of study and anticipated doctrinal problems that would be
raised at licensure. So valuable were such lists that Bellamy proposed to Hopkins in 1756 that they co-author a book of theological
questions "to assist young Students in the Study of Divinity."[50]
While the work was never completed, the correspondence between
these two theologians in the 1750's and 1760's contains a number
of theological questions and answers which were undoubtedly passed
along to students.[51]

With the list of questions in hand, the student turned to his
teacher's library in search of orthodox and heretical works dealing
with a particular subject. The libraries of ministers were small,
so that students did not read extensively into most theological
problems. Certainly Edwards's works were carefully analyzed,
and by the late eighteenth century the writings of Bellamy and
Hopkins were added to provide the reading staple of students.

When a student exhausted the minister's reading material on
a theological question, he composed a dissertation that he hoped
would demonstrate his understanding of the subject. For an hour
or two in the afternoon or evening, the instructor would leave his
study to join his pupils in a discussion of their reading and writing.
As students read compositions and posed questions, the teacher
offered criticism, suggested subtle points, and interpreted passages
of scripture. Of course, many candidates thus absorbed the peculiar emphases and interpretations of their teacher, which they

carried into their public ministry. But students were taught that God progressively shed "further light" on scripture and doctrine, and teachers impressed upon their young scholars the obligation to continue to seek theological knowledge as preparation for the millennium.

A teacher usually took an interest in the spiritual life of the candidates under his supervision. Both students and instructors understood the importance of experiencing conversion prior to ordination, and one or the other usually initiated private discussions on the subject. When Hopkins sent Jonathan Edwards, Jr., to study in Bethlehem, Connecticut, in 1766, he wrote Bellamy telling him the son of the great theologian "will take it kindly if you converse with him particularly about his personal religion and act the part of a father to him, in freely giving him your best counsel and advice."[52] While the two ministers undoubtedly took a special interest in young Edwards, students in general were to be treated with the same fatherly concern that Hopkins and Bellamy experienced in Northampton.

Readings, dissertations, and discussions attended each theological question until the candidate completed a system of divinity. With several months of concentrated study a candidate could ground himself in systematic divinity and present himself for licensure. Hopkins, for example, spent only about three months at Northampton and another month studying on his own before he was licensed to preach. Many students supplemented their formal theological training with periods of independent reading away from the schools of the prophets. Once a candidate completed the study of a system of divinity, he moved on to the preparation of sermons. Students were taught the difference, at least in theory, between theologizing and preaching. Ideally, the pulpit was not to be a forum for analyzing abstruse theological problems. Teachers instructed students to follow an extemporaneous style of preaching that avoided unnecessarily flowery language and metaphysical reasoning. Nathanael Emmons insisted that his students prepare sermons "which all could understand, which none could dislike, and which some of the best judges could admire."[53] Students like Hopkins who were already licensed to preach but continued to study under a minister found opportunities to deliver sermons in neighboring churches and occasionally were called upon to fill their teacher's pulpit.

Aspirants to the ministry from modest backgrounds found the cost of education in schools of the prophets within their means. The more fortunate candidates secured temporary teaching positions that financed the cost of their training. Ministers did not charge tuition, for the preparation of evangelical ministers was considered an obligation of their office. Moderate sums were assessed for room and board. "Have lived very happily at Dr. [Stephen] West's, and I hope received much good instruction," Thomas Robbins wrote in his diary after completing his course of study. "Parted with him at night affectionately. Board twelve weeks, sixteen dollars."[54] Robbins had earned his money teaching school, but most students paid for their education in other ways. Some tutored boys for college while they pursued their own studies. Others, such as Emmons, tutored the children of their instructor in return for room and board. Still others performed various farm tasks, which their teachers were reluctant to undertake, in place of formal charges. Thus, in return for spending a limited amount of time with his students, an instructor received additional income and relief from concern with his secular affairs. A candidate often began his study of divinity under financial hardship and finished his preparation with the hope, as Thomas Robbins expressed it, of being "able to support myself."[55] The system flourished well into the nineteenth century because it met the needs of both students and teachers.

The course of study and the teaching methods in the schools of the prophets were passed along from generation to generation. Bellamy's students began their own schools using their teacher's practices as a guide. In turn, the second generation of instructors provided models for another group of graduates who became theological teachers. Residence in schools of the prophets, then, facilitated the emergence of a group consciousness within the New Divinity movement. Students graduated with common doctrinal concerns, clerical habits, and attitudes toward the role of the ministry. They renewed friendships begun at Yale and established new relationships which persisted throughout their ministerial careers. Some students even found future spouses in the daughters of their teachers or in the sisters and other female relatives of fellow students. Consequently, the schools of the prophets were a source of in-law kinship ties, which further unified the New Divinity movement.[56]

Living together, the New Divinity men rediscovered their common social backgrounds, shared their experiences at college, and tightened the bonds that promoted their social consciousness. While attending the schools of the prophets they heard of openings in the expanding backcountry of New England. The schools themselves may have functioned as clerical placement centers where destitute churches or congregations in temporary need of a minister could make contact with a supply of eager candidates. In any case, calls for preachers came, especially from western New England, and the New Divinity men gradually filled many of the new pulpits that opened in the backwoods.

THE CALL OF WESTERN
NEW ENGLAND

IN the decades after the Awakening conservative Calvinism became entrenched in the small hamlets and villages of western New England, making the area an intellectual counterpoise to the emerging secular and liberal culture of eastern Massachusetts. Three of the New Divinity movement's most important theologians — Jonathan Edwards, Samuel Hopkins, and Stephen West — as well as a number of other, less prominent Consistent Calvinist ministers[1] held pastorates in rural Berkshire County in the decades after the Awakening. A short distance across the Massachusetts border in Bethlehem, Connecticut, another powerful New Divinity divine, Joseph Bellamy, preached Consistent Calvinism and wrote theological tracts and tomes. Throughout the eighteenth century Bellamy's Litchfield County was not only the training center for New Divinity recruits but also the numerical stronghold of the movement. In 1792, for example, there were twenty Consistent Calvinists in Litchfield pastorates, more than in any other county in Connecticut.[2] Consistent Calvinism was frequently referred to as the Litchfield or Berkshire divinity. In particular, the theological opponents of the movement preferred these labels, for the geographical identification suggested that the New Divinity was a provincial and unsophisticated school of thought.

Several factors contributed to the rise of Consistent Calvinism to a position of dominance in western New England. Litchfield and Berkshire counties were the last areas of Connecticut and Massachusetts to be settled. The northwest corner of Litchfield County, for example, was not even officially opened to settlement until 1738. During the 1740's and 1750's, the development of Litchfield and Berkshire counties was seriously hindered as the

New England frontier became a scene of conflict in the territorial struggle between the English and the French-Indian alliance. With the winding down of the French and Indian War in the early 1760's the settlement of western New England accelerated. Land-hungry settlers began to converge on Litchfield County from the Connecticut River towns to the east and from the coastal towns to the south. From Litchfield County these mobile Yankees pushed across the colony boundary line into Berkshire County, where they joined migrants from the Connecticut River towns in Massachusetts.[3] The residents of the growing backwoods settlements established churches that created new clerical opportunities.

Just at the time western New England began to grow in earnest, the New Divinity men began to graduate from Yale and search for clerical openings. The mere existence of opportunities in the backcountry did not automatically mean that ministers would be secured. In the years after the Awakening the expanding population of New England and the establishment of new churches outstripped the available supply of clergymen. Most young clerics were able to choose from among several calls to settle in the ministry. In the prevailing ecclesiastical economy, the small, remote, low-paying backcountry churches of Litchfield and Berkshire counties were in weak bargaining positions for the limited supply of clergymen. But for pious young ministers weaned from worldliness by conversion and by repeated admonitions against the danger of an unconverted ministry, western New England represented a challenging missionary field offering a suitable opportunity for self-denial.

In addition to young missionaries, another group of Consistent Calvinists settled in the western New England wilderness. Older, established New Divinity ministers who were dismissed from their pastorates as a result of local disputes, and who were therefore unacceptable to many Congregational societies, were drawn to the small, poor churches of western New England. Still, churches in Litchfield and Berkshire counties did not simply tolerate Consistent Calvinism out of necessity; many backwoods Congregationalists welcomed the conservative theology of the New Divinity men.

In 1724, for £460, three barrels of cider, and thirty quarts of rum, the Colony of Massachusetts obtained from the Housatonic Indians title to a large tract of mountainous and thickly forested land which eventually became Berkshire County. Two years later, a settling committee of the General Court granted a portion of this wilderness to a group of proprietors whose job was to promote the orderly development of the region by organizing the first township. The settlement had not advanced far beyond a frontier outpost when it was incorporated in 1733 as the town of Sheffield. Fur traders, solitary migrants from Westfield, and even entire families made their way to the town, but the lack of a road leading into the Berkshire hills and the conflict with the Dutch from New York who claimed the land impeded the development of the community. Disagreements with the Dutch were so serious that, in 1727, the settling committee prohibited further migration to the area, a position which remained in effect until 1733. Prospects for the town brightened in 1735, when authorities cut a narrow road east through the wilderness to Westfield. At the same time the inhabitants organized the First Congregational Church of Sheffield.[4]

During the 1730's settlers began to move up the Housatonic River to an area north of the town, which was known as the village of Housatonic. In 1741 these northern inhabitants of Sheffield petitioned the General Court for the right to build a meetinghouse and hire their own minister. Although the lower township objected, the Housatonic petitioners were granted parish privileges in 1742 and appointed a committee "to provide some suitable person or persons to preach the Gospel Word among us, in order for his settlement in the ministry."[5] Hopkins responded to the call of the parishioners and arrived in the village on July 2, 1743. Undoubtedly, he had prior knowledge of the physical rawness of the town as a whole and of Housatonic village in particular, so that he was not overwhelmed by what he encountered on that first day. Few roads were laid out in Housatonic, and those he did find were hardly more than wide paths winding through the wilderness. The village contained thirty families, numbering about two hundred people.[6] Many of the residents lived in small, crude log houses. No steepled, white church added a touch of dignity to the settlement; indeed, the meetinghouse which had been erected in 1742 was as roughhewn as the other buildings in Housatonic. On Sunday morning, one day after his arrival, Hopkins found himself preaching in an unpainted, barn-like structure approximately forty-five feet long and thirty-five feet wide. On the top of this frontier meetinghouse stood the frame of a steeple and belfry that the settlers had neither the money nor the desire to complete until 1745.[7]

In Hopkins's eyes the coarseness of many of the people exceeded even the physical crudeness of the town. "Took a Walk today in the Woods and as I returned went into the tavern," he recorded in his diary after preaching for several weeks. "Found a Number of Men there, who believe I had better been somewhere else. Some were disguised by drink. It appeared to be a Solemn Place. The Circumstances of this Place appear more and more doleful to me. There seems to be no Religion here." A few months later his first impressions had been confirmed. "They are a very wicked people," he admitted, "but I can't tell them of it."[8] Hostility and indifference to Hopkins stemmed in large measure from a strong Dutch faction in the village. Culturally and religiously antagonistic toward Yankees and New England Calvinism, the Dutch migrants from New York opposed Hopkins from the beginning of his ministry in Housatonic.

In spite of this opposition, Hopkins preached to the inhabitants throughout the summer and fall of 1743, occasionally leaving the village to fill another pulpit. In September, just as he turned twenty-two years old, the residents issued a call for Hopkins to settle over them. They agreed to a £60 settlement and a salary of £35 which would increase each year until it reached £45. While the salary was acceptable, Hopkins objected to the amount of the settlement, which he felt was inadequate to build a house and a barn. When the people agreed to provide logs and stones for a house, he accepted the call, and the ordination was set for December.[9]

But still Hopkins had doubts and fears about his future in Housatonic. "I feel very much discouraged about entering the work of the ministry," he wrote two weeks prior to his ordination. "They are a contentious people and I fear I am no way qualified for such a work."[10] Jonathan Hubbard, pastor of the church in the lower township, assumed the responsibility for gathering a church. In traditional Congregational ecclesiology, the church consisted of those people who had experienced conversion and who consequently enjoyed the privileges of full church membership, including participation in the Lord's Supper. The congregation, on the other hand, was comprised of worshippers who were un-regenerate and not entitled to communion or other privileges that members of the church enjoyed. Although it usually included only a small minority of the membership, the church was the corner-stone of Congregational polity. Gathering a church, that is, organ-izing a group of converted people, preceded the ordination of a minister. Thus, Hopkins was alarmed when Hubbard had dif-ficulty finding Housatonic inhabitants who were willing or able to become members of the church. Less than a week before or-dination a church had not been formed, and Hopkins himself circulated through the settlement in search of converted frontiers-men. Instead he discovered increased cause for pessimism:

> I find some people very backward, and one told me he did not like my preaching. . . . The way looks very dark before me. I am, it is most probable, going to run myself into innumerable Difficulties by settling among this people. I dare not that there is one mail [sic] Christian among them, and most of them [are] opposers to divine grace and the power of Godliness.[11]

Finally, on December 28, 1743, Hopkins was ordained in the presence of the five members of the newly formed Second Con-gregational Church of Sheffield.[12]

During the next several years his days and energy were in-vested in sustaining the religious life of the church. Nevertheless, he did find time to start a family. In 1748 he married Joanna Ingersoll, the daughter of a Housatonic resident, and shortly thereafter the first of their eight children was born.

For a fifteen-year period beginning in the mid-1740's, the hardships of frontier life and the religious indifference of many Housatonic residents combined to debilitate Hopkins's spirit, hinder the progress of his church, and unsettle his domestic life. From 1744 to 1763, England and her American colonies were in an almost constant state of war with the French and their Indian allies. The people of Housatonic, Stockbridge, and other exposed towns in western Massachusetts and Connecticut lived under the fear of attack by the enemy. This threat not only discouraged new settlers but it also frequently disrupted the daily lives of the in-habitants of western New England. Some residents turned their homes into small forts by reinforcing walls and doors with thick planking. Often alarms were sounded that sent settlers fleeing on a moment's notice to the nearest fortified house, where frightened groups of people would huddle until the threat passed. On other occasions, warnings provided enough time for settlers to retreat to the protection of a nearby fort. Sometimes the members of Hopkins's church refused to leave the fort to attend Sunday services, and he preached to them with guns at their sides and surrounded by soldiers. Occasionally worship at the meetinghouse was interrupted by news of Indian attacks a few miles away. "On the Lord's [day] P.M. as I was reading the psalm," Hopkins wrote to Joseph Bellamy in 1754, "news came that Stockbridge was beset by an army of Indians, and on fire, which broke up the assembly in an instant. All were put into utmost consternation — men, women and children crying 'What shall we do? not a gun to defend us, not a fort to flee to, and few guns and little ammunition in the place.' " Soon the retreating inhabitants of Stockbridge were in sight, and Hopkins reported that "some presently came along bloody, with news that they saw persons killed and scalped."[13] Shortly after this attack, Hopkins moved his family to the more secure town of Canaan, Connecticut.[14] Housatonic was constantly filled with soldiers who were pursuing Indians or traveling through the area to do battle with the French in Albany or Canada. Troops often lodged at Hopkins's church or stayed overnight in his home.

All of these circumstances crippled Hopkins's ministry and upset the organized religious life of the town. While real threats often prevented Sunday worship, inhabitants sometimes used the specter of Indians as an excuse for not attending church. Especially during bad weather and at harvest time, large numbers of settlers failed to attend Sunday services. Regularly during the 1750's, Hopkins preached to a less than half-filled meetinghouse.[15] As the number of worshippers declined, Hopkins's discouragement mounted. "This Day finishes eleven years since I was ordained to the Work of the ministry," he recorded in his diary on December 28, 1754; "how poorly it has been spent, God knows! [I] have had no success! [I] have reason to be greatly ashamed. . . . God only knows my misery."[16] The dire prospects that he had seen ahead of him while preaching as a candidate and at the time of his ordination had now become the daily reality of his life in Housatonic. Before his ordination he could have accepted more promising calls, and in light of conditions on the frontier in the 1740's and 1750's he certainly could have justified abandoning his church for another, more secure pastorate. But he persisted in Housatonic for twenty-five years because he saw himself as a selfless missionary to western New England.

What Hopkins and other New Divinity men had learned from the sermons and treatises of Edwards, and also from personal conversations while studying under him, was that a converted minister must not only defend the Awakening theologically but he must also personify the practical piety and self-sacrificing zeal that were among the distinguishing marks of conversion. "When there is light in a minister consisting in human learning, great speculative knowledge and the wisdom of this world," Edwards argued in *The True Excellency of a Gospel Minister*, "without warmth and ardour in his heart, and a holy zeal in his ministrations, his light is like the light of an *ignis fatuus*, and some kinds of putrefying carcasses that shine in the dark though they are of a stinking savour."[17] When in his own ministry and in his advice to ministers and congregations in ordination sermons Edwards deemphasized the importance of traditional pastoral duties and warned of the danger of secular concerns interfering with the work of the ministry, he intended to free clergymen not only for theological speculation but also for revivalism and missionary work. Edwards developed his interpretation of the role of the ministry as a corrective to what he saw as the complacency and worldliness of unconverted ministers on the one hand, and the smug Antinomianism of evangelicals on the other.[18] Self-denying zeal became a hallmark of the Edwardsian clergy. Edwards warned his followers that they were "not to expect outward ease, pleasure and plenty." As he learned at Northampton, a minister could not even "depend upon the friendship and respect of men; but should prepare to endure hardness, as one that is going forth as a soldier to war."[19]

Edwards sitting in his study composing theological dissertations provided a model for one dimension of the New Divinity ministry, and David Brainerd preaching to Indians in western Massachusetts and later in Pennsylvania and New Jersey, as tuberculosis gradually drained life from his body, supplied a model for another. The missionary's death gave Edwards an occasion to illustrate to his disciples the self-sacrificing piety that a dedication to the ministry demanded. His *Life of Brainerd* published in 1749 undoubtedly renewed Hopkins's resolve to remain in Housatonic. Brainerd's religion, Edwards maintained, "did not consist only in experiences, without practice." Nor did Brainerd's spirituality lead to "merely a practice negatively good, free from gross acts of irreligion and immorality"; rather, it promoted "a practice positively holy and Christian . . . making the services of God, and our Lord Jesus Christ, the great business of life. . . ." The lesson to be learned from Brainerd's life held special meaning for the despondent Hopkins: "And his example of laboring, praying, denying himself and enduring, with unfainting resolution and patience, and his faithful, vigilant, and prudent conduct in many other respects, . . . may afford instruction to missionaries in particular."[20]

Upon entering the ministry, Hopkins dedicated his life to the service of Christ in language that Edwards and Brainerd would have found inspiring. He renounced the world and vowed to live a life of self-denial. "It is done," he confided to his diary. "I am no more my own, but give myself away to God, to be his forever."[21] Just prior to his ordination, when nearly six months of preaching in Housatonic convinced him that nearly insurmountable obstacles lay in the path of his ministry, Hopkins expressed the commitment of a missionary: "My Courage is increased about settling here in the Work of the Ministry being willing to go where God calls me, knowing that this Life is not the place for happiness."[22] In later years he would express in theological terms the self-sacrificing, missionary piety that sustained his residence in Housatonic. His doctrine of disinterested benevolence was not the disembodied theory of a cloistered theologian, but a formal statement of a religious and psychological impulse that he exhibited from his earliest years in the ministry.

In Hopkins's view, Housatonic offered two outlets for missionary efforts. First, the New Divinity men feared that the frontier might be lost to the forces of infidelity and immorality. As Hopkins and other leaders of western Massachusetts stated in a petition to the King in 1762 to establish a college in the area, the expanding population and the growth of settlements in the backwoods aroused the concern that the inhabitants of frontier New England were "in danger of growing up barbarous and uncivilized, unless furnished with men of learning to serve 'em in a civil and religious character."[23] Drawing on New England's traditional communal perspective, which emphasized corporatism, personal restraint, and simplicity, the New Divinity men hoped to fashion the primitive settlements of western New England into model Bible commonwealths.

Western New England also provided the New Divinity men an opportunity to convert Indians. When Hopkins accepted the call to Housatonic, he surely realized the possibility of working with the nearby settlements of Indians. His uncle, Samuel of West Springfield, was a committed and well-known Indian missionary who must have encouraged his nephew's interest in the tribes of western New England. In 1755 the uncle published *An Address to the People of New England*, which called for Christian treatment of the Indians, and *Historical Memoirs Relating to the Housatonic Indians*, which detailed the history of the Stockbridge mission. From almost the beginning of his ministry in Housatonic the nephew devoted considerable time and energy to missionary activities among the Mohican Indians at Stockbridge and the Indians of the Six Nations in New York. Like most white missionaries Hopkins showed little sympathy and respect for the culture and mode of life of the Indians. He attempted to impose his own values on the subjugated natives of America. But he did recognize the economic and political exploitation of the Indians, and he fought to secure their rights and to protect them from totally insensitive white settlers and speculators.

The Stockbridge mission, seven miles from Hopkins's church, had been established in 1735 as part of a reservation for the Mohican Indians who had deeded their land to the colony. Samuel Hopkins of West Springfield was among those most responsible for the endeavor. John Sergeant, then a tutor at Yale, accepted the call to preach to the Indians and labored at Stockbridge until his death in 1749.[24] During the 1740's Samuel Hopkins of Housatonic became a frequent visitor to the mission. He often preached to the Indians when Sergeant was called away from Stockbridge. Upon the death of Sergeant, the Commissioners of Indian Affairs in Boston joined with the white and Indian residents of the settlement to invite Hopkins to become the new minister of the Stockbridge mission. "And the Indians sent a particular messenger to me," he later claimed, "to entreat me to come and be their minister."[25] Hopkins rejected the offer and recommended in his place Jonathan Edwards, who had recently been dismissed from his

Northampton church. Edwards accepted the position and ministered to the Indians until 1758, when he left to assume the presidency of Princeton. Stephen West, whom Hopkins helped convert to the New Divinity movement, then took charge of the mission until 1775.

During the forty years from the establishment of the mission to the end of West's ministry, the original intentions of the organizers of the settlement were gradually subverted and the plight of the Indians steadily worsened. Under Sergeant's plan, the Indians were to be kept as isolated as possible from the corrupting influences of white settlers while they were learning English and being converted to Christianity. Sergeant established the first of many proposed schools in which Mohican children were taught useful arts along with reading and writing. The adults erected houses, cultivated farms, and learned trades. Although the Indian population slowly expanded under Sergeant, the success of the experiment was short-lived.

The position of the Stockbridge Indians deteriorated during the French and Indian War. The French attempted to win the support of the Mohicans by warning them that, as Jonathan Edwards described it, "the English were on a design of exterminating the Indians within their reach."[26] As the Mohicans looked around them in the 1750's and 1760's they found evidence substantiating French claims. The population of Stockbridge swelled with ambitious English and Dutch settlers and fur traders. "When the white people purchased [our land] from time to time of us," the Stockbridge chiefs informed the Indian Commissioners in 1754, "they said they only wanted the low lands. . . . But now we see people living all about the hills and woods, although they have not purchased the land. When we inquire of the people who live on these lands what right they have to them, they reply to us that we are not be be regarded and that these lands belong to the King."[27] Sergeant and the Mohicans watched helplessly as Ephraim Williams (uncle of the well-known "river god," Israel Williams of Hatfield) and his relatives ignored Indian land titles, confiscated acre after acre, and invited friends and settlers from the Connecticut River towns in the east to move to Stockbridge. The Williams family had been instrumental in Edwards's dismissal from Northampton, and when the theologian came to the mission, Ephraim opposed his attempts to speak on behalf of the Indians.

After watching the activities of the clan in Stockbridge for two years, an embittered Edwards remarked that the Williamses, "by their natural disposition . . . , are sufficiently apt to engross all power, profit and honour to themselves."[28]

The Indians also suffered at the hands of British soldiers who made little distinction between peaceful and hostile tribes, viewing the Stockbridge inhabitants as uncivilized savages on a footing with the allies of the French. When the Indians protested their treatment by the Williams family and the troops, stories spread of conspiracies to massacre white settlers and of the subsequent escape of the Mohicans to Canada.[29]

Shortly after the end of the war in 1763, the mission was on the verge of failure. Once the frontier was secured, settlers began pouring into the small towns of Berkshire County. The Mohicans' lands became prey for the English and Dutch, and rum became a popular tool of exploitation. In numerous letters to the Commissioners of Indian Affairs, in Boston, Hopkins pleaded the case of the Mohicans. "The sights that are seen among them every day," he wrote to Commissioner Andrew Eliot in 1767, "are enough to make the compassionate heart of a true Christian bleed." The Stockbridge Indians were largely drunkards, Hopkins reported. "They are consistently idle, and of course poor and many almost starved, which leads them . . . [to] live on those who have something, and even to steal from them." Most of the time the Indians ravaged about for food "as the hungry wolves in the wilderness."[30]

During the 1760's Hopkins made several proposals to protect the Mohicans from the white settlers and to salvage the missionary experiment. He suggested the separation of the two races and the passage of laws which would avoid the manipulation of the Indians by the whites and "prevent their getting into debt, and alienating their lands." Justice for the Indians also required the reopening of their school and the appointment of a new teacher. Unless these reforms were begun immediately, Hopkins warned the Indian Commissioners in 1767, the mission would collapse.[31]

Hopkins and Stephen West attempted to implement the first of the proposed measures. The two New Divinity ministers sought the approval of the Commissioners in Boston and the members of West's congregation for the establishment of a separate church for the Indians. Under this plan West would continue to preach to the white settlers, and Jonathan Edwards, Jr., would become the new missionary to the Mohicans. Hopkins felt assured that Edwards would accept the call and urged the Commissioners to extend the offer as soon as possible.[32] But neither the Commissioners nor the town took immediate action on the proposal. Hopkins's concern for the Indians was not shared by most townspeople who wished, he wrote, "to have the Indians with them, that they may make tools of them to carry their points in town affairs."[33] In 1773, however, the General Court, with the support of the Commissioners, passed a bill that attempted to protect Indian landholdings by limiting both the amount of money Indians could borrow and the amount for which they could be sued by whites. Two years later the long-planned division of West's church occurred. He handed the care of the Indian members of his congregation over to John Sergeant, Jr., son of the original missionary. The younger Sergeant had studied under West for several years with the intention of assuming responsibility for the Indians when the separation took place. West continued as the minister of the whites while Sergeant revitalized the Indian school.[34]

Hopkins's interest in Indian missions was not confined to Stockbridge; it extended to the New Light missionary experiments in other parts of New England and beyond. He followed closely the progress of Indian boys studying under Bellamy in Bethlehem. He communicated with Eleazar Wheelock, seeking information on the development of Wheelock's newly established Indian school in Lebanon, Connecticut.[35] In his correspondence with Bellamy, Wheelock, and the Indian Commissioners, Hopkins stressed the need for official sanction, coordination, and financial support of the various missionary experiments. Frequently he sought young men who possessed the dedication of "disinterested missionaries."[36] Gideon Hawley was such a young man who was recruited and encouraged by Hopkins, Bellamy, and others to fulfill an important mission to the Indians.

Hawley graduated from Yale in 1749, studied briefly under Bellamy, and in 1750 traveled to Stockbridge to pursue his theological preparation under Edwards and to serve as a teacher in the Indian School. He soon became the central figure in a New Divinity plan to send missionaries to the Indians of the Six Nations in New York. After gaining experience and demonstrating his commitment in Stockbridge and in western New York, Hawley was recruited to be the first of what were to be several missionaries who would carry the gospel to the Six Nations. In 1753 Hawley journeyed to Boston, where he consulted with the Indian Commissioners and completed planning for the mission. A year later, he began his pilgrimage into the wilderness, following in the footsteps of Brainerd, Hopkins, and other disciples of Edwards.[37] He remained with the Indians for two years, occasionally returning to western New England to seek advice and information from Hopkins, Edwards, and Bellamy. As a result of the French and Indian War, Hawley was forced to abandon his mission in 1756, and the following year he accepted a call to serve the Wampanoag Indians at Mashpee, Massachusetts, on Cape Cod.

Although the war was not over, by 1760 conditions in the land of the Six Nations had improved sufficiently for Hopkins to begin efforts to reestablish the mission. In a series of letters to Hawley and the Indian Commissioners, Hopkins urged renewed support for the endeavor. "Mr. Hopkins appears to be engaged in the important affair of propagating the Gospel among the Six Nations," Hawley wrote to Commissioner Andrew Oliver in 1761, "and to have them at Heart in every letter he writes." Hopkins urged officials to recruit and train missionaries and interpreters. He advised Hawley and the Commissioners to support only an individual who was willing "to sacrifice his all in the world for the good of the Indians. . . ." Following the example of Wheelock's school, Hopkins proposed to educate young Indians in New England so that they might return to the Six Nations as missionaries and interpreters. English youngsters also would be sent to the Indians to learn the Mohawk language, and the most intelligent and pious of this group were to be provided with a college education to prepare them for missionary work among the Six Nations. Hopkins recommended John Brainerd, brother of the famous missionary, as the individual most qualified to assume responsibility for all work with the Six Nations and offered to write to Brainerd and seek his opinion on the position.[38]

By 1762 many of the lessons of the Stockbridge experiment were clear, and the success of Wheelock's school suggested new approaches to missionary work. As he studied the operation of missions in New England, received letters from West, Hawley, and Wheelock, and recalled the ideas of John Sergeant, Sr., Hopkins refined his own plan for a mission among the Six Nations in order to avoid many of the pitfalls that plagued the Stockbridge mission. The plan which Hopkins communicated to the Commissioners through Hawley in 1762 called for a boarding school "furnished with proper mothers and mistresses . . ." and a farm stocked "with all things necessary to carry it on in the best manner." All the mechanic arts would be taught, with "the boys to be schooled certain hours each day, and to work certain hours under a mother or mothers; and the girls to be taught all sorts of women's work." Except for missionaries and instructors, whites would be barred from the self-sufficient settlement. When the young Indians had been Anglicized, educated, and converted, they would assume control of the mission. This course of action, Hopkins insisted, "will tend to make them *the people*, and prevent their viewing themselves as *underlings*, despised by the English &c. which would be of very ill consequences, and even frustrate the whole design." Hopkins envisioned a series of Indian Bible commonwealths dotting the land of the Six Nations and then spreading to other Indian territories. "In this way," he concluded, "all the barbarian nations on this continent may be civilized in a century, and Christianity established among them."[39] In short, the work would be completed by the time the millennium commenced in America. Hopkins's persistence prodded official interest in missionary efforts to the Indians of the Six Nations, and his calls for "disinterested missionaries" to prepare the way for the millennium helped attract pious young men to the cause. But needless to say, the wilderness home of the Six Nations, like the vernal wood of western New England, was not transformed into a holy commonwealth.

Hopkins's missionary work on behalf of the Indians in the 1750's and 1760's demonstrates that social concern did not become a part of his ministry late in life only after he witnessed the brutalizing slave trade in Newport.[40] Early in his clerical labors he was confronted by the reality of white men exploiting people of another race. Whatever the psychological sources of his self-effacing ethics or of his often paternalistic advocacy for social outcasts, Hopkins's commitment to social justice for Indians and later for blacks was clearly influenced by the practical piety and millennial expectation stimulated by the Great Awakening.

In his autobiography Hopkins recalled that when Christian duty called him to Housatonic in 1743, he found it objectionable

to move so far from Edwards. At the time he would have preferred to settle within closer traveling distance of Northampton,
so that he would be able to enjoy Edwards's friendship and continue theological studies under him.[41] In Housatonic he felt isolated from his mentor. Hopkins's sense of separation diminished
greatly in 1750 when Edwards moved to Stockbridge. At least
once a month Hopkins made the half-hour ride on horseback to
the mission. Frequently Bellamy journeyed to Housatonic to accompany Hopkins to Stockbridge. Sometimes the theologians reversed the itinerary, with Edwards riding to Housatonic to travel
side by side with his disciple to Bethlehem.

The Stockbridge residence was the most productive period of
Edward's life. In spite of the problems between the Indians and
whites and the constant intrusion of the war, Edwards managed
to spend long hours in his study and to produce several of his
most important works. With the exception of the *Religious Affections* published in 1746, Edwards's most influential treatises belong to the Stockbridge years: *Free Will* (1754), *The Nature of
True Virtue* and *Concerning the End for Which God Created the
World* (both written in 1755 but not published until 1765), and
Original Sin (1758). In conferences with his two leading disciples
on the New England frontier, Edwards sought criticism, refined
his arguments, and further imparted his theology to his former
students.

Hopkins and Bellamy functioned as Edwards's editors. "Mr.
Bellamy came to my house last Tuesday," Hopkins noted in his
diary in 1756, "with whom I went to Stockbridge and staid there
two nights and one Day, to hear Mr. Edwards read a Treatise
upon *The last end of God in the Creation of the World*."[42] Bellamy's
students sometimes supplied the pulpits in Bethlehem, Housatonic, and Stockbridge so that the three ministers might meet to
discuss a theological work in progress. Edwards also encouraged
the novice theologians to take part in New England's doctrinal
warfare. "I have not quite finished the Remarks upon the Winter
evening, but I am grown proud of them," Hopkins informed
Bellamy in 1758, describing the progress of his first published
work. "Mentor has heard them and commended them and offered
to be the first subscriber if I would draw up proposals for printing
them."[43] It was doubtless with thoughts of such intellectual contact

that Hopkins refused the offer to settle over the Stockbridge Indians and recommended "mentor" in his place.

But a more compelling reason lay behind Hopkins's action on Edwards's behalf, which further illuminates the pattern of the New Divinity's rise to dominance in western New England. As Hopkins noted in his biography of Edwards, the professional future of the Northampton divine appeared gloomy after his dismissal in 1750, "considering how far he was advanced in years; the general disposition of people who want a minister to prefer a young man who has never been settled, to one who has been dismissed from his people; and what misrepresentations were made of his principles through the country. . . ." Approaching fifty years of age and burdened with the support of a family, Edwards began seriously to consider the uninviting prospect that his future in the ministry might be limited to filling vacant pulpits. Yet, Hopkins reported, Edwards "was not inclined or able to take any other course or go into any other business to get a living."[44] In light of these facts, Hopkins saw the Stockbridge mission as a clerical refuge for Edwards.

Under circumstances similar to Edwards's, a number of New Divinity ministers who carried the stigma of dismissal were drawn to the unattractive pulpits in western New England, joining newly licensed missionaries in the task of establishing Zions in the wilderness. The backcountry of Litchfield and Berkshire counties became a haven for conservative ministers whose theology and social shortcomings made them odious to churchgoers in more cultured and populous areas. David Perry of Harwinton, Connecticut, for example, was dismissed from his congregation in 1783 and settled a year later in Berkshire County. For the next thirty years he preached his version of Consistent Calvinism in the small town of Richmond. The ecclesiastical career of Ephraim Judson of Taunton, Massachusetts, was similar. His congregation dismissed him in 1791, and he retreated into Berkshire County. At Sheffield, Judson preached the New Divinity without further difficulty until his death in 1813.[45] The clerical career of Jonathan Edwards, Jr., also included a pastorate in western New England. After a dispute with his New Haven congregation in 1795, Edwards was dismissed from the church and accepted a call to Colebrook, Connecticut, in Litchfield County near the Massachusetts border.[46] For some dismissed New Divinity ministers the backwoods churches of western New England turned into clerical way stations. The elder Edwards, for example, was called to the presidency of Princeton from Stockbridge. Most New Divinity men, however, did not manage to overcome the stigma of dismissal, and they finished their careers in the backcountry. In either case, when many New Englanders closed their meetinghouses to New Divinity men, the residents of the backwoods, often faced with the choice of a Consistent Calvinist or no minister at all, opened their pulpits.

But more than practical necessity contributed to western New England's support of the New Divinity men. Many members of the small, isolated, agricultural congregations of Litchfield and Berkshire counties welcomed the conservative theology espoused by Edwards's followers. The New Divinity was a Connecticut movement that originated with ministers who had been raised on that colony's historically conservative Calvinism, and who had been educated at Yale, a school that institutionalized the orthodox theological perspective of "the land of steady habits." Berkshire County developed as a cultural province of Connecticut with similar conservative theological inclinations. Especially after the French and Indian War, large numbers of Connecticut migrants settled in western Massachusetts, and as a result Berkshire County became linked socially and intellectually to Connecticut. The residents of the Berkshire hills preferred ministers from back home who were trained at New Haven, rather than Massachusetts ministers who were educated at Cambridge. Of the first thirty-eight Congregational ministers ordained in Berkshire County, twenty-six were graduates of Yale.[47]

Included in the orthodoxy that settlers and ministers brought to western Massachusetts was a plan of church government unique to Connecticut. The Saybrook Platform established in 1708 provided for a semi-presbyterian or associational ecclesiastical structure. County associations comprised of all ordained ministers controlled local church affairs, such as licensing, ordaining, and dismissing ministers. The county ministerial associations were organized into a general association governing the ecclesiastical life of the entire colony.

The implementation of the Saybrook Platform enabled the New Divinity men to reinforce and to advance the strength of their movement in western New England. When residents wished to settle a minister, they followed the provisions of the Saybrook Platform and sought the advice of local clergymen. Because they were the clerical pioneers of western New England, the New Divinity men dominated the ministerial associations of the region. In western Connecticut Joseph Bellamy, who was referred to as the "Pope of Litchfield County" by reason of his seniority and reputation, controlled the local association of ministers. As pulpits opened in the area and churches sought his advice, Bellamy recommended his students who were steeped in the New Divinity. In Berkshire County the ministers were not officially organized into an association until 1763, but Hopkins, Bellamy, and Edwards served as an informal association, with considerable sway over the churches.[48] Once the small county association was established, Hopkins and even Bellamy continued to exert influence over Berkshire churches and to approve only ministers who they believed were theologically sound. When the First Church of Sheffield was attempting to settle a minister in 1767, for example, Hopkins wrote to Bellamy informing him that word began to spread "that Sheffield might not get a minister unless he was in a straight line from Great Barrington to Bethlehem. This being spread, some began to say, 'we shall never get a minister so long as Messrs. Bellamy and Hopkins are our advisers.' "[49]

In the final analysis, then, the orthodox theological outlook and ecclesiastical practices of Litchfield and Berkshire counties, the practical considerations that made the area a haven for dismissed ministers like the Edwardses, and the missionary commitment that attracted men such as Hopkins converged to win western New England to the New Divinity movement. From their backwoods retreats the Consistent Calvinists launched a theological counter-offensive against liberal and moderate Calvinists which reverberated through New England's churches and affected the social and intellectual life of the region for at least two generations.

chapter four

A "PAPER WAR"
OF THEOLOGY

FOR two decades prior to the outbreak of the American Revolution, New England ministers waged a "paper war" that,
in the words of one of the participants, "raised disputes to the
greatest height, divided towns, broke societies and churches, alienated affection among dear brethren, etc."[1] By the time the
descendants of the Puritans braced themselves for a more bloody
war with the mother country, the intellectual life of their churches
had become as fragmented and afflicted with contention as the rest
of their society. The familiar appeals for harmony and peace traditionally addressed to townspeople by the ministers of New England were now delivered by the laity to the clergy. As one critic
wrote to the *Connecticut Courant* in 1771,

> Would God that all Christ's ministers would cease
> Their paper war, follow the prince of peace,
> Forebear to wrangle with their scribbling pens,
> And show the world that Christians can be friends.[2]

The major battles of New England's paper war were the result of
a three-way struggle among Old Light Calvinists and the supporters of the new theological parties that became gradually distinct in the 1750's: the liberal Calvinists and the New Divinity
movement. The starting point of all three groups was New England's century-old doctrinal orthodoxy — the covenant theology.[3]

American Calvinists adopted the covenant scheme from Reformed theologians in Europe. There were two major interpretations of the covenant in Calvinist thought. One understanding
of the covenant, flowing out of Genevan Calvinism, held that it
was an unconditional promise: God had made a covenant or prom-

ise to save a portion of mankind, but there were no conditions attached to this promise. Man was totally dependent upon God and could do nothing to influence his salvation. Some Reformed theologians, however, saw the covenant not as an unconditional promise but as a conditional agreement or contract for salvation that made God's dealings with man more rational than the totally arbitrary determinism of Genevan Calvinism.[4] In this view, man was not completely passive in regeneration; he had some role to play — some conditions to fulfill — before God granted him saving grace.

The covenant theology of seventeenth-century New England was a synthesis of the contractual and unconditional Calvinist theological traditions.[5] As a means of grappling with the problem of spiritual regeneration, this synthesis was dependent upon a complex doctrine of preparation for salvation. Covenant theologians argued that man must prepare his heart for regeneration by using the means of grace — Bible reading, prayer, and church attendance — and by living a moral life. Although such activities did not guarantee redeeming grace, they were preconditions for God's free bestowal of it.

While New England Calvinism combined the contractual and unconditional covenant traditions, it did not exercise a monolithic orthodoxy. Puritan ministers differed in the degrees of emphasis they placed on the contractual and unconditional nature of the covenant. The contractual elements in their theology did not lead to a progressive moralization of the covenant in the course of the seventeenth century. Rather, from the late 1630's, after the rout of the Antinomians who rejected the doctrine of preparation and who upheld the covenant as a totally unconditional promise, New England Calvinism developed as a synthesis of the two covenant theological traditions.

As a result of the Great Awakening and the growth of Arminianism in the middle of the eighteenth century, the synthesis came asunder. The experimental religion of the revival stressed God's absolute sovereignty, man's spiritual inability, and the instantaneous nature of rebirth. Thus, the Awakening's New Lights placed renewed emphasis on the covenant as an unconditional promise, while Old Light opponents of the revival attempted to maintain a more traditional balance of conditional and unconditional elements in the conversion process. After the revival, liberal

Calvinists began to Arminianize conversion by stressing its conditional nature, that is, by enlarging the role of human effort. They suggested, for example, that the diligent use of the means of grace would lead directly to salvation. Such different approaches to the covenant theology were at the heart of the religious disputes that comprised New England's doctrinal paper war.

The theological structure of New England Calvinism became even more complex with the development of the New Divinity movement in the late 1750's and 1760's. The New Divinity men, like other New Lights, reasserted the view of the covenant as an unconditional promise. They formulated what they referred to as "consistent" Calvinism to distinguish it from the "conditional" Calvinism of Old Lights and liberals. But unlike other New Lights, the New Divinity men endeavored to extend, not simply to restate, the Reformed interpretation of the covenant as an unconditional promise. Samuel Hopkins's theological contributions to New England Calvinism were original and radical extensions of this Reformed tradition. First, he argued that God's sovereignty was so absolute that He did not merely permit sin, He willed it. Second, he held that regeneration was so unconditional that an awakened sinner who used the means of grace was more vile and worthless in God's eyes than an unawakened sinner who ignored these means. Finally, he developed a doctrine of disinterested benevolence, which required man to be so self-denying and submissive to God that he ought to be willing to be damned for the glory of God and the good of mankind.

When the paper war began in the late 1750's, Hopkins was an obscure country parson and the New Divinity had not developed as a distinct theological school. Within a decade, however, Hopkins formulated and publicized the first two of his novel theological interpretations, achieved recognition as the intellectual heir of Jonathan Edwards, and became the leader of a vigorous New Divinity movement. Hopkins the theologian emerged with the New Divinity. Indeed, by 1769 the two had become virtually synonymous.

After having opposed the revival, Old Light Calvinists compounded their unrighteousness in the eyes of the Edwardsians when in the 1750's they urged caution in combating Arminianism and other liberal Calvinist heresies that were winning clerical adherents in New England. An incident in the middle of the decade reveals the Old Light reluctance to purge unorthodox thought by launching a public attack on its spokesmen. In 1755 Jonathan Mayhew published a book of sermons in which he openly criticized the doctrine of the Trinity. "Christians ought not, surely, to pay any such obedience or homage to the Son," he boldly asserted, "as has a tendency to eclipse the Glory of God the Father; who is without Rival or Competitor."[6] A year later an English anti-Trinitarian tract, Thomas Emlyn's *Humble Inquiry*, was re-published in Boston. These two events deeply disturbed Jonathan Edwards, who wrote Edward Wigglesworth, Hollis Professor of Divinity at Harvard, urging him to take the lead in publicly rebuking such obvious heresy.[7] Wigglesworth responded to Edwards and urged a more circumspect course of action. While he agreed with Edwards that Mayhew's volume of sermons and Emlyn's work contained unorthodox interpretations, he felt that an open controversy was not needed to counter the objectionable doctrines. After all, Wigglesworth pointed out, ministers in Boston continued to defend the divinity of Christ from the pulpit and in the press. Under no circumstances should either of the two works be allowed to precipitate a public dispute, for, Wigglesworth warned Edwards, "If the controversy be once begun, perhaps neither I nor you, sir, who are much younger, will live to see the end of it."[8]

Wigglesworth expressed the prevailing Old Light attitude toward theological controversy. As socially secure spokesmen for the Congregational establishment who looked upon themselves as members of a highly professional elite,[9] Old Lights attempted to avoid anything that threatened to erode the authority and prestige of their calling. Public disputes over theology, like the emotional excesses of revivalists, were unbecoming to the clerical profession. Of course doctrinal disagreements would arise, but, Ezra Stiles argued in 1760 in *A Discourse on the Christian Union*, ministers were to rely upon the "gentle force of persuasion and truth not parties"[10] to resist heresy. In the Old Light view, private corre-spondence with ministers who had taken unorthodox positions, the reissuance of standard orthodox works, and the publication of new orthodox discourses would serve as theological firebreaks to pre-vent the spread of heresy. If theological disagreements persisted, Old Lights could still present a united front to the laity by refusing to acknowledge reality publicly. Thus Stiles, in the midst of the paper war in 1760, insisted that theological harmony characterized New England Congregationalism. Echoing widespread affirmations of communal harmony and consensus by embattled town leaders in the eighteenth century, Stiles denied the existence of doctrinal divisions in the clerical community. "From some considerable acquaintance with the ministers of New England, I cannot perceive any very essential difference in their opinions respecting the fundamental principles of religion," he reported. "I may be mistaken — but their different manner and phraseology in explaining the same principles appears to me to be their chief difference."[11]

In the view of the New Divinity men, the reluctance of Old Lights to engage in theological controversies and to root out Arminians merely confirmed that the moderate Calvinists were, as Hopkins put it, "moderate" or "semi-Arminians."[12] The evangelicals' stress on the covenant as an unconditional promise enabled the New Divinity men to make such an assessment. From this hyper-Calvinist perspective, many of the contractual or conditional aspects of the Old Lights' covenant theology appeared to be semi-Arminian. Indeed, the New Divinity men argued, the covenant theology of the Old Lights had established the preconditions from which fully developed Arminian heresies emerged in the middle of the eighteenth century. After discrediting their theological opponents, the New Divinity men proclaimed themselves New England's only authentic, consistent Calvinists.

The paper war began in earnest in the 1750's when New Lights in Connecticut initiated a movement to unmask full-fledged and "semi-Arminians." In 1753, for instance, President Clap of Yale instituted an "orthodoxy act," which empowered him and the college's fellows to examine, and punish if necessary, any official of Yale suspected of unorthodox views.[13] Churches began requiring ministers to sign confessions of faith, and doctrinal tests for admission were introduced into church covenants. Ministerial consociations in Connecticut carefully probed the theological positions of clerical candidates before granting licenses to preach or approving ordinations. This campaign to guard against heresy by screening ministerial candidates led to one of the first skirmishes in the paper war — the hotly contested Wallingford controversy.

In 1758 a majority of the First Church of Wallingford, Connecticut, agreed to call James Dana (Harvard, 1753) to settle over them. The church had been without a pastor since the death of Samuel Whittelsey in 1752. Dana came with the recommendation of Harvard President Edward Holyoke, but he was unable to satisfy the New Lights in the church who posed theological questions to the candidate and found his answers evasive. With strong suspicions that Dana held Arminian errors, the dissenting New Lights appealed to the New Haven Consociation, which claimed jurisdiction over the case under the terms of the Saybrook Platform. The ministers of the Consociation proposed that Dana not be ordained until they had an opportunity to question him and establish his orthodoxy. But a majority of the First Church called an ordaining council comprised of Old Lights who ignored the Consociation and ordained Dana. In turn, the New Haven and Southern Hartford Consociations joined in withdrawing official recognition of the majority and their pastor and approved the minority as the legitimate church. Dana and his supporters, although barred from future activities of the Consociation, persisted in their defiance of ecclesiastical authorities.[14]

"Nothing makes So Great a Noise in these parts as the late ordination of Mr. Dana at Wallingford,"[15] Joseph Bellamy reported shortly after the controversial minister was installed. A bitter disupute in the press ensued in which Old Lights defended the actions of the ordaining council and questioned the value of doctrinal tests and confessions of faith. The position of the Old Lights was summed up by one anonymous contributor to the public debate who claimed to be a layman: "Ministers were meant to be instruments of peace, and not to be devouring one another and engaged in name-calling."[16] Several New Lights rushed tracts into print that warned of the spread of heresy, underlined the importance of doctrinal tests for clergymen as well as for prospective church members, and upheld the actions of the Consociation.[17] In a brief pamphlet published in 1760, Joseph Bellamy spoke for the New Divinity men. Bellamy was one of the most vigorous supporters of doctrinal creeds, which he used to make the Litchfield Consociation perhaps the most orthodox in Connecticut. Strict confessions of faith were necessary, Bellamy believed, because Old Lights preaching on probation often concealed the Arminian tendencies of their theology from congregations. After ordination an Old Light might take "the greatest care to express himself so as that his secret sentiments should not be discovered." Consequently, it would be difficult for his church "to strip off his false colours, and get legal proof of his true character." Turning to the Wallingford controversy, Bellamy argued that the whole affair "might have been settled in an hour or two" if Dana had been willing to make a doctrinal confession to the church or the Consociation. If Dana's faith was sound, Bellamy asked, why was he so reluctant to make a full public statement of his theology?[18]

The debate over the ordination of Dana and the value of written creeds continued into the early 1760's; however, the focus of the paper war shifted away from ecclesiastical practices designed to halt the spread of heresy to the nature of the heresies themselves. Samuel Hopkins had not become embroiled in the Wallingford dispute, but he was to enlist in this second, theological phase of the paper war. Indeed, his theological contributions would place him at the center of the controversies.

As early as the mid-1740's, scattered Arminians in New England had attacked the traditional Calvinist interpretation of the doctrine of original sin. But disagreement over this cornerstone of Calvinism did not become widespread until 1757, when Samuel Webster (Harvard, 1737), minister of Salisbury, Massachusetts, published a work entitled *A Winter-Evening's Conversation upon the Doctrine of Original Sin*. . . . Webster rejected the idea that Adam's guilt was imputed to mankind. Man was morally responsible only for his own actions because "*Sin and guilt* . . . are *personal* matters." God was too benevolent and holy to bring men into the world naturally depraved. People who subscribed to this view, Webster argued, made God the author of sin.[19]

Public replies to a *Winter-Evening's Conversation* came from several corners of New England, encouraging liberal Calvinists in eastern Massachusetts such as Charles Chauncy to spring to Webster's defense. The numerous pamphlets that the controversy generated focused on the problem of why God created a world in which sin existed.[20] Hopkins tackled this problem in his first major work, *Sin, thro' Divine Interposition, an advantage to the Universe*, which was published in 1759.

Hopkins's volume was far from simply an abstract, polemical contribution to the theological paper war. He had delivered the sermons on sin to his Housatonic congregation two years prior to their publication. The sermons dealt with one of the critical religious problems confronting New Lights in the 1750's: How to reconcile the optimistic millennialism stimulated by the Awakening with the disheartening reality of a society that had returned to a pre-revival state in which the number of conversions was small and contention and materialism were widespread. Furthermore, the prospect of a prolonged war with the French and Indians added to the dismay of the New Lights in the 1750's.[21] As Hopkins noted in *Sin . . . an advantage to the Universe*, Calvinists in the 1750's were in danger of falling into despair, because it appeared that "Satan and wicked Men prevail, and the World lies, as it were, in Ruins, and looks no more like God's World. . . ."[22]

Hopkins endeavored to reassure Calvinists that history was proceeding according to God's plan and despair was unwarranted. In so doing, he modified the traditional Calvinist interpretation of the relationship of human sin and suffering to divine sovereignty. While emphasizing the absolute sovereignty of God, Reformed theologians had tried to avoid making the Deity the author of sin by turning to the concept of "permission." God did not cause sin; rather, as Joseph Bellamy put it in the *Wisdom of God in the Permission of Sin* published in 1758, "God's permitting sin consists merely in not hindering it."[23] Hopkins was dissatisfied with this resolution of the problem, because the concept of God's permission of sin did not convey fully enough the absolute sovereignty that He exercised over the world. Thus, Hopkins argued that God did not simply permit sin but "he willingly suffered it to take place."[24]

Why had God "willingly" brought sin into the creation? Hopkins answered with the argument that God "is willing Sin should take Place for the sake of . . . the great Good it will be the occasion of producing."[25] Reformed theologians had traditionally argued that God was able to use sin for his own purposes, some of which were intelligible to man. God permitted evil in the world, for example, as a way of showing men their natural depravity and dependence upon divine grace, thus making the work of redemption a more glorious affair than it would have been if God had not permitted sin in the world. Hopkins stretched this position to its logical limits by insisting that the world was "a *much better world*, than it would have been, had not Sin and

Misery entered into it." God was so absolutely sovereign "that all Sin which takes place among Men from the Fall of the first created pair, to the End of the World, shall some Way or other be over-ruled by God to answer some good End."[26]

Hopkins anticipated the charge that his work gave people a license to sin. Hence, he impressed upon his readers the fact that from man's perspective the nature of sin was unchanged. It was still a moral evil. It was only from the sovereign perspective of God, who "over-ruled" sin, that it became good, not in its nature but in its "*consequences.*"[27]

Therefore, Hopkins reassured evangelical Calvinists in 1759, there was no reason for a true Christian to abandon his millennial expectation, even "tho Sin abounds and threatens to bear all down before it, and every thing is to his View in the utmost Disorder and Confusion." Calvinists were not to despair but to "confide in [God's] infinite Wisdom and Goodness, and set their Hearts at rest."[28] Even the growth of heresies and the paper war were not causes for alarm. God had "willingly suffered" not only sin to enter the creation but heresy as well, Hopkins argued several years after the publication of his work on sin. Heresies and the paper war they produced were, like sin, advantages to the universe because they aroused interest in theology and stimulated a search for religious truth. In Hopkins's view God's plan called for "every important truth . . . [to] be canvassed, and disputed out, as the best way to have [it] established to the greatest advantage: And that is one end he designs to answer by suffering heresies to arise and almost every truth in its turn, to be called into question and opposed."[29]

Clerical disputes over sin continued into the early 1760's, but Arminians began to attack Calvinism at other points, carrying the paper war into new theological areas. As a result of the publication of two sermons by Jonathan Mayhew in 1761, the role of human effort in the conversion process became the new issue around which controversies swirled. In *Striving to enter in at the strait gate . . . , And the Connexion of Salvation therewith, proved from the Holy Scriptures*, Mayhew stressed the spiritual efficacy of the means of grace and thus portrayed salvation as a conditional agreement.

New England covenant theologians had traditionally encour-aged the unregenerate to use the means of grace and to prepare their hearts for the reception of God's grace. From English and Continental sources the New Englanders had adopted a complex doctrine of preparation for salvation which drew on the two theological interpretations of the covenant as an unconditional promise and as a conditional agreement. Most covenant theologians held that God's promise of salvation operated in three principal stages. First, God issued an "external" call to sinners which awakened them to their sins and turned them toward God. The "first grace," which God bestowed in the "external call," was absolutely unconditional; God called whomever he wished and a sinner could do nothing to influence his fate. However, awakened sinners were then obliged to prepare their hearts for an "effectual" or converting call by using the means of grace. While these preparatory efforts were prerequisites for converting grace, covenant theologians still protected the sovereignty of God by arguing that the fulfillment of these conditions did not obligate God to make an effectual call.[30] Sanctification completed the conversion process. After external and effectual calls, a regenerate individual led a sanctified life of spiritual exercises and holy actions.

Strict predestinarians in Europe and New England, emphasizing that man's covenant with God was an unconditional promise, had resisted both the concept of the external call and the doctrine of preparation for salvation on the grounds that they were steps in the direction of substituting a covenant of works for a covenant of grace. Man's ability could be gradually enlarged, they argued, to the point where preachers and laymen would come to believe that preparatory effort would lead directly to salvation.[31]

This was the heretical position that Mayhew seemed to take in *Striving to enter in at the Strait Gate*. "God undoubtedly strives with sinful men," Mayhew wrote, "by his word, his spirit, and the dispensations of his providence; awakening them to a sense of their guilt, misery and danger, antecedently to their striving, or doing any thing tending to their salvation. . . ."[32] Mayhew described what spokesmen for the doctrine of preparation identified as the external call, and thus his arguments were within the bounds of New England orthodoxy. But he went on to imply that anyone who answered the external call and who strove after salvation by using the means of grace would be saved. "However free the Grace of God is," Mayhew wrote, "it is manifest that he has required something of us in order to [bring about] our salvation."[33]

Mayhew's sermons did not cause an immediate controversy. While his position was implicitly Arminian, his statements were carefully worded, and their heretical implications were often obscured by his use of orthodox language. Hopkins issued the first public answer to Mayhew in 1765, four years after the publication of the sermons. He confessed that he had not seen Mayhew's work until sometime after it was published, but part of the delay in refuting it stemmed from Hopkins's expectation "that some able hand would undertake an answer."[34] When no one rose to defend orthodoxy, Hopkins accepted the task. His response to Mayhew, *An Inquiry into the Promises of the Gospel*, was crucial to the development of the New Divinity movement. The work not only dealt with all the hyper-Calvinist theological issues that the Awakening raised — the absolute sovereignty of God, the total depravity of man, his inability to influence his salvation, and the instantaneous nature of rebirth — but it also broke new theological ground and raised for the first time charges that Hopkins was preaching "new divinity."

Hopkins began his *Inquiry* by simply reasserting the strict predestinarian position on the doctrine of preparation and on the covenant as an unconditional promise. "The spirit of God in regenerating men," Hopkins wrote, "operates not as a promised gift or agent; but regeneration is affected as an unpromised favor."[35] He suggested that there was no such thing as an external call or preparation for salvation. He reduced the conversion process to two stages: regeneration (the effectual call), in which man passively received God's grace, and active conversion (sanctification), which manifested his salvation in holy exercises and actions. Striving after holiness, Hopkins argued, followed God's bestowal of "effectual" or saving grace. Salvation was so unconditional, he informed Mayhew, that there was "nothing which the unregenerate may be supposed to do, in order to obtain a new heart."[36]

Up to this point Hopkins had merely restated the essentials of strict predestinarian Reformed theology. But near the end of his *Inquiry* he made a radical extension of this tradition which aroused charges of "new divinity" and won for his theology the label Hopkinsianism. New England ministers — including strict predestinarians such as Cotton Mather who gave little value to preparatory activities — followed the Westminster Confession and the Savoy Declaration and urged sinners to use the means of grace.

The English divines who drafted the Westminster and Savoy creeds taught that although the means of grace could not bring about regeneration, "neglect of them is more sinful and displeasing to God."[37] This position was acceptable to strict predestinarians as well as to preparationists. The two groups disagreed over the spiritual importance of preparatory activities, but both agreed that the awakened sinner who used the means of grace was less odious and vile in God's sight than the unawakened sinner who did not use them. Hopkins reversed this accepted interpretation. An awakened sinner lived in a state of conviction — aware of and burdened by the guilt of his sins. In this sense, Hopkins pointed out, an awakened sinner's spiritual agonizing made him more miserable than an unawakened sinner in a state of security. But, Hopkins insisted, the awakened sinner was also more miserable than an unawakened sinner in the eyes of God, for while intellectually he was awakened to his sins, his heart continued "obstinately to reject and oppose salvation offered in the gospel." Thus an awakened but unregenerate sinner "does in some respects, yea, on the whole, become not less, but more vicious and guilty in God's sight the more instruction and knowledge he gets in attendance on the means of grace."[38]

Covenant theologians agreed that the awakened sinner did not grow in virtue or earn merits toward his salvation by using means. What he gained was an intellectual conviction of his sinfulness and an understanding of the need for redeeming grace. Yet if this knowledge did not lead to conversion, Hopkins maintained, the awakened sinner became more guilty and odious in God's eyes than the unawakened sinner who did not have the benefit of this knowledge. Indeed, Hopkins argued that the sins of an awakened but unregenerate believer were more serious than the sins such an individual committed "when he lived in security and the neglect of the means of grace," that is, in a spiritually unawakened state.[39] Finally, returning to an orthodox strict predestinarian position, he insisted that the unregenerate were still obliged to use means; for although their efforts were spiritually worthless and God's grace was unconditional, He was more likely to convert awakened than unawakened sinners.

Thus Hopkins sought merely to underline the unconditional nature of saving grace and the moral inability of natural man. He achieved his purpose but in a theologically provocative way. In

70

combining standard and new strict predestinarian arguments, Hopkins's *Inquiry into the Promises of the Gospel* virtually abandoned the Reformed theological tradition that viewed the covenant as at least partly a conditional agreement. Consequently, from several corners of New England and from the middle colonies as well inquiring voices began to question whether his "consistent" Calvinism was not in fact a "new divinity."

Hopkins's interpretation of the moral state of awakened sinners became the focal point of the paper war in the late 1760's and early 1770's. In particular, Old Lights feared that his radical depreciation of unregenerate moral ability would alienate the vast majority of Congregational worshippers who led moral lives and used the means of grace but who had not experienced conversion. When Hopkins's views began to win clerical support in the late 1760's, peace-seeking Old Lights were transformed into reluctant controversialists.

In *An Inquiry concerning the State of the Unregenerate under the Gospel*, published in 1767, Jedidiah Mills of Stratford, Connecticut, initiated the attack on Hopkins. He began by apologizing to his readers for involving himself in theological polemics and admitted his "great aversion to public debates in divinity, unless duty require [them]. . . ." Mills dismissed Hopkins's view of the awakened sinner as an absurd novelty. Repeatedly in his tract, Mills attempted to discredit his foe by raising the charge that Hopkins was advocating new divinity. "I must say," Mills wrote, "the divinity here exhibited, appears to me *strange* and new; never before advanced in the Christian world, by any divine of tolerable sense and reputation, so far as my acquaintance reacheth."[40] From 1767 on, the theological school of Hopkins, Bellamy, and their followers was known as the New Divinity.

In two works published in 1769, one of which was a direct response to Mills, Hopkins restated his interpretation of the moral state of awakened sinners.[41] At this point, William Hart of Old Saybrook, Connecticut, replaced Mills as Hopkins's major antagonist. Hart had previously debated with Bellamy the issues involved in the Dana controversy. With this experience behind him, Hart was chosen to speak for the Old Lights and to "bear a public testimony against the dangerous errors which are spreading among our churches. . . ."[42] In 1769 Hart published *A Sermon of a new kind, never preached nor ever will be; containing a Collection of Doctrines belonging to the Hopkintonian Scheme of Orthodoxy. . . .*[43] Hart added little in the way of substance of Mills's charges, but his work popularized the terms Hopkintonianism or Hopkinsianism, which became interchangeable with the epithet new divinity. By 1769, then, opponents of the New Divinity recognized the backwoods minister from Berkshire County as the theological leader of the movement.[44]

For several reasons, Hopkins achieved similar recognition within the New Divinity movement itself by the late 1760's. Before his death, Jonathan Edwards appears to have chosen Hopkins as his theological heir. On his way to Princeton in 1758, Edwards stopped at Housatonic and placed a large body of manuscripts in his disciple's hands, granting him permission, Hopkins informed Bellamy, to "take what I please."[45] After Edwards's death the same year, Sarah Edwards, following instructions her husband had given her, put all of his manuscripts and library under Hopkins's care. "And Mrs. Edwards solicited me to write the life of Mr. Edwards," Hopkins reported in his autobiography, "to be published with a number of sermons, to be selected from his manuscripts."[46] During the 1760's, with the help of his brother Daniel, Joseph Bellamy, and New Divinity minister John Searle, Hopkins edited several of Edwards's works, and he published his biography of the famous divine in 1765.[47] As a result of his close friendship with Edwards, his unsurpassed knowledge of the theologian's writings, his editorial labors, and his own publications in the 1760's, Hopkins won the respect and leadership of the New Divinity men. This recognition was confirmed in 1767 when the Consistent Calvinists at Princeton attempted to continue the Edwardsian tradition at the college by securing Hopkins's appointment as professor of theology.

Close ties between the New Side Presbyterians (as opposed to the Old Side, anti-revival Presbyterians) in the Synods of New York and New Jersey and the Edwardsians of New England had existed since the Awakening. Edwards, Hopkins, and Bellamy frequently corresponded with Samuel Buell, Samuel Davies, and other prominent New Side clergymen. Evangelical New Englanders often sent their sons to Princeton, and sons of Presbyterians in the middle colonies frequently enrolled at Yale. In the decades after the Awakening, New England ministers and ideas dominated the New Side party, culminating in the appointment of Edwards as president of Princeton.[48] In 1767, the Edwardsian trustees united with Jonathan Edwards, Jr., then a tutor at the college, in an effort to bring Hopkins to the Princeton faculty. The younger Edwards was a particularly loyal supporter of Hopkins, having spent nearly a year reading theology and studying his father's manuscripts at Housatonic. He agreed to journey to Hopkins's parsonage and personally ask the theologian to accept the position. Other Princeton New Divinity men wrote to Joseph Bellamy requesting that he use his influence to persuade his friend to come to Princeton.[49] But the plan was thwarted when the Scotch-Irish faction at Princeton succeeded in appointing one of their own ministers to the professorship. Nevertheless, the efforts of the Edwardsian forces on Hopkins's behalf demonstrated that he wore the New Divinity's mantle of leadership.

The New Divinity movement grew significantly in the 1760's. By 1767 it had a name and a clear theological identity. Moreover, beginning in the 1760's and continuing up to the eve of American independence, the New Divinity movement attracted a large proportion of the Yale graduates who entered the Congregational ministry. A considerably smaller but still significant number of Princeton graduates during these years also became New Divinity ministers.[50] It was the growing clerical popularity of the movement and not simply its doctrinal novelties that alarmed Old Lights in the 1760's. In one of his pamphlets attacking "Hopkinsianism," William Hart admitted that if only Hopkins espoused the doctrines expressed in his works on the unregenerate, "I would not trouble myself with any attention to them; but as they are embraced and taught by too many, I will a little remark upon them." He felt that Hopkinsianism was "breaking in upon us as a flood. . . ."[51]

Old Side and moderate evangelical Presbyterians took more drastic measures than Old Light Calvinists in New England to prevent the spread of the New Divinity. In 1767 one Presbyterian supporter of Hopkins wrote to Bellamy with information suggesting a campaign against the New Divinity was imminent: "We begin to be suspected of refining too far, and of sifting that thing called Metaphysics or Common sense, which is so awful to the schemes, or rather no schemes, of so many moderns."[52] At Princeton, newly appointed President John Witherspoon initiated a drive in 1768 to rid the school of Consistent Calvinism. The administration attempted to shield students from the novel doctrines by suppressing the books of New Divinity men. Consistent Calvinist sympathizers secretly read the works of Hopkins and Bellamy and then cut out title pages in order to circulate the books among other undergraduates.[53] Disgusted with the actions of the Princeton authorities, Jonathan Edwards, Jr., and Joseph Periam, two New Divinity tutors, left the college shortly after Witherspoon's installation as president. A few years later when Periam applied to the Synod of New York for a license to preach, he was refused on the grounds that he maintained that God was the author of sin. The New Divinity Presbyterian minister who had recommended Periam to the Presbytery was then charged with heresy.[54] Other Consistent Calvinists found themselves in similar positions in the decade preceding the American Revolution.

In spite of such organized opposition, the New Divinity movement continued to grow until the outbreak of the Revolutionary war disrupted the lives and engaged the passions of New Englanders. "The New Divinity, so prevalent in Connecticut will undo the Colony," Charles Chauncy complained to Ezra Stiles in 1771. " 'Tis a Scandal to Yale College, and those who have the government of it, that they retain there and teach their students, the very quintessence of pagan fatality with all its genuine consequences."[55] Moderates and liberals were at a loss to understand the appeal of Consistent Calvinism to the younger generation of clerics and ministerial candidates. In many respects, the New Divinity was the intellectual vogue of the 1760's and '70's which attracted the metaphysically inclined because it demanded rigorous logical consistency.[56] Hopkins implied as much in 1765 when he referred to the typical "Unhappy . . . young student of divinity" who was usually advised by established ministers "against meddling with metaphysical subjects, and dark, abstruse matters. . . ."[57] Still, the New Divinity was much more than simply a theological vogue; it was also a protest movement with particular appeal to young, pietistic ministers. The New Divinity men were sharply critical of the established ministry, of the development of Puritan theology, and also, as we shall see, of the evolution of New England society.[58]

Consistent Calvinism was not a fleeting post-Awakening theological fad that burned itself out with dry, metaphysical tinder. From its substantial beginnings in the decade or so before American independence, the New Divinity would develop into a major, and in some respects dominating, movement within New England Congregationalism. But for a brief period in the late 1760's liberal and moderate Calvinists found just cause for confidence that the movement was short-lived. In 1769 Samuel Hopkins, the theological successor of Edwards, the redoubtable leader of the Consistent Calvinists, was dismissed by his Housatonic congregation. Hopkinsianism had become so rarefied and out of touch with reality, the story went, even backcountry farmers could no longer tolerate it.

chapter five

THE NEW DIVINITY AND
THE CHURCHES

THE development of doctrinal parties with opposing approaches to covenant theology in the middle of the eighteenth century animated the intellectual life of New England's churches. Not since the first decade of New England history was theology debated with such zeal. Not since the Antinomian crisis of the 1630's were charges of heresy so prevalent nor the boundaries of New England Calvinism so sharply disputed. Not since the first generation of Puritans experienced the shift from dissenting sect to established church, symbolized by the Half-way Covenant, was the ecclesiastical structure of Congregationalism so altered. Now the strife-ridden established church assumed a pluralistic cast as theological parties made a mockery of New England's communal socio-religious ideals. While the old causes of church disputes — salary problems, ecclesiastical practices, and clerical incompetence — remained, theology emerged as a critical issue in quarrels between ministers and congregations with a degree of fervor that had not been experienced in over a hundred years. The doctrinal creeds and confessions of faith instituted in the 1750's precipitated numerous ecclesiastical controversies, some of which were similar to the Wallingford affair.

Furthermore, when the New Divinity men developed a position on church polity from their theology in the 1750's, the seventeenth-century debate over the Half-way Covenant was revived. Just as New Divinity theology maintained a sharp distinction between saints and sinners, refusing to recognize the moral worth of an intermediate, awakened sinners category, so too New Divinity ecclesiology rejected the idea of a middle way in church membership. In Hopkins's view, the spiritual condition of so-called Half-way members and of awakened sinners was comparable; both groups were composed of the worst kind of hypocrites — individuals who took steps toward God but whose hearts continued to resist saving grace.

The theology and ecclesiastical practices of the New Divinity men embroiled them in church disputes. Very few of the congregations who dismissed their New Divinity pastors, however, were in western New England. Samuel Hopkins's departure from Great Barrington in 1769 was one of the rare instances when backcountry Congregationalists turned a Consistent Calvinist out of a pulpit. Old Light and liberal Calvinists persisted in believing that, as Charles Chauncy put it to a credulous Ezra Stiles in 1769, Hopkins "preached away almost his whole congregation at [Great] Barrington . . . ."[1] While his theology and rejection of the Halfway Covenant contributed to his dispute with his parishioners, Hopkins's dismissal after twenty-five years of service did not represent a repudiation of the New Divinity by his church.

The dynamic growth of Berkshire County did not take place until after the end of the French and Indian War in 1763. Still, in the two decades between the granting of parish privileges to the residents of Housatonic in 1742 and the incorporation of the settlement as Great Barrington in 1761, the town grew significantly, shedding much of its unwrought appearance and moving beyond the rudimentary stage of a frontier society. The population of the settlement jumped two-and-a-half times between 1743 and 1761, largely as a result of new settlers from older towns in Connecticut and Massachusetts as well as from New York. Roads were laid out, new homes were erected, and the services of a doctor and lawyer were available.[2] Hopkins's church shared in the growth of the town. The meeting house, which was only partially constructed during the first years of Hopkins's ministry, was completed in 1748. Moreover, from time to time in the 1740's and 1750's small numbers of worshippers joined the church, and on occasion, when the war was off in the distance, Hopkins reported that he preached to "a pretty full Congregation."[3]

The theological content of Hopkins's sermons did not emerge as a divisive issue in his church until the late 1750's when he began to formulate the New Divinity. In 1757 and 1758 Hopkins preached three sermons on sin which formed the basis of his controversial work *Sin . . . an advantage to the Universe*. Hopkins's line of argument did not arouse widespread opposition in the church, but it did outrage one member — Israel Dewey, a recently settled migrant from Westfield. Dewey met privately with Hopkins and challenged the theologian's explanation of God's purposes in bringing sin into the creation. The pastor and his parishioner continued their debate in correspondence, and in 1759 Dewey published a work titled *Letters to the Reverend Samuel Hopkins . . .* . Dewey charged that Hopkins's interpretation of sin as a means for good was "pregnant with a train of the most deformed Monsters that ever were born in the Kingdom of Irreligion." Dewey informed Hopkins that he felt it his "Duty and Interest, to oppose you, so long as you oppose the Truth. . . ." He went on to issue a stern challenge to the theologian: "But if I live, and you don't dismiss your Principles, you may rationally expect I shall oppose you; and endeavour your Dismission, unless I can learn the Knack of believing Contradictions. . . ."[4]

Public knowledge of this heated theological controversy led opponents of the New Divinity to conclude that Hopkins had gradually "preached away" his congregation in the 1750's and 1760's, culminating in his dismissal in 1769.[5] Undoubtedly Dewey had support in the town and church, particularly among members of the Dutch faction, which had opposed Hopkins from the beginning of his ministry; but Dewey made little progress toward securing Hopkins's dismissal. Perhaps in frustration, Dewey carried his opposition to extremes in 1758 when he interrupted Hopkins's Sunday sermon. As a result the church decided that Dewey "should be dealt with for disorderly behavior in time of preaching."[6] On the larger issue of Hopkins's theology, which was the basis for Dewey's outburst, a clear majority of the church sided with their pastor. When Dewey admitted the impropriety of his behavior in order to avoid public censure, the church hesitated to pardon him and endorsed Hopkins's New Divinity: "But whereas he [Dewey] has declared before the brethren of the Church, that it was an article in his belief *that it was not upon the whole best that sin should take place in the world*, and had in unjustifiable ways opposed the Doctrine of God's decrees, the Church voted to defer this [pardon] to further Consideration." Finally, the church agreed not to censure Dewey "but only to publically admonish him before all the brethren, to be more modest and earnestly seek further light as we look upon him . . . [as] ignorant and much out of the way."[7] Neither in the Dewey controversy nor in more serious challenges to Hopkins in the 1760's was theological opposition alone strong enough to bring about his dismissal.

The abandonment of the Half-way Covenant proved to be a more divisive issue among Hopkins's parishioners than his theology. Instituted in 1662, the Half-way Covenant had become a widely accepted custom in New England by the eighteenth century. The Half-way Covenant not only extended baptism to the children of the regenerate; more importantly, it provided that upon reaching parenthood baptized but still unconverted worshippers could offer their own children for half-way membership. The Half-way Covenant began as an accommodation of the Puritans' pure church ideal to social reality. It was a clerical proposal designed initially to create a new sense of religious community by including in the church the large number of outwardly moral but unregenerate New Englanders. Within a short while, however, the Half-way Covenant became part of a movement which has recently been called a "renaissance of sacramental piety." Confronted with a growing body of unregenerate half-way members in the late seventeenth and early eighteenth centuries, some ministers began to stress the role of baptism in conversion. They came to see this sacrament as an important means of grace, and they urged half-way members to strive after holiness and to fulfill the promise of salvation that baptism offered. Edwards's grandfather, the famous Solomon Stoddard, took this sacramentalism one step further; he held that the Lord's Supper was also a means of grace, and therefore it was not to be restricted to the regenerate.[8]

The Half-way Covenant, open communion, and sacramentalism came under attack during the Great Awakening. Revivalists reasserted the pure church ideal which recognized only one category of membership — full sainthood. Moreover, the New Lights' stress on the instantaneous nature of rebirth and on man's inability to influence regeneration encouraged a depreciation of all means of grace, including the sacraments. In short, the revival stimulated a reformation of church polity in New England.

Among the issues that led to Jonathan Edwards's dismissal from Northampton were his rejection of the Half-way Covenant and the open communion practices of Solomon Stoddard. In two works published in 1749 and 1750, Edwards defended his position and laid the foundation for the New Divinity movement's opposition to the Half-way Covenant in the 1750's and 1760's. In the first place, Edwards argued, sacraments were not converting ordinances but seals or privileges of the covenant open only to the regenerate. Simply living a scandal-free life did not entitle one to receive communion or to present one's child for baptism.[9] Second, Edwards maintained, God recognized only one visible church comprised of the regenerate. Advocates of the Half-way Covenant and the open church concept (the idea that everyone — whether regenerate or unregenerate — who lived a moral life belonged to the church) were wrong in viewing the church as composed of two distinct groups of internal and external covenanters: "One company consisting of those who are *visibly gracious* Christians, and *open professors of godliness*; another consisting of those who are visibly *moral livers*, and only profess common virtues, without pretending to any spiritual experience in their hearts."[10] Third, since there was only one church and regeneration was the entrance requirement, Edwards insisted that an individual needed to make a profession of faith that he had received redeeming grace before he could be admitted to the church and be allowed to participate in the Lord's Supper or have his child baptized. But Edwards tempered his position by urging ministers and churches to exercise caution and restraint when judging professions of faith. Since only God knew for certain who the saints were, any attempt by man to establish totally pure churches free of hypocrites was misguided. Professions of conversion should be taken on good faith, Edwards recommended, because the experience of saving grace "cannot be certainly known by any but the subject himself." Edwards dismissed as enthusiasm the efforts of the Separate Congregationalists to form absolutely pure churches by relying on a "discerning light" which permitted one saint to recognize another.[11]

Hopkins and Bellamy adopted their teacher's views, implemented the Edwardsian plan of church polity in Housatonic and Bethlehem, and defended their ecclesiastical practices against critics. In the early 1750's Bellamy became the first non-Separating Congregationalist minister in Connecticut to renounce the Halfway Covenant. Many of his theological students followed his example, so that by the late 1760's, after the New Divinity movement had gained a significant number of clerical recruits, the Edwardsian approach to church polity became a controversial issue in New England and initiated yet another phase of the paper war. In a series of dialogues published in 1769 and 1770, Bellamy defended, elaborated on, and popularized the Edwardsian position. He was disturbed by the increasing number of worshippers in New England who joined the church under the Half-way Covenant but who failed to follow infant baptism with adult conversion. Too many New Englanders remained content with the membership status that Bellamy's dialoguing parishioner sought: "I knew myself to be unconverted. I meant to own the covenant, as the phrase is, and have my children baptized; but I had no design to profess godliness, or to pretend a real compliance with the covenant of grace."[12] The practical effect of offering baptism and communion to such hypocrites, Bellamy stressed, was to discourage rather than to encourage conversions. Consequently, what Christ intended to be sealing ordinances of regeneration were in fact undermining the covenant of grace. Revivals and experimental religion would not prosper, Bellamy suggested, until churches abandoned both the Half-way Covenant and open communion.[13]

Not only evangelical Christianity but pristine Puritan tradition demanded the repudiation of these practices. If one searched the earliest history of New England, Bellamy argued, no evidence of a Half-way Covenant or of open communion could be found. Both practices were of relatively recent origin, not part of Puritan tradition, and certainly not sanctioned by Scripture. Finally, while insisting on a profession of faith as a prerequisite for church membership, and thus for participation in the sacraments, Bellamy followed Edwards in urging ministers and churches to exercise "a judgement of charity, regulated by the word of God" when listening to declarations of conversion by candidates seeking admission.[14]

The New Divinity movement's ecclesiology became as controversial as its theology. Hopkins reported to Bellamy from Boston in May 1769 that the ministers in eastern Massachusetts were disturbed by the reopening of the old dispute over the Half-way Covenant: "[they] are sorely displeased that you have set it agoing in Connecticut."[15] Two months later a former student of Bellamy's informed him that his first *Dialogue on the Half-way Covenant* had aroused "a general alarm [in Boston], for fear the churches will be ruined."[16] Some New Divinity men became entangled in bitter disputes with church members who resisted, sometimes successfully, the abandonment of the Half-way Covenant. Other Consistent Calvinists, such as Bellamy, had little difficulty instituting an Edwardsian polity in their churches. Still others, like Hopkins, were able to implement the new ecclesiastical plan but only at the cost of alienating factions in their parishes.

Hopkins discarded the Half-way Covenant shortly after Edwards began to reevaluate the Stoddardean polity of his Northampton church in the mid-1740's. As early as 1752, in a letter defending his position written to a supporter of the Half-way Covenant, Hopkins reported that "There are a considerable number of Parents within the Bounds of my parish whose children are not baptized, the most of whom would I suppose gladly get their children baptized if they might have it done on such [Half-way Covenant] terms."[17] He employed standard Edwardsian arguments to justify his refusal to baptize these children, but he also added a point of his own. Simply living a moral life did not entitle one to the sacraments. Practitioners of the Half-way Covenant were misled when they talked about unscandalous people. No matter how moral their lives, all unregenerate people were scandalous. In fact, as Hopkins pointed out in an argument similar to his view of the moral state of the awakened sinner, if a person led a moral life but continued to oppose regeneration in his heart, he was "wholly more scandalous and wicked than an open Drunkard" or a whore.[18] How then could the sacraments be offered to such a person?

Not all of Hopkins's parishioners accepted his ecclesiastical views and practices. But although the abandonment of the Half-way Covenant was a more controversial issue than Hopkins's theology, no open rift occurred in the church in the 1750's. Opposition to Hopkins's theology and ecclesiology was centered in the Dutch faction in Housatonic. This conflict was more ethnic than theological or ecclesiastical. Culturally unsympathetic to Yankee Puritanism, the Dutch petitioned around 1759 to have the meeting house opened to a Reformed minister who spoke their own language. When this request was denied, some of the Dutch residents stopped attending Hopkins's services. These protesters were in defiance of colonial law which compelled church attendance. Consequently, Sheffield authorities (Housatonic was still only a parish in that town and came under its jurisdiction in civil matters) ordered the lawbreakers to travel into town where they were placed in the public stocks and forced to suffer public ridicule.[19] In the punishment of the Dutch and in the earlier Israel Dewey dispute, the town and the church clearly demonstrated their support of Hopkins. Indeed, shortly after these controversies the parishioners voted him salary raises in two successive years.[20] Still, on several counts Hopkins had made enemies in Housatonic. In the 1760's the anti-Hopkins factions united and ultimately succeeded in bringing about his dismissal.

Hopkins's troubles began when Housatonic was incorporated as Great Barrington in 1761. Up until this date the residents of the village simply had parish privileges — that is, they could use their portion of the ministerial taxes of Sheffield to support their own minister. The church was charged with the responsibility of fixing and collecting Hopkins's salary, there being no town meeting or independent civil authority in Housatonic because the parish was under the jurisdiction of Sheffield.[21] After incorporation of the parish, the Great Barrington town meeting controlled the amount of Hopkins's salary as well as its collection. Incorporation enhanced the political power of Hopkins's opponents. While Housatonic merely had parish status, Hopkins's foes were a distinct minority in Sheffield town affairs. Once a separate and a smaller town meeting was established in Great Barrington, however, the members of the anti-Hopkins faction were in a much stronger political position, especially after they drew new recruits from the Dutch and English settlers who arrived in the 1760's.

Hopkins continued to have the strong support of the full church members who numbered upwards of one hundred in 1761.[22] It was in the town meeting, which included both church members and non-members, that opposition to Hopkins surfaced. Gradually, beginning in 1761, his enemies withdrew financial support of him. Each year the town meeting voted Hopkins a salary, but his opponents delayed or refused to pay their portion of the ministerial taxes and authorities were lax in enforcing collection. By the middle of 1762, Hopkins's salary for the previous year had still not been paid in full. Deeply discouraged, Hopkins addressed a letter to the members of his church reaffirming his dedication to them but realistically evaluating his circumstances in the town. He informed the church that he doubted the townspeople would "afford me a sufficient maintenance, so as to put me under proper advantage to give myself wholly to the work of the ministry among you; but that most had rather part with me, than comply with this."[23] Since he had a large family to support and since he had been offered the pastorate of the church in Halifax, Nova Scotia, he wished to settle the question of his future in Great Barrington immediately. Therefore, he sent a letter to the selectmen asking that a town meeting be called to deal with the inhabitants' attitude toward him in general and the problem of his financial support in particular.[24]

Anticipating the results of the town meeting, Hopkins began to make preparations to move with his large family to Halifax. But he had to alter his plans when his supporters appeared to carry the town meeting held on June 4, 1762. The voters approved a resolution stating "That the Rev'd Samuel Hopkins is so acceptable to the Inhabitants of this town in the work of ministry that they are willing to receive him in that capacity still and afford him a reasonable and competent maintenance."[25] The townspeople agreed to raise his salary to £80 as compensation for existing arrears.

This victory was short-lived, however, for in 1762 a group of English and Dutch settlers organized an Anglican Church in Great Barrington which siphoned financial support away from Hopkins and the Congregational Church. From time to time the Society for the Propagation of the Gospel sent missionaries to Great Barrington, and on other occasions an Anglican clergyman from Litchfield County preached to Hopkins's opponents, administered communion, and baptized the children that Hopkins refused to accept on half-way terms.[26] The Society for the Propagation of the Gospel bore much of the financial burden for these services, and undoubtedly Hopkins was right when he claimed that "a number [of townspeople] turned churchmen, apparently and some professedly, to get rid of paying anything for the support of the gospel."[27]

But most Anglican worshippers resisted paying ministerial taxes because they were in fact contributing to the construction of their own house of worship. By the end of 1764, the edifice was completed. "I have visited Great Barrington and the parts adjacent in October last," the Anglican clergyman serving the residents reported to the S.P.G. in December 1764, "and shall, if God permits, set out directly for that place, in order to open a very elegant and large church which those people have erected at great expense and whilst laboring under the severest ill treatment from their brethren dissenters."[28] At the same time that their church was completed, the Anglican worshippers requested and received from town authorities the right to apply any ministerial taxes they paid to the support of their own minister.[29]

As the Anglican church progressed Hopkins's fortunes waned. Not once in the 1760's was his yearly salary paid in full. Instead, each year Hopkins added a new arrearage to what was already owed him, and he struggled to provide for his large family. To no avail, members of Hopkins's church raised their voices at town meetings, protesting the authorities' disregard for the maintenance of their minister. Only voluntary contributions by New Divinity supporters outside of Great Barrington who were aware of his plight eased Hopkins's financial hardship and enabled him to remain in the town as long as he did.[30]

Hopkins's New Divinity was not solely, or even primarily, to blame for his deteriorating circumstances in Great Barrington. Certainly his theology and more importantly his ecclesiastical policies alienated some townspeople. But his more serious problems with the Dutch were cultural and would have been difficult for any Congregational minister to resolve. Furthermore, conflict with taxpayers over church finances was a common problem for the Congregational clergy in the eighteenth century. It was an important reason why the ministry became increasingly less attractive to college students from upper-class backgrounds.[31] Small, poor towns often resisted raising ministers' salaries, with the result that the clergy were unable to keep up with inflation in the eighteenth century. It was also not uncommon for parishioners to fall into arrears when it came time to pay yearly ministerial taxes. Sometimes ministers were forced to sue towns for back pay.[32]

The financial plight of the clergy worsened with the growth of new settlements with parish privileges in the eighteenth century. As people in outlying districts won the right to hire their own preacher and apply their ministerial taxes to his support, the inhabitants in the center of a town had to bear a greater financial burden to maintain their minister. Fewer worshippers meant higher church taxes. Then, too, the spread of Anglican and Baptist churches drained the religious tax pool even further. Thus, in the middle of the eighteenth century a minister voiced a familiar complaint about "the unhappy times we are fallen into in the Ingratitude of most of the people of the Country to their Ministers, very few besides the Boston ministers being able to Support themselves with what they Receive from their People."[33] Similarly, at the height of his troubles Hopkins wrote to Bellamy asking plaintively, "Where is there a clergyman that is well maintained? Where then is there a congregation that will maintain me?"[34]

Under these circumstances, many clergymen sought secular supplements to their salaries. Some ministers were little more than acquisitive Yankees dressed in clerical garb, while others turned to land speculation, farming, and tutoring in order to support growing families. The development of these two groups of secular-minded clerics profoundly influenced New Divinity attitudes toward the ministry. Secular involvement came to be seen as one of the chief shortcomings, and one of the distinguishing signs, of unconverted ministers. Edwards advised his followers that they were not to fall into the pattern of the unregenerate clergy: "Ministers should be diligent in their studies, and in the work of the ministry . . . , giving themselves wholly to it; taking heed to themselves that their hearts be not engaged, and their minds swallowed up, and their time consumed, in pursuits after the profits and vain glory of the world."[35] When Edwards preached at the ordination of one of his followers, he usually exhorted the church members to free their minister "from worldly cares, and the pressure of outward wants and difficulties, to give himself wholly to his work. . . ." He warned the laity not to repeat the error of so many churches — subverting the work of the clergy by "necessitating your minister by your penuriousness towards him to be involved in worldly cares. . . ."[36] Thus when Hopkins's supporters proposed that their minister expand his farming beyond his parsonage lots in order to offset losses of salary, the loyal disciple of Edwards rejected the suggestion.

Even if Hopkins had been willing to cultivate more land to support his family, it would have been difficult for him to continue preaching, for by 1766 his foes openly admitted their determination to drive him from the pulpit. At this time another issue was added to the complex accumulation of grievances that Hopkins's opponents held against him. When political disputes with England broke out in the mid-1760's, Hopkins emerged as a vocal supporter of the rights of the colonists and further alienated the Anglican faction in the town. Hopkins became a pawn in an ensuing political struggle with people he identified as Tories. "Town affairs engross the thoughts of many," Hopkins notified Bellamy on March 16, 1766. "The battle is to come next Monday, they say. If the Tories get the victory, which they are zealous to do, the town will be in ruins, and I must soon leave preaching here, it is probable."[37] The annual March meeting for the election of town officers was declared illegal on a technicality, and the inhabitants were not called together again until July. When the business of the crucial meeting was concluded, Hopkins knew the end of his ministry at Great Barrington was at hand. On July 26, 1766, he informed Bellamy of the results:

> Last week we had a town meeting which lasted three days. The spirits of each party were raised to a very high degree. In the issue, the Tories carried the day, and have got all town affairs in their hands, just as they had before; with this aggravation, that now they have a vastly higher degree of resentment against me and the party that adheres to me, than before. They say they will uphold a great part of my salary, if not all, and it appears they intend to get me out of town. Query: Since my salary seems to be the great bone of contention, the strife at bottom being about money, (Who shall have the government of the money voted for preaching, or in a word, whether the Dutch, &c. shall pay any part of my salary?) had I not better give my salary up and if those who adhere to me will not maintain me by subscription, either leave them or preach *gratis*?[38]

From 1766 until his dismissal in 1769, Hopkins received only negligible amounts of money from the townspeople. By 1768 he claimed he was owed over £138 in back salary.[39]

Still, the members of the First Congregational Church would not allow Hopkins to leave his pulpit. In 1767, for example, he requested that his supporters call an ecclesiastical council to review his situation and make a recommendation to the church. Technically a council, like a Consociation, could only convene, gather the facts, and issue a recommendation on which the church then voted. But Hopkins wanted the church to accept the council's decision as determinative. Furthermore, the council itself would be dominated by Bellamy, West, and other local ministers who were personal friends and theological allies of Hopkins. In short, Hopkins was attempting to ensure his own dismissal. Understandably, the church at first balked at the arrangement and refused to call a council. Given the divisions in the town, they argued, if Hopkins departed it would be almost impossible to persuade another minister to fill the vacant pulpit.[40]

By the end of 1768, however, Hopkins's predicament had apparently aroused enough sympathy among the members of the church that they agreed to call the ecclesiastical council. In January 1769 the clerical and lay representatives of several neighboring churches convened at Great Barrington and after hearing the testimony of Hopkins and the members of the church came to a speedy conclusion: "It appears that they [the townspeople] have neither paid him his salary according to Covenant nor attended his public ministry according to Divine institution, but have been greatly Deficient in both respects, which by this in our opinion [they have] forefeited all further claims on him as their Minister in point of Justice, especially as no objection against Mr. Hopkins, his doctrines or practice is made by any."[41] In short order, Hopkins's twenty-five year pastorate of the church was terminated. When the council concluded its business the church unanimously voted "hearty thanks to Mr. Hopkins for this faithful service in years past and wishing the Divine Blessing may always attend him, thro life and asking a remembrance in his prayers till death."[42]

Hopkins had not come to the Massachusetts frontier twenty-five years earlier brimming with optimism — a twenty-two year old minister setting out to convert the world. Rather, he had arrived in Housatonic as a sober, even dour, Puritan who believed that "this life is not the place for happiness."[43] His experience in Great Barrington — the rude introduction to frontier life, the hardships of the French and Indian War, the abortive attempts to protect and convert the Indians, and the contention and impoverishment leading up to his dismissal — all reinforced the stern perspective that Hopkins had brought with him in 1743. Yet the sense of personal pessimism which was the distinctive feature of his temperament, and which was a key element in his theology, did not lead to passive acceptance of the world, or to social despair. Suffering and self-denial were redemptive; they were essential elements of disinterested service in the cause of Christ. Indeed, just as his theology was characterized by paradoxical doctrines, so too his life and ministry were distinguished by the paradox that only outward suffering appeared to bring him inner peace. Enduring pain either as the result of radical self-denial (Saturdays were a total fast day for Hopkins) or from championing an unpopular cause (such as the opposition to the Half-way Covenant or more significantly his antislavery stance in Newport, a center of the slave trade) seemed to bring him psychological security and spiritual happiness by giving him confidence in the disinterestedness of his motives. Furthermore, as he reassured Christians in *Sin . . . an advantage to the Universe*, personal suffering and unhappiness were not cause for *social* pessimism; God, in all His sovereignty, turned individual unhappiness and suffering to His advantage to promote the establishment of His kingdom in the world. Thus Hopkins's theology shielded him from social despair. His personal defeat was not translated into a setback for the kingdom of God.

Before leaving Great Barrington Hopkins initiated a suit against the town for back salary. In 1771 the inhabitants were ordered to pay their former minister £145 in arrearages.[44] Three years later, when Revolutionary mobs were roaming the Litchfield County countryside attacking British sympathizers and symbols, a group of Connecticut patriots crossed into Massachusetts with their sights set on Hopkins's Anglican opponents in Great Barrington. "Their wrath fell chiefly upon the Rev. Mr. Bostwick and David Ingersoll, Esq.," Rev. Samuel Peters reported. "The former was lashed with his back to a tree and almost killed. . . ." The mob then destroyed Ingersoll's house, stole his possessions, and "brought him almost naked into Connecticut upon the back of a horse." And this special hatred of the Anglicans in Great Barrington, Peters noted, was fueled by memories of their opposition to Hopkins and his Congregational supporters in the 1760's.[45]

The history of the Congregational Church in Great Barrington after Hopkins's dismissal confirmed the fears of those who had been reluctant to call an ecclesiastical council in the late 1760's. The Church did not obtain a successor to Hopkins until 1787, and this minister remained in the town only until 1790. The church was again without the services of a minister for sixteen more years. In 1794 Hopkins and William Patten, then pastor of the Second Church in Newport, Rhode Island, visited Great Barrington, where as Patten described it, religion was in a deplorable state.

The people were without a minister, nor was there any convenient place to assemble for public worship. Dr. H. inquired if his former meeting house could not be fitted for the purpose for one Sabbath, but it was found to be impracticable, as the windows were broken, the door had fallen down, and the floor had long since been occupied by sheep, who resorted to it from the common at night, and in storms. . . . It was common for those who regarded the Sabbath and public ordinances to go to other towns to enjoy them. . . .[46]

In the light of the future history of the church, Hopkins developed doubts concerning the wisdom of his having left Great Barrington. Had he accepted the suggestion of his supporters, Hopkins self-servingly recalled in his autobiography, and sacrificed time in his study for time in the fields, he would have been able to provide more than adequately for his family. Such a course of action, he maintained, "would have been greatly to my *worldly* advantage," but it would have hindered his work as a minister.[47] Thus, in characteristic fashion, Hopkins claimed that self-denial and not self-interest lay behind his willingness to leave Great Barrington.

The overwhelming majority of New Divinity dismissals took place outside the supportive surroundings of western New England. Most of these disputes were less complicated than Hopkins's difficulties in Great Barrington, and they usually resulted from one or more of three issues: the Half-way Covenant, theological disagreements, and church finances. The case of John Bacon, a New Divinity graduate of Princeton in 1765, is illustrative. Bacon was installed in the Old South Church in Boston in 1769. Shortly thereafter, as the result of a discussion with Hopkins, Bacon became convinced that the Half-way Covenant was improper, and he abandoned the practice in the church.[48] By 1774 the church was in an uproar as parishioners voiced their disagreement with elements of Bacon's theology as well as with his stand on the Half-way Covenant. Church meetings became the forum for heated theological discussions with Bacon on the disputed points.[49] Finally, a majority of the members voted to request Bacon's dismissal, justifying their decision on his rejection of the Half-way Covenant and on the fact that he had "preached and held forth

Doctrines and Sentiments which we esteem Erroneous, and which are diverse from, and contradictory to, the Doctrines and Sentiments we have recited from the [church's] Confession of Faith aforesaid."[50] Bacon admitted that he had departed from the Confession he had signed before his settlement. But, he explained, he had no intention of deceiving the church at the time of his candidacy. Rather, "upon further consideration and searching the holy Scriptures, I have been fully convinced that I was then in Error. . . ."[51]

In Plymouth, similar issues entangled Consistent Calvinist Chandler Robbins in a protracted controversy with the First Congregational Church. The church called Robbins in 1759 after failing for several years to settle a minister. Before the church proceeded with ordination, the members obliged Robbins to agree to "the New England Confession of faith commonly received in these Churches or Exhibit one in writing to the Satisfaction of the Church."[52] This occurred in 1759, before the systematic formulation of the New Divinity. Robbins had earlier studied under Bellamy and adopted his teacher's theological sentiments. When Bellamy published his first *Dialogue on the Half-way Covenant* in 1769, Robbins attempted to convince his church to abandon the practice. For the next three years, church meetings were filled with debates on Robbin's proposal and the theology which underlay it. Led by a prominent parishioner and sometime preacher, the church resisted Robbins's altering of what they saw as a traditional practice. In an ensuing local pamphlet war Robbins's "new scheme"[53] came under heavy attack. By the middle of 1772 the membership had become so divided and the controversy so disruptive of town life that for the sake of peace the church voted to terminate further discussion of the issue. Robbins admitted that a majority of the church "continued to be of the Opinion that the *Old Practice*, as tis called, was right. . . ."[54] Nevertheless, the church members did not initiate dismissal proceedings, perhaps because they feared they would not be able to agree on a successor to Robbins. The unregenerate who sought baptism for their children waited until Robbins was out of town and approached the pastor's substitute. Thus while dissatisfaction persisted Robbins avoided dismissal.

Many Consistent Calvinists who were involved in church disputes, however, were less fortunate than Robbins. Few New

Divinity ministers went as far as David Sanford (Yale, 1755) who divided his Medway, Massachusetts, church "by conscientiously inserting in his Chh gov't. as a term of Admission that we profess we are willing to be damned for the Glory of God and the Good of the Universe."[55] But controversy seemed to follow some Consistent Calvinists nearly everywhere they went. David Avery, for example, graduated from Yale in 1769, and after studying theology received a call to a newly organized township in Gageborough, Vermont, in 1773. Three years later he voluntarily left the church to serve as a chaplain in the Revolutionary army. In 1778 he preached as a candidate in Newburyport, Massachusetts, but the church never offered him a settlement. Two years later he answered the call of a destitute church in Vermont and remained for only three controversial years. From the beginning of Avery's candidacy a faction in the church had reservations concerning his theology and voted against his installment. His opponents, who were largely Separate-Congregationalists, then insisted that Avery submit to lay ordination, and he refused. With the approval of his supporters, Avery became pastor of the church without ever being officially installed. The controversy raged for the next three years, with the attack on Avery shifting from his denial of lay ordination to his preaching on the doings of the unregenerate, the atonement, and free will. Avery finally resigned in 1783, and was installed over the church in Wrentham, Massachusetts, between Boston and Worcester. In a short time he was dismissed from this congregation, and for much of the remainder of his ministerial career he resorted to filling vacant pulpits on a temporary basis.[56]

In Taunton, Massachusetts, at about the same time, the New Divinity views of Ephraim Judson (Yale, 1763) contributed to his dismissal. For two years prior to Judson's ordination in 1780, his church had unsuccessfully attempted to settle a minister. Throughout the 1780's a group of members opposed Judson's ministry, culminating in his dismissal in 1790. The controversies in the church, Judson informed the council called to consider his fate, stemmed partly from financial problems and the desire of outlivers for a new meetinghouse and "partly from a dislike that a few influential characters have to the doctrines that are preached."[57]

Nor did Ephraim's brother, Adoniram (Yale, 1775), experience any more success in nearby Malden. Called to the North

Parish during the 1780's, Judson was warned by his opponents that his ordination would constitute "an effectual barrier in preventing the mutually wished for union of the two parishes in this town . . . and will probably terminate in the ruin of both." Judson's foes prevented his ordination until 1787. When Judson was finally installed, his opponents, who objected to "Settling a Minister of Bade [sic] Hopkintonian principals [sic]," separated from the church. After the division dissatisfaction continued, and Judson was dismissed in 1791.[58]

A number of other New Divinity men were involved in church disputes which led to their dismissals. Yet historians have exaggerated both lay opposition to the New Divinity and the movement's contribution to the ecclesiastical disorder of mid-eighteenth-century New England. The ecclesiastical history of the New Divinity is only a slightly more contentious story than that of the Congregational clergy as a whole in the middle of the eighteenth century. Recent studies of the Congregational ministry document a significant escalation of serious church disputes and of clerical dismissals in the eighteenth century. A minister's chances of having a major conflict with his church increased from 22 to 47 percent between 1700 and 1740. Furthermore, from 12 percent during the first decade of the century, the proportion of Congregational ministers who were dismissed from churches at least once surged to 27.5 percent between 1740 and 1760; and the rate of dismissal rose even higher in subsequent decades.[59] Such clerical-lay contention derived not only from an increase in salary problems but from the theological and ecclesiastical controversies which the revival and New England's paper war provoked. Moreover, the relatively high rates of dispute and dismissal, like the financial problems of the clergy, were important reasons for the declining appeal of the ministry as a profession in the middle of the eighteenth century.

The percentage of New Divinity men who were dismissed from their churches is not markedly higher that the dismissal rate for the Congregational ministry as a whole. Thirty-four percent of the Consistent Calvinists were dismissed at least once. Many New Divinity men, such as Joseph Bellamy, Nathanael Emmons, Levi Hart, John Smalley, and Benjamin Trumbull, to name only a handful, served fifty-and sixty-year pastorates over single churches. For too long historians have read the history of the New

Divinity movement through the eyes of such clerical representatives of the Standing Order as Ezra Stiles, who claimed in 1793 that "none of the Churches in New England are New Divinity, this commodity being monopolized by a Selective but increasing body of the Clergy." There were no more than "two or 3 persons or individuals . . . to a parish who are in the New Theology," Stiles insisted.[60] While the rapid growth of the New Divinity on the clerical level during the 1760's and 1770's outpaced its adoption by the laity, the churches of New England were far more receptive to Consistent Calvinism than Stiles suggested. Indeed, between 1766 and 1769 four churches offered pastorates to Hopkins.[61] To the dismay of liberals and Old Lights, he answered the call of the First Congregational Church of Newport, Rhode Island. The opponents of the New Divinity were prompted to take action to prevent the ordination of the movement's leader in their midst.

chapter six

A PURITAN IN BABYLON

WHEN in the middle of the winter of 1769 Hopkins preached for the last time from the pulpit that had supported his sermon notes and Bible for twenty-five years and bade farewell to his church, his situation was not unlike the one that confronted his theological teacher, Jonathan Edwards, nearly twenty years earlier. A forty-seven-year-old, dismissed minister who was scorned by liberal and moderate Calvinists faced an uncertain future if he decided to pursue a career in the ministry. Like Edwards after he was dismissed from his Northampton church, Hopkins was burdened with the support of a large family and was temperamentally unsuited for most worldly occupations. At least he possessed a house and land at Great Barrington which had been deeded to him as part of the terms of his settlement in the town. Out of necessity, Hopkins began seriously to consider putting more effort into cultivating his farm land, since now that he was no longer a pastor he would not have to worry about stealing time from the work of furthering God's cause. With the help of his sons, Hopkins could farm his land and provide for his family, while occasionally filling vacant pulpits and waiting until God revealed whether there was still a clerical role for him to play in the establishment of a Christian kingdom in America.

As he mulled over the future, much of the old pastoral routine continued through the winter. Dismissal could not be allowed to hinder his work in progress: an answer to Jedidiah Mills's pamphlet criticizing his position on the state of the unregenerate. Then, too, a weekly sermon had to be prepared because the destitute church twelve miles away in North Canaan, Connecticut, requested his services until the parishioners settled a minister. During the week he secluded himself in his study and on weekends rode on horseback to Connecticut.[1]

By the early spring both his writing and interim preaching assignment had been completed, and he set out on a social visit to Boston. When he arrived in the city he was informed that the Old South Church was in need of a minister to replace its aged and ailing pastor, Joseph Sewall. Old South was one of the most theologically conservative churches in Boston, numbering among its membership a small group of worshippers who embraced Hopkinsianism. Sewall would eventually be succeeded by New Divinity minister John Bacon, but in the spring of 1769 the Hopkinsians in the Old South Church proposed that Hopkins be invited to preach as a candidate for the position. The Hopkinsians in the Old South Church were not strong enough, however, to overcome the opposition of a majority of the membership. While he preached to the church during April and May, his candidacy was prevented, he reported, when "some of the leading men in the Church being opposed to it, exerted themselves in opposition to it, and took measures effectually to prevent it."[2]

But the stay in Boston brought a firmer offer from the New England backcountry. A representative from the newly organized settlement in Topsham, Maine, who had journeyed to Boston in search of a minister for the inhabitants, invited Hopkins to return with him on the approximately one hundred fifty mile journey to the frontier township. Other dismissed ministers, Hopkins discovered, were settling in northern New England, especially in Maine which was then a district of Massachusetts. Hopkins informed Joseph Bellamy, who undoubtedly communicated the information to his students, that "there are a number of congregations in that neighborhood that are vacant."[3] The northern frontier, like much of western New England, consisted of new settlements with small churches offering low salaries to any clerical takers they could find. Hopkins agreed to preach to the church in Topsham, but if he entertained any thoughts of permanently settling over the inhabitants they were quickly dispelled upon his arrival in the township early in June. The new settlement reminded him of Housatonic in the 1740's. He found "the people ignorant and generally stupid in matters of religion; and no church or professors of religion in the town."[4]

Nevertheless, his preaching was well attended, and he was quickly offered a call to the church. Acceptance would have meant a renewal of his earlier missionary commitment and all the hard-

ships that such a decision entailed: the demands of sustaining and
nurturing a small, frontier church and of contending with irre-
ligious, backwoods elements; the prospect of a small, inadequate
salary (often paid in kind rather than in money) to support his
wife and eight children; the problems involved in clearing the
land and gathering the stone and lumber to construct a new parsonage. In light of his family circumstances, age, and previous
service in Great Barrington, Hopkins explained defensively in his
autobiography, he concluded that Christian duty did not require
him to accept the offer of the Topsham settlers. The position was
more suitable for a young man, he told them, who without the
care of a large family could dedicate all his time and energy to
the religious life of the town and mature with the church and the
settlement.[5]

As for his own future, Hopkins decided "that it would be my
duty to live with my family at Great Barrington, and cultivate my
farm for a living, rather than to settle at Topsham, or any place
like that; . . . unless I would have some better prospect of settling
in the ministry."[6] Hopkins fasted and prayed, beseeching God
for guidance. "The chief thing I propose to seek God for today,"
he noted in his diary in mid-June while he was still preaching in
Maine, "were, first, his direction and smiles, with regard to my
future circumstances and usefulness in the world; with respect to
which I have a variety of exercises, which would fill a volume
were they all recorded; secondly, for my Christian friends and
thirdly for the church of Christ, &c." While reflecting on his
personal predicament Hopkins was sometimes overwhelmed with
a sense of his worthlessness and utter dependence on God. At
times during private devotions this Puritan intellectual and rigorous metaphysician was unable to contain his emotions. One Sat-
urday before he was scheduled to preach to the people of Topsham,
a pre-Sabbath ritual of fasting and praying brought on a particularly intense emotional reaction: "I was in tears a great part of
the day," he recorded in his dairy, "so that I was obliged to shut
myself up, not fit to be seen."[7]

As he was about to leave Maine early in July and return to
his family in Great Barrington, Hopkins received a letter from
the First Congregational Church of Newport inviting him to
preach as a candidate to the parishioners of the seaport. Doubtless,
Hopkins saw this offer as the answer of Divine Providence to his

self-effacing devotions. He set out for Newport directly from the Maine backwoods. The next year would be a turning point in Hopkins's ministerial career. His most important theological and reform work lay in the future. With the call to Newport he began the second, and the most productive, half of his career in the ministry. But first he had to overcome the efforts of his clerical opponents to undermine his call to the church. At first liberal and Old Light Calvinists were surprised that Hopkins had been invited to preach as a candidate in Newport. Next they were disturbed when they learned that Hopkins had been offered a settlement. They then became determined not to stand by idly while the members of the respectable First Church dignified the New Divinity by installing the movement's leader as their pastor.

On July 21, 1769, Hopkins arrived in Newport and entered a social and cultural world totally removed from the rural, small-town society so familiar and comfortable to him. In nearly every external detail the fashionable seaport contrasted with Waterbury and even more starkly with Great Barrington. Where formerly he had gazed from his father's fields or his parsonage window upon the furrowed land and rolling hills of western New England, his view from the First Church's parsonage fixed upon Newport harbor and ships sailing into port or off to the horizon. Where the hills of western New England reinforced the isolated and provincial atmosphere of the area, the ocean exposed Newport to contacts from around the world. The seaport was the fifth largest city in the American colonies, boasting 11,000 residents by 1775. While the population of the city was preponderantly English, its inhabitants included French, Spanish, Italian, and Jewish merchants who established permanent homes in Newport and who combined with over 1,200 black residents to give the seaport a cosmopolitan character.[8]

Agriculture played a relatively insignificant role in the economy of the compact city crowded on the waterfront. Rather, commerce and all its ancillary businesses and trades occupied Newporters' working days. The city's harbor teemed with activity, as trading vessels constantly sailed out to other colonial ports and to the British West Indies loaded down with a variety of products from food to candles and horses. From these destinations, with bills of exchange and other food products, the Newport ships headed to London and Liverpool to trade for manufactured items, clothing, and other goods to be imported into the American colonies. Often Newport shipmasters steered their vessels to the coast of Africa, where in exchange for rum they secured slaves to barter away on return voyages to the West Indies and colonial ports. Indeed, rum had become so important to the economic life of Newport that no less than sixteen distilleries operated in the city.[9]

The system of trade that Newport merchants had built up over several decades paid handsome dividends for many individuals. A wealthy merchant aristocracy lorded over the social life of the seaport. The fortunes and social needs of the commercial gentry spawned elegant mansions, exclusive clubs, fashionable balls, and the numerous decorated carriages that traveled the city's streets. Hopkins arrived in Newport in the middle of the summer — the height of the social season. Each year from late spring to early fall, the city's permanent aristocracy welcomed wealthy summer residents from the Carolinas and the West Indies who sought relief from the stifling heat at home. The culturally-minded members of the seaport gentry met regularly at the Redwood Library, designed by Peter Harrison and presided over by Ezra Stiles.[10]

The social life of many of Newport's less intellectual residents revolved around the city's thirty-four taverns. Interspersed among the numerous public drinking places were the seaport's diverse houses of worship: two Congregational and two Baptist societies; an Anglican and a Moravian church; a Quaker meeting house; and a Jewish synagogue.[11] The rustic, withdrawn, and ascetic Hopkins was ill-prepared to accept and adjust to the tolerant, commercial, refined, and, in his eyes, decadent society that he encountered in Newport.

But the members of the First Congregational Church were prepared to accept him. By tradition the society was theologically more conservative than the neighboring Second Church of Ezra Stiles, which had separated from the First Church in 1729 in a dispute with the pastor over his refusal to administer communion. Within a short while the Second Church established a reputation for its theological moderation and the worldly prosperity of many of its communicants. In addition to wealth and social prestige, Stiles's society dwarfed the nearby First Church in size. Whereas the membership of the Second Church approached seven hundred,

Hopkins's society had just over two hundred worshippers—seventy full church members (fifty of them women) and an additional one hundred thirty-five in the congregation. First Church's previous minister, William Vinal, had been dismissed in 1768 after twenty years of service. Failing health, which Vinal attempted to remedy with large amounts of Newport rum and other alcoholic spirits, had debilitated the religious life of the church for a number of years. The dwindling membership finally called a council in 1768, and the minister honestly faced his problems and asked for a dismissal. [12]

From the end of Vinal's ministry in September to the following July when Hopkins arrived in Newport, the church obtained the services of nearby ministers who were willing to preach for a Sabbath or two and sustain the religious life of the parish until a candidate could be found. The conservative theological sentiments of the church members inclined them to invite ministers sympathetic to Edwardsianism. During most of that time the vacant pulpit was supplied by Punderson Austin and Ephraim Judson, two young Connecticut clergymen who were theological followers of Hopkins. [13] Undoubtedly, the parishioners learned of Hopkins's availability through one or both of these Consistent Calvinists.

To Hopkins's surprise, the church seemed willing to accept his theological views. Exactly a month after his arrival in Newport, Hopkins's brief candidacy appeared to be over. On August 21 the membership convened and voted "That this Congregation do joyn this Church in inviting the Reverend Mr. Samuel Hopkins to settle in the Pastoral office over us & that the persons chosen by the Church for that purpose be desired to wait on him in the Name of Chh & of this Congregation with information of our concurrence with the Church in the invitation." [14] Five days later the parishioners voted Hopkins a salary of £70 sterling, a parsonage, and firewood. Immediately Stiles communicated the information to Hopkins's opponents, explaining away the actions of the First Church and laying the foundation for attempts to reverse the offer. "The Reverend Mr. Hopkins has a call from the Chh late the pastoral care of the Reverend Mr. Vinall," Stiles informed Noah Welles, minister of the First Church in Stamford, Connecticut, on August 26. "His peculiarities give some uneasiness; & there is far from being unanimity. However as the Chh is small, he will probably persuade a majority to submit to his baptismal Restrictions. If I find him of a Disposition to live in honourable Friendship, I shall gladly cultivate it."[15]

While there was little doubt that Hopkins would accept the call, he decided not to give the committee an immediate answer but to return to Great Barrington, discuss the offer with his family, and then make a decision. He left Newport near the end of August and did not return until late October. Now he entered the seaport with renewed dedication to the ministry. He had not only found an audience receptive to his theology, but he had also been offered a settlement that would enable him to support his family.

His hopes were quickly dashed, however, when the ordination committee notified him that the church was not ready to proceed with his installation, because the members were now sharply divided over his call. The committee suggested that he withhold a formal answer to the church's offer and continue to preach on probation until the issue could be resolved.[16] In Hopkins's two-month absence he had lost much of his support in the church and congregation, a development largely due to the machinations of his clerical opponents.

Moderate and liberal Calvinists conveyed their dismay at the prospect of Hopkins's settling in Newport to Ezra Stiles, whom they attempted to enlist in a campaign to prevent the ordination of the leader of the New Divinity movement. "Mr. Hopkins, I think, expects to settle among you," Chauncy Whittelsey, Old Light minister of New Haven's First Church wrote to Stiles in the middle of September. "I esteem him a man of good sense but I don't at all like the Cast of his Divinity. . . ." Furthermore, Whittelsey warned, "his notions of Baptism, if he insists upon them, will increase the Chh of England, or your Congregation, perhaps both."[17] A short while later liberal Calvinist Charles Chauncy expressed similar objections to Hopkins's ordination. "I'm sorry with my whole soul, that Mr. Hopkins is likely to settle at Newport," he confided to Stiles. "I have a much worse opinion of his principles than of Sandeman's. He is a troublesome, conceited, obstinate man. . . . He will preach away all his congregation at Newport, or make them tenfold worse than they are at present. I wish his installment could be prevented."[18]

A number of clerical opponents of the New Divinity in Connecticut agreed with Whittelsey and Chauncy on the importance of preventing Hopkins's ordination at Newport. William Hart, who earlier in the year had published his *Brief Remarks* strongly criticizing the New Divinity, was commissioned to write a new pamphlet aimed particularly at the unregenerate and designed to lay bare the fatal consequence of Hopkins's position on the state of awakened sinners. In this way, Hopkins's opponents hoped to turn the congregation of the First Church against him. Hart's anonymous essay, *A Sermon of a New Kind*, together with his *Brief Remarks* circulated among the parishioners during Hopkins's two-month absence from Newport. The author confessed that he was serving as a spokesman for "sundry gentlemen of good judgment, and moral taste" who had met and "expressed a desire to have such a kind of discourse published as the following. . . ."[19] Whittelsey later admitted to Stiles that he was one of the "gentlemen" who had planned and encouraged the publication of the pamphlet.[20] Clearly, Hopkins's call to Newport, coming at the end of a decade of steady growth for the New Divinity movement, alarmed the rationalist clergy. In striking out at Hopkins, the Old Lights were attempting to discredit and deal a setback to the burgeoning movement.

In *A Sermon of a New Kind* Hart repeated the points he had made in his *Brief Remarks*, intensifying under the cover of anonymity his ridicule of Hopkinsianism and his appeal to the unregenerate to recognize the absurdity of this "new divinity." "So you see," Hart informed his unregenerate but churchgoing readers after quoting extensively from Hopkins's works, "I am [so] restrained by this scheme of doctrines, that I can't consistently and without great absurdity, expect or exhort you to believe and repent, unless you are first regenerated."[21] The pamphlets had the desired effect on the congregation of the First Church, as Hopkins now began a second, drawn-out, and contentious candidacy.

Hopkins retained considerable support among the full church members who continued to endorse his ordination and who labored to remove the newly raised objections against him. The core of the church and the locus of Hopkins's aggressive backing was a women's praying society established during the Great Awakening and numbering approximately fifty members by 1769. The women held weekly meetings at which they prayed, discussed theology, listened to the spiritual problems of members, and arranged for the collection and distribution of alms. Hopkins remained in New-

port without his family and clung to the hope of eventual installment largely because, of the women's society. In an extensive and
revealing correspondence with the two leaders of the women's
group — Sarah Osborn and Susanna Anthony — he described his
despondent state. "I find I have a strong, and even unconquerable
desire to spend my life at N.P. — I am loth, very loth, to be
rejected," he admitted to Miss Anthony on November 15. "It is
dreadful to think of being rejected as a minister of Christ, hated,
discarded for his names [sic] sake," he wrote, assuming a sacrificial pose. "But I cannot reconcile myself to be rejected in any
other way."[22] Two weeks later he confided to Miss Anthony that
this new controversy combined with all the earlier disputes had
drained his vigor: "I often think, with a sense of pleasure, of
settling down on my farm, and spending the rest of my days in
sweet obscurity."[23]

Throughout the fall and winter Hopkins continued to preach
on probation, while his women supporters were "violently engaged," as Stiles saw it, in gathering votes for a new call.[24] In
the middle of February 1770 Hopkins wrote dejectedly to his
close friend Levi Hart of Preston, Connecticut, that he did not
now expect a call. The church was "truly in a broken situation,
more so than you imagine, I believe," he reported to Hart. "A
number are cordial & zealous in my favor, a few against me &
a considerable number indifferent; most, I believe, say that if I
leave them, the congregation will be broke up."[25]

Hopkins's supporters scheduled a meeting at the end of February to settle the question of renewing the church's call to him.
This news quickly traveled to Connecticut. "Pray inform me,"
Whittelsey requested in a letter to Stiles on February 26, the day
appointed by the First Church to decide Hopkins's future in Newport, "whether Mr. Hopkins is likely to settle in your Vicinity,
and how his peculiar Sentiments are relished by the more sensible
among you." A rumor was circulating in Connecticut, Whittelsey
notified Stiles, that the pastor of Newport's Second Church had
fallen under the spell of Hopkins's New Divinity.[26] This belief
was based in part upon the fact that Stiles refused to work actively
against Hopkins's ordination. When the scheme of the moderate
Calvinists to deny Hopkins his installation over the First Church
began to crumble, accusing fingers were pointed at Stiles for failing to do all in his power to prevent the dreaded result.

To be sure, there was no substance to the suspicions that Stiles's opinion of Hopkins and the New Divinity had changed. In fact, Hopkins's actions while preaching on probation in Newport added to Stiles's disapproval of him and his Consistent Calvinist followers. When Hopkins administered communion and performed a baptism prior to his ordination, Stiles viewed it as another example of New Divinity disregard for ecclesiastical order. "It was formerly in the last century," he remarked, "a great Doubt in New England whether a Minister might occasionally administer Baptism & the Lds Supper in any Chh but his own."[27] Yet in spite of new objections to Hopkins, the peace-seeking Stiles remained unwilling to participate in the campaign to block Hopkins's call for fear of antagonizing his First Church neighbors who supported the New Divinity theologian. While secretly hoping that Hopkins would not be installed, Stiles assumed an outwardly neutral stance throughout Hopkins's long probationary period, simply reporting to other interested parties the progress of affairs in the First Church. As a result, he estranged many of his liberal and moderate Calvinist friends.

The February meeting of the First Church did not produce a new call to Hopkins. The women's society and the other adherents of Hopkins in the First Church did not comprise a majority of the membership. Although indifference had replaced much of the earlier hostility to Hopkins, his backers concluded that he still did not have sufficient support to warrant their calling for a vote on renewing the church's call. The meeting ended with the suggestion that Hopkins be informed of the unlikely prospect of his ordination. This assessment was confirmed on March 12 when the church did take a vote on the question of reissuing the previous offer to Hopkins. Thirty-three members favored Hopkins's ordination but thirty-six opposed it.[28]

The ordination committee communicated the results to the disappointed candidate and requested that he now give a formal answer to the call of the previous August. "Tho I am willing to spend my life among you in the service of Christ and your souls . . . ," Hopkins wrote to the church a week later, "as the case now stands, according to your public transactions . . . I am obliged to give my answer in the Negative; and now informe [sic] you that I intend to leave you as soon as I can conveniently."[29] On the same day that he addressed his formal answer to the church, Hopkins, adopting a disinterested pose, delivered a farewell sermon to the congregation. He insisted that "he held no doctrines, the substance of which he had not preached to them before they gave him a call. . . ."[30] He went on to express a concern for the future of the church, but did not suggest that the members reconsider their vote. By the following Sunday he planned to be back in Great Barrington with his family, making the first of many anticipated spring preparations for cultivating his farm.

But events quickly reassured Hopkins that God had not called him from the backwoods of northern New England only to allow the forces of darkness to defeat him in a sin-laden town so badly in need of Calvinist preaching and moral reform. Hopkins's farewell sermon apparently had an unexpected — miraculous, Hopkins believed — impact on his opponents. His calculatedly temperate sermon moved many of his women supporters to tears, and, what is more important, it reversed or neutralized a part of the opposition to him (like "the blowing of rams' horns" destroying the walls of Jericho, he later rhapsodized).[31] The day after he bid farewell to friends and foes, he was notified that three men who had opposed his ordination now wanted him installed as their pastor. "They were brought to this by my farewell sermon," Hopkins recorded in his diary. "It is said this sermon had greater effect than all my preaching before. Some who have thought it not best for me to stay, now appear zealous for my staying." Hopkins took little credit for this turn of events, attributing it to the hand of God. "How greatly are my obligations increased to trust in God . . . and [to] follow him in the dark," he reflected. "What matter for praise and gratitude."[32]

Hopkins's pious women supporters deserved much of the credit for salvaging his call to the church. The leaders of the praying society had worked continuously to change the minds of those church members who were opposed or indifferent to Hopkins. The sobs of these supporters during Hopkins's composed farewell sermon contributed to its effect on the congregation. Hopkins's advocates undoubtedly used the sentimental discourse to persuade or shame some of his antagonists into dropping their opposition to him. When a new church meeting was called to order one week after Hopkins's farewell address, many of his opponents were absent. With no negative votes and only two abstentions, the members reissued their offer to Hopkins to settle over the church.[33]

No one in Newport followed the events in the First Church with keener interest than Ezra Stiles. From time to time friends in the neighboring church apprised him of the congregation's disposition and previewed the business of forthcoming meetings. In his diary Stiles recorded his impressions of the Hopkins controversy. After the church's second call Stiles observed, with considerable accuracy although with some exaggeration, that there was still significant opposition and indifference to Hopkins's ordination. Only about "30 families or one quarter of the Society," Stiles reported, were ardently in favor of Hopkins's installation.[34] Stiles's account suggests that Hopkins's farewell sermon did not have as dramatic an effect on his opponents as he came to believe. Yet in spite of lingering objections to the New Divinity minister, there was no mass departure of dissatisfied members from the First Church after his ordination. While perhaps an obstinate family or two quit the First Church when Hopkins was installed, neither Stiles's church nor Newport's Anglican Church prospered as a result of his ordination. Although Stiles continued to have doubts about the effect of Hopkins's ministry on the religious life of the seaport, he agreed, over the objections of the members of his own church, to deliver the sermon at his theological opponent's ordination in April. Consequently, Stiles further alienated his fellow Old Lights who had worked secretly and skillfully to defeat Hopkins.

After Hopkins took charge of the First Church on April 11, 1770, there remained only one piece of unfinished business involving the protracted dispute over his call: an answer to William Hart and in effect to all the clerical and lay opponents of the New Divinity. For a number of weeks in the midst of the controversy Hopkins had been working on a reply to Hart. Whether or not he had ultimately succeeded in Newport, the movement which had developed a public identity largely as a result of Hart's publications deserved a public defense. Indeed, the New Divinity men planned and propagated Hopkins's apology just as the Old Lights had Hart's diatribes. "When it is finished," Hopkins wrote to Stephen West on January 12, 1770, "I am to send it to Mr. [Levi] Hart of Preston and he will get it printed, if he and Mr.

Austin approve it."[35] New Divinity plans called for the systematic distribution of the work. Copies were to be given to the Connecticut clergy on election day in May. Joseph Bellamy, Jonathan Edwards, Jr., and Levi Hart assumed responsibility for distributing additional copies of Hopkins's work to the laity in different parts of the colony.[36] In this way, there would be a wide dissemination of Hopkins's vindication of the New Divinity on the home ground of the movement.

Animadversions on Mr. Hart's Late Dialogue in a Letter to a Friend appeared in print on schedule. Hopkins concentrated on removing the reproach attached to the term "new divinity." "It is at least *possible*," he maintained, "that there is some truth contained in the bible, which has not been commonly taught; yea has never been mentioned by any writer since the apostles: And whenever that shall be discovered and brought out, it will be new." It was equally possible that the Consistent Calvinists were making such "new discoveries." "If so, unhappy and very guilty will be the man who shall attempt to fright people," and to arouse their opposition to truth "by raising the cry of New Divinity." Nevertheless, Hopkins insisted, for the most part Consistent Calvinism was not theologically new. It was "really a revival and improvement of sound Calvinism, being founded on the scriptures, and the doctrine of total depravity; and . . . [it] cannot be opposed consistently upon true calvinistic principles."[37] In a brief postscript Hopkins followed the same line of argument in refuting the charges of Hart in *A Sermon of a New Kind*.

Now Hopkins set about to revitalize the once flourishing religious life of the church. He started a weekly lecture series and established regular meetings for catechizing the young people in the parish. At meetings during his first year, he persuaded the membership to revise the church's covenant so that it would reflect New Divinity theology. He also secured the members' cooperation in altering the church's admission rules, bringing them into conformity with New Divinity ecclesiology.[38] The next several years of Hopkins's ministry were productive and devoid of any serious strife between pastor and parishioners. Small accessions to the church and congregation were recorded each year, and the number of full members climbed to well over one hundred by the opening of the Revolutionary War.[39]

The admiring members of the women's society provided a

constant source of moral, intellectual, and even financial support to Hopkins. When at afternoon teas, Hopkins found himself the center of attention and the solicitous women willing to do anything in their power to aid their minister, he was reassured that he had found one of the few churches in New England where a clergyman still commanded respect and deference. The five-year period from his ordination to the beginning of military conflict with Great Britain in mid-1775 marked the most stable and personally satisfying period of Hopkins's career in the ministry. "While you are all in quarrels in Connecticut, and *Hopkintonians* are cursed with bell, book, and candle," he wrote to Bellamy in 1771, "Divine Providence has led me out of the noise; and provided a quiet retreat, where all is peace, and I receive more kindness from the hands of my friends in one year than I ever received in my life."[40]

Hopkins's ordination, his rebuttal to the Old Lights, and his pastoral success in Newport, however, did not still the pen of William Hart. Late in 1770 he responded to Hopkins's *Animadversions* with *A Letter to the Reverend Samuel Hopkins*. But more importantly, Hart devised a new strategy for discrediting the New Divinity, a strategy that required him to go back to Jonathan Edwards's theology in order, as he put it, to lay "the axe to the 'root of the tree.' "[41] Hart and Hopkins agreed on at least one point — namely, that Edwards's *Dissertation on the Nature of True Virtue*, published posthumously in 1765, had provided the New Divinity movement with a major theological statement of the evangelical Calvinism of the Awakening that served as the foundation upon which Edwards's followers constructed their doctrinal systems. Thus, in 1771 Hart published a volume highly critical of Edwards's the *Nature of True Virtue*. In reply Hopkins wrote a major theological work, *An Inquiry into the Nature of True Holiness* (1773), in which he advanced his original doctrine of disinterested benevolence. Hopkins's interpretation of disinterested benevolence, however, was far from simply an abstract, metaphysical response to his theological foe. It was, in part, a protest against the social values of Newporters and a critique of the development of New England society. In Hopkins's mind, Newport, with its grasping merchants, indulgent way of life, and idle diversions, symbolized the moral dangers in the course that New England society was following.

chapter seven

DISINTERESTED BENEVOLENCE:
A Theology of Social Reform

AT the Yale commencement of 1741, Samuel Hopkins had listened attentively as Jonathan Edwards confronted the problem of the authenticity of the Awakening in light of what many people saw as the false piety and emotional excesses that it carried in its train. Five years later in the *Religious Affections*, Edwards attempted to make a clear theological statement that would simultaneously define geniune spiritual sentiments, silence rational critics of the revival, and expose the fraudulent religious enthusiasm it had unleashed. But a decade after the Awakening the question of the spiritual validity of its experimental religion remained as problematical as ever. The American debate over the nature of true virtue represented another effort by rationalists and evangelicals to settle the issue of what constituted truly spiritual affections. In this sense, Edwards's interpretation of true virtue was the theological "root" of his pro-revival experimental religion and of the New Divinity movement as well.

As the evangelical pietism underlying America's revival was transatlantic in scope, so too the debate over its validity and thus over the nature of true virtue took place in an international context. Indeed, much of the American controversy turned on the defense and refutation of European rationalist thought and the European development of natural theology: the position that man had the natural ability to understand scripture, judge right from wrong, and attain salvation. In the middle of the eighteenth century, such natural theology was popular among liberal and moderate Calvinists who used it to bolster and extend the conditional elements in their covenant theology that recognized the role of human effort in conversion.[1] To evangelical Calvinists, however, the natural theology of the rationalists seemed to undermine not only the doctrine of total depravity but also the experimental religion of the Awakening and the belief that true virtue could only result from God's unconditional gift of grace. In the *Nature of True Virtue* Edwards came to the defense of the supernatural theology of the revival. He attempted to refute the natural theology of the rationalists by incorporating elements of their moral philosophy into his own thought.

Edwards's approach proved unacceptable to his leading disciple. While in fundamental respects Hopkins was a follower of Edwards, he nevertheless found serious flaws in his mentor's theology. Specifically, Hopkins concluded that Edwards's interpretation of true virtue was deficient on several counts. Not only did it make unnecessary concessions to rational moral philosophers, but it tended toward abstraction, mixed aesthetics with ethics, and did not provide an adequate spur to social action.

Although written in 1755, during the midst of his Stockbridge exile, Edwards's *Nature of True Virtue* did not appear in print until 1765. In 1771 William Hart published his *Remarks on President Edwards's Dissertation concerning the Nature of True Virtue*. Hart intended his work to be a final moderate Calvinist assault on the theology of the Awakening. He wanted to demonstrate how the New Divinity as a whole and Edwards's concept of true virtue in particular were "wrong, imaginary and fatally destructive of the foundation of morality and true religion." Hart was especially disturbed that Edwards had replaced the biblical God with the abstract metaphysical concept of "Being in general." Furthermore, Hart argued, a penchant for metaphysics and aesthetics had allowed Edwards to deny that social morality was true virtue and to "involve practical religion . . . in a cloud." Most of Edwards's *True Virtue* was vitiated, Hart suggested, because he had confused aesthetics with ethics.[2]

Criticism of the *Nature of True Virtue* by Hart and others helped clarify for Hopkins the deficiencies in Edwards's ethical theory and convinced him that his own work should be an improvement on, not simply a defense of, Edwards. Hopkins focused on Edwards's interpretation of Being in general as one of the central areas in need of improvement. "True virtue," Edwards began his dissertation, "most essentially consists in benevolence to *Being in general*." Edwards tied the elusive concept of true virtue to what Hart denounced as "an idolatrous" object. "When I say true virtue consists in love of Being in general," Edwards pointed out, "I shall not be likely to be understood that no one act of the mind or exercise of love is of the nature of true virtue, but what has Being in general or the great system of universal existence, for its direct and immediate object. . . ." While Edwards seemed to equate Being in general with God, he described an ultimate reality different from traditional notions of the Deity. God was not only "the *head* of the system [of universal being] and the chief part of it," but the source of all being.[3] Hopkins found this conception of Being in general both amorphous and abstract. He attempted to correct Edwards by redefining Being in general as "God and our neighbors," that is, God and mankind.

Hopkins was also dissatisfied with Edwards's handling of the subjective nature of true virtue. Love of Being in general, Edwards argued, originated in a "relish," "propensity," or "inclination" of the will or heart. In short, true virtue was essentially a matter of motivation. While natural principles governed the will of an unconverted person, through regeneration an authentic Christian had a benevolent affection implanted in his heart which motivated him to love Being in general.[4]

At this point, critics such as Hart charged that Edwards transformed his analysis into a discussion not of ethics but of aesthetics. To ask what is the nature of true virtue, Edwards wrote, "is the same as to enquire what that is which renders any habit, disposition, or exercise of the heart truly beautiful."[5] The major alteration produced by regeneration, and thus the distinguishing feature of true virtue, Edwards concluded, consisted in a "comprehensive view" of spiritual reality which the saint relished and loved for its beauty.[6] Edwards's overly aesthetic interpretation of true virtue was another element of his theology which Hopkins undertook to improve.

Both Hopkins and the critics of *True Virtue* saw that Edwards's emphasis on the beatific nature of regeneration militated against worldly action. Edwards left an ambiguous legacy for Christian ethics. In the 1740's he had attempted to counteract a new wave of revival-inspired antinomianism by insisting upon the importance of evangelical activity as a fruit of conversion.[7] But a decade later New England's religious life had changed dramatically, and the emphasis of Edwards's theology changed with it. A sharp decline in conversions put an end to the antinomian menace. Anti-revival rationalism now posed the major threat to evangelical Calvinism. Indeed, it seemed to Edwards that the spiritual delights of regeneration had been largely forgotten. In this sense, the dominant theme of *True Virtue* — that regeneration culminates in relishing the beauty of Being in general — was intended as an antidote to rationalist thought.

Yet more than theological strategy accounts for the aesthetic argument of *True Virtue*. Edwards frequently dwelled on the spiritual beauty of regeneration, attempting to capture intellectually the "inward sweetness" that he described in his "Personal Narrative."[8] But at times he saw the need to uphold the claims of Christian social ethics. Nowhere is the conflict in Edwards's thought between quietism and activism better revealed than in the *Religious Affections*. Holy action is the last of the twelve distinguishing signs of conversion that he discusses in the *Religious Affections*. Many of the other marks of God's grace are existential states and aesthetic perceptions. Sign four, for example, describes a new consciousness: "Gracious affections do arise from the mind's *being* enlightened, richly and spiritually to apprehend living things." In sign ten Edwards foreshadowed the argument of *True Virtue*: "Another thing wherein those affections that are truly gracious and holy differ from those that are false is beautiful symmetry and proportion."[9]

The aesthetic side of Edwards's thought put theological obstacles in the way of evangelical activism.[10] In Hopkins's view, the quietistic emphasis of *True Virtue* made Edwards vulnerable to the charge that he had involved practical religion in a cloud. Edwards's detailed descriptions of the subjective nature of regeneration, when combined with the mystical quality of his concept of Being in general, encouraged passive contemplation and rapt otherworldliness. Through his doctrine of disinterested benevolence Hopkins endeavored to remove the ambiguity in Edwards's theology on the issue of ethics. The cause of religious reform profited from this shift.

When Edwards did discuss social morality in *True Virtue*, he made it clear that he was talking about an inferior, secondary order of virtue and beauty. Hopkins found Edwards's analysis of secondary virtue the most deficient part of his ethical theory. In Hopkins's judgment, it was objectionable in general because it borrowed too much from the views of contemporary moral philosophers whose thought was essentially rationalistic and in particular because it embraced a concept of self-love that was ethically as well as spiritually dangerous.

Edwards's interpretation of secondary virtue incorporated the views of such exponents of natural theology as the Earl of Shaftesbury and the Scottish philosopher Frances Hutcheson.[11] Well before the Awakening both moral philosophers laid the foundation for later rationalist critiques of the revival and its theological implications. Responding to the moral cynicism of Thomas Hobbes, Shaftesbury and Hutcheson rested their sanguine hopes for mankind on belief in an innate "moral sense" capable of regulating the behavior of individuals without the need for supernatural grace. Man's reason and conscience or moral sense, Shaftesbury argued, enabled him to distinguish right from wrong and to incline naturally toward virtue. This moral sense, Hutcheson maintained, was tied to disinterested benevolence. Hence natural man was capable of disinterested benevolence. Evil and sin derived not from natural depravity but from an uninformed reason or an underdeveloped moral sense.[12]

Many eighteenth-century moral philosophers reacted to Hobbesian pessimism by basing the regulation of social behavior on another natural faculty in man — self-love. Not always carefully distinguishing this principle from selfishness, advocates of natural theology described it as an inclination to seek one's own happiness and avoid misery. Moses Hemmenway, an Old Light critic of Edwards and the New Divinity who adopted the view of most rational, "common-sense" philosophers, and of most moderate and liberal Calvinists as well, defined self-love in reply to Hopkins in 1772 as "that affection or propensity of heart to ourselves, which causes us to incline to our own happiness." Rationalists contended that self-love did not conflict with the public good. It was a form of enlightened self-interest in which individual happiness was part of the public good. Selfishness, Hemmenway argued, was a much narrower affection; it was "a regard to ourselves and our own good exclusive of all regard to others or their good."[13]

In short, self-love, like man's reason and moral sense, was a natural principle implanted in human nature by God; upon it, both true virtue and social order were established. For some "sentimental" eighteenth-century moral philosophers like Hutcheson and Shaftesbury, self-love merely supplemented the moral sense in creating social order; for other "hardheaded" theological utilitarians such as Thomas Rutherford, Professor of Divinity at Cambridge University, and Adam Smith, self-love replaced the moral sense as the primary natural faculty influencing and controlling human behavior.[14] For both groups, however, virtuous human conduct as well as social order resulted from the operation of the natural principle of self-love.

Edwards attempted to counter such moral philosophy by arguing that natural principles played an important role on the level of secondary virtue. Not true virtue but an inferior form of virtue resulted from the operation of reason, conscience, moral sense, and even self-love. To Hopkins's disappointment, Edwards agreed with many rationalists that "self-love is a principle that is exceeding useful and necessary in the world of mankind." Self-love may promote social harmony, Edwards asserted, because unregenerate men "are most affected towards, and do most highly approve, those virtues which agree with their interest most, according to their various conditions in life."[15] What Edwards was saying in his attempt to assimilate the natural theology of the rationalists into his ethical theory was that God had provided for the organization of society on the basis of a kind of virtue and beauty inferior to true virtue and its beauty. While the realization of a thoroughly virtuous social order depended upon mass revivalism, the realization of a basically harmonious society did not have to wait for a new Awakening, because natural principles such as reason, moral sense, and self-love were at work in the world. Even though the human race suffered from natural depravity, Edwards reminded the readers of *True Virtue* that "the present state of mankind is so ordered and constituted by the wisdom and goodness of its supreme Ruler, that these natural principles for the most part tend to the good of the world of mankind."[16] The abrupt termination of the Awakening, his dismissal from Northampton, and his unflagging belief in natural depravity did not lead Edwards into social despair. For God had obviated the problem of social chaos in the world by controlling man's corrupt nature — although certainly not modifying it, since only regeneration could accomplish that — through such natural principles as reason, conscience or moral sense, and self-love. "These principles," Edwards pointed out, "have a like effect with true virtue in this respect that they tend several ways to restrain vice and prevent many acts of wickedness."[17]

To Edwards, secondary virtue established negative moral goodness as the normative ethical state of natural man. "By negative moral goodness," Edwards wrote, "I mean the absence of true moral evil." Although secondary virtue "be not of the nature of real positive virtue or true moral goodness, yet it has a negative moral goodness, because in the present state of things it is evidence of the absence of that higher degree of wickedness which causes great insensibility or stupidity of conscience."[18] This interpretation directly contradicted Hopkins's view of the moral state of the awakened sinner. In Edwards's ethical theory there were degrees of negative moral goodness. The more an unregenerate person enlarged his circle of benevolence short of love to Being in general, the more negative moral goodness he possessed. In contrast, Hopkins and his followers argued that such an individual grew progressively worse in God's sight.

Edwards created a continuum of virtue with gradations of morality. At one end of the continuum he located the divinely entranced, regenerate saint, ruminating over the beauty of true virtue or love of Being in general. At the opposite end he placed the totally selfish individual who sinned "not only against a spiritual and divine sense of virtue but . . . also against the dictates of that moral sense which is conscience."[19] The real moral reprobate, in other words, was the natural man who failed to live up to the standards of even secondary virtue. Calvinists of all shades as well as rational moral philosophers like Shaftesbury and Hutcheson recognized a dissolute, selfish sinner. The misunderstanding between rationalists and evangelicals, Edwards suggested, originated in the middle of the ethical continuum with people whose lives exemplified secondary virtue and negative moral goodness. The difficulty was that in practice the virtue of these moral persons resembled true virtue. "Approbation of conscience," Edwards explained as an example, "is the more readily mistaken for a truly virtuous approbation because by the wise constitution of the great Governor of the world, when conscience is well informed and thoroughly awakened, it agrees with him fully and exactly as to the object approved, though not as to the ground and reason of approving."[20] Trying objectively to differentiate true virtue from secondary virtue was comparable to attempting to distinguish between invisible and visible saints. At bottom the difference was not external but resided in the motive or inclination of the heart or will.

Rationalist moral philosophers like Shaftesbury and Hutcheson, Edwards implied, allowed themselves to be seduced by the fact that true and secondary virtue resembled each other in practice. But Edwards, as a son of New England Puritanism, readily accepted and understood God's use of natural-supernatural analogies: "And it pleases God to observe analogy in his works, as is manifest in fact in innumerable instances; and especially to establish inferior things in an analogy to superior."[21] God often used the natural world to present an image of the supernatural. Thus, in assuming the appearance of ultimate spiritual and aesthetic reality, secondary virtue and beauty had "a tendency to assist those whose hearts are under the influence of a truly virtuous temper, to dispose them to the exercises of divine love, and enliven in them a sense of spiritual beauty."[22]

Hopkins discovered a number of defects in Edwards's concept of secondary virtue. He feared that while Edwards had denied the rationalists' contention that natural man was capable of true virtue, he had nevertheless conferred theological legitimacy on natural principles. Hopkins was especially alarmed by Edwards's acceptance of self-love. It appeared to him that Edwards's position played into the hands of the rationalists who, by distinguishing self-love from selfishness, were developing a moral philosophy that was facilitating the transition from communal to individualistic social ethics. The concept of self-love as differentiated from selfishness served as the underpinning of the rationalist clergy's social thought in the second half of the eighteenth century. Their "realistic" social perspective held that the best possible society and the greatest good to the greatest number would result from the operation of self-love, that is, from the individualistic pursuit of happiness.[23] Hopkins's identification of all virtue with disinterested benevolence was an attempt to shore up traditional social thought and block the advance of self-love theories. His radical call for self-denial, in conjunction with his efforts to amend what he saw as the abstract and aesthetic qualities of Edwards's interpretation of true virtue, broadened the theological base for social reform within the New Divinity movement.

In 1773 Hopkins entered the theological paper war over the nature of true virtue with the publication of *An Inquiry into the Nature of True Holiness*. Whereas Edwards had located true virtue in exalted consciousness, Hopkins placed it in elevated social behavior. Consequently, evangelical activism superseded mystical quietism. In this respect, as well as in several others, Hopkinsianism did indeed liberalize Calvinism — or, as one critic of the New Divinity prefers to put it, moralize Edwardsianism — and look forward to modern humanized religion.[24] But the weight of theological tradition prevented an easy slide into Enlightenment humanism. The social ideals which Hopkins's *True Holiness* endorsed, for example, were reactionary; that is, the work marshaled old and new theological arguments to reaffirm the legitimacy of New England's communal values against lay desertion and clerical compromise.

Edwards described Being in general as a comprehensive ontological reality, and true virtue as an aesthetic perception of this universal being. Hopkins, on his part, stressed that Being in general was the tangible reality of God and our neighbors. As a result, Hopkins saw true virtue as more an ethical than an aesthetic ideal. Universal benevolence or "love to God and our neighbors including ourselves . . . or friendly affection to all intelligent beings"[25] constituted Hopkins's definition of true virtue.

On the question of God's moral nature and its relationship to true virtue, Hopkins Arminianized Edwards's thought. For Edwards, God's glory did not depend upon His benevolence toward His creatures. Although God desired man's happiness, His "goodness and love to created beings is derived from, and subordinate to his love of himself." While self-centered existence was morally reprehensible in man, Edwards argued, it was appropriate in the Deity. God did not exercise disinterested benevolence toward earthly beings; rather, He loved Himself as the "chief part" and source of all being. Though he acted benevolently toward mankind, He was not morally obliged to promote their happiness.[26]

In contrast, Hopkins maintained that God was not a self-centered Deity but a benevolent governor whose glory depended upon the happiness of mankind.[27] Disinterested benevolence was His primary moral attribute: "the holiness and perfection of God *and* His people consists, so much at least, in disinterested benevolence that there is no moral perfection without it *in God or the creature*."[28] Hopkins joined liberal Calvinists such as Jonathan Mayhew and Charles Chauncy in linking divine perfection to human happiness. Mayhew, for example, argued that benevolence was God's principal moral characteristic: God is not a selfish, "ambitious Being who desires the praise & homage of his creatures"; rather He is "an infinitely good One who aims at making them happy without any selfish end."[29] Hopkins agreed that disinterested benevolence was such an important part of God's moral nature that he had always to act in accordance with the moral interests of His creatures.

As Hopkins's views of divine benevolence suggest, the New Divinity was Janus-faced. The New Divinity men looked backward and endeavored to revive a strict Calvinist theological perspective by reaffirming the Reformed interpretation of the covenant as an unconditional promise. Yet Hopkins and his followers advanced a liberal Calvinist concept of the benevolence of the Deity. In New Divinity theology, natural man was depraved, spiritually unable to influence his regeneration, and utterly dependent upon God. But though God ruled absolutely, He did so with benevolent, disinterested intentions toward His creatures. This liberal Calvinist side of the New Divinity was absent from or restrained in Hopkins's early theological works and was not fully developed until his treatise on *True Virtue*. The argument for the benevolence of the Deity was outlined briefly in his *Sin . . . an advantage to the Universe*. God's "willing" sin into existence and then overruling it for good was not only an act demonstrating His absolute sovereignty; it was "an Act of Benevolence to the Universe in which he sought the good of Being in general." Hopkins added, "The Holiness of God primarily consists in *LOVE*, or Benevolence to himself, and to the creature; in the exercise of which he seeks his own Glory and the happiness of the creature: or in one Word, he seeks the Good of the *UNIVERSE*, as comprehending both Creator and Creatures."[30] Ultimately, Hopkins's belief in the benevolence of the Deity led him to adopt a liberal Calvinist interpretation of the atonement.[31] Thus the New Divinity evolved into a novel synthesis of hyper-Calvinist and liberal Calvinist doctrines.

Edwards would not have recognized his concept of Being in general or the God of his Calvinism in Hopkins's *True Holiness*. On these two points Hopkins had greatly altered Edwards's thought. But Hopkins's most important refashioning of Edwards's definition of true virtue — and Hopkins's major contribution to an evangelical theology of social reform — consisted of the opposition of disinterested benevolence to self-love. Here he not only parted ways with Edwards but dismissed out of hand the natural theology of European moral philosophers and of New England rational Calvinists. Hopkins refused to give even the slightest theological sanction to the self-interested behavior which he saw undermining New England society, particularly that of Newport.

Hopkins contended that no middle ground such as secondary virtue and beauty existed between true virtue and selfishness. Every human being's heart was filled with either totally self-interested or totally disinterested affections, and a gulf existed between these moral states which only the Holy Spirit could close. Before presenting this view in the debate on the nature of true virtue, Hopkins had advanced it in different form in his argument that the awakened sinner was no further along the road to salvation than the unawakened sinner. Hopkins confidently rejected Edwards's claim that the secondary virtue which natural principles produced was morally and socially valuable even though it fell short of true virtue. He insisted that secondary virtue and the "negative moral goodness" it established in the world were irreconcilably opposed and in no way analogous to the disinterested benevolence of true virtue: "There is, however, a great difference and opposition in these two kinds of affections. . . . This selfish affection, though extended to the whole community with which the selfish man is connected, is at bottom nothing but love to himself. This is the foundation and center of his love. He in reality loves nothing but himself and regards others wholly for his own sake."[32] Hopkins created a complete disjunction between true and secondary virtue, because every affection that fell short of disinterested benevolence was rooted in selfishness. He argued, for example, that self-love, far from restraining wickedness, "is the source of all the profaneness and impiety in the world; and of all pride and ambition among men; which is nothing but selfishness acted out in this particular way."[33]

Hopkins's strictures on self-love in *True Holiness* led ultimately to the most famous tenet of his theological system: a regenerate person must be willing to be damned for the glory of God. "He therefore cannot know that he loves God and shall be saved," Hopkins argued in *A Dialogue between a Calvinist and a Semi-Calvinist*, written in the late 1780's and published posthumously in 1805, "until he knows he has that disposition which implies a willingness to be damned, if it be not most for the glory of God that he should be saved."[34] In other words, one could not avoid damnation except by being willing to be damned. Lay and clerical opponents of the New Divinity tore this doctrine out of context and used it to portray Consistent Calvinism as an absurd system. Hopkins's position becomes intelligible, however, when it is related to the eighteenth-century debate on the nature of true virtue and to what the New Divinity men saw as a crisis of social thought in New England.

After rejecting Edwards's contention that natural principles, including self-love, resembled true virtue and brought secondary virtue into the world, Hopkins reassessed the larger role of self-love in his mentor's theology. Few New Englanders other than Hopkins had access to the unpublished writings of Edwards that supplemented *True Virtue*. In these manuscripts Hopkins found Edwards arguing that self-love not only produced secondary virtue but that it operated on the level of true virtue. "That a man should love his own happiness," Edwards noted in *Charity and Its Fruits*, written in 1738 but not published until 1851, "is as necessary to his nature as the faculty of the will is; and it is impossible that such a love should be destroyed in any other way than by destroying his being."[35] Self-love, like the will, was a faculty common to all members of the human race. The converted as well as the unconverted were moved by it to desire their own happiness. The essential difference was that the regenerate, having gained a new disposition of the heart, identified their interest and happiness with love of Being in general. On the basis of this view of self-love, which was grounded in Lockean sensationalism, Edwards found it inconceivable that a person could be willing to be damned. In "Miscellany 530," Edwards stated the matter clearly: "Love to God, if it be superior to any other principle, will make a man forever unwilling, utterly and finally, to be deprived of that part of his own happiness which he has in God's being blessed and glorified, and the more he loves Him, the more unwilling he will be. So that this supposition, that a man can be willing to be perfectly and utterly miserable out of love to God, is inconsistent with itself."[36] Regeneration disposed the faculty of self-love to relish, delight, and seek happiness in eternal harmony with God. While not going as far as theological utilitarians, Edwards did argue that "wicked men do not love themselves enough"[37] or else they would seek their own eternal happiness by avoiding sin.

Hopkins countered by arguing that a Christ-like disposition for self-denial, rather than an inclination flowing from self-love to identify ultimate happiness with Being in general, was the hallmark of true virtue. He rejected all ethical theories that approved self-centered inducements to salvation: "To give up our temporal interest, worldly interest, for the sake of eternal happiness, wholly under the influence of self-love, is as real an instance of selfishness as parting with all we have now, to possess a large estate next year."[38] Love of God and neighbor and not the saving of one's soul became the core of Hopkinsianism. The true Christian must lose himself in a cause higher than his own salvation — namely, the temporal and eternal well-being of others.[39] Thus the most peculiar tenet of Hopkinsianism, and the one most offensive to the rational mind, reinforced the social activism which his redefinition of Being in general and his criticism of secondary virtue encouraged.

Taken together, Hopkins's innovations in the theory of true virtue represented an important shift away from the equivocal theological legacy of Edwards on the issue of worldly action in the direction of an emphatic endorsement of social reform.[40] Where Edwards saw true virtue as essentially a matter of right affections, Hopkins viewed it as right actions. God's moral law, Hopkins concluded, "leads us to consider holiness as consisting in universal disinterested good will considered in all its genuine exercises and fruits, and acted out in all its branches toward God, and our neighbor."[41]

In reinterpreting true virtue as radical disinterested benevolence, Hopkins was not simply responding to Edwards's positions. He was also attempting to furnish a corrective to the increasingly fashionable theological notion of self-love. In the eighteenth century, self-love was defined with the same range of implications it had displayed in Edwards's theology, in that it was at times viewed as a mediating moral state between selfishness and true virtue, while at other times it was considered part of true holiness itself. In either case it appeared to the New Divinity men to be a doctrine that promoted and legitimized avaricious, egoistic patterns of behavior. Their apprehensions had considerable justification, for the concept of self-love proved to be an intellectual way station on the road to a full-fledged theory of self-interest. By removing much of the moral obloquy attached to egocentric behavior, it eased the passage from traditional communal ideals to a new ideology of individualism and self-interest. As the rational clergy saw it, the idea of self-love brought about greater coherence between social theory and social reality. At the same time, they argued, it denied the legitimacy of naked self-interest (selfishness) and would create a more stable social order since, in theory at least, self-love would promote the public good. The notion of self-love lent those structural forces in eighteenth-century New England that encouraged individualistic, self-centered behavior — economic and demographic expansion, and land hunger — a theoretical argument that may have allowed many people to allay feelings of guilt for having violated social tradition and to rationalize self-interest. This was particularly true in commercial areas, where by the 1760's New England's crisis in social theory was adjusted and a modified corporate ethic (self-love) coexisted with naked self-interest.[42] Yet, as the recent work of several historians has suggested, in spite of such changes in social values, the rural New England world in which the New Divinity men originated and which supported their theological movement clung to an idealized corporate perspective that made even relatively minor social changes seem like radical departures from historical tradition.[43]

The 1750's and 1760's in New England have been described as "a period of experimentation in social theory because everyday experience confronted people with the problem" of contriving "a new rationale for the social order."[44] The New Divinity men saw present and potential dangers in such experimentation. Liberal and Old Light Calvinists drew their self-love social theories directly from rational moral philosophers like Shaftesbury and Hutcheson. Many New Lights, on the other hand, gave self-love a role in human behavior based upon the views of Edwards in

True Virtue.[45] It remained for the New Divinity men to protest what they saw as theological concessions to selfish social behavior.

To this theological task Hopkins brought a strong sense of moral urgency. In growing numbers ministers chose "to represent the hopes and fears, joys and sorrows, and all the exercises of the Christian as wholly selfish, and treat all of the doctrines and duties of christianity in this light," he protested. "How common to find arminians, neonominists, professed calvinists, antinomians, or whatever name they may bear, and however they may differ in other things all agreeing in this!"[46] The New Divinity men held that self-love ethical theories, whether Edwardsian or Hutchesonian, were contributing to the failure of communal ideals. As Hopkins reasoned, "if no person can renounce his eternal interest, in opposition to a selfish regard to it, there is no such thing in nature as self-denial, or public disinterested affection."[47] Furthermore, if the new social morality was anchored in egocentricity, then the truly benevolent man was required to battle that false morality in all its social manifestations. Hopkins's theology obliged him to oppose the emergent values of commercial Newport; in particular, it inspired his assault on slavery and the slave trade.

The idea of disinterested benevolence was not exclusively of New England origin. Francis Hutcheson, George Whitefield, John Wesley, and the Quakers, for example, all developed notions of benevolence in the eighteenth century that inspired the crusading reformers of the next century.[48] No other theory of disinterested benevolence, however, not even that of Edwards, approached the self-denying idealism of Hopkins's views. Consequently, many of New England's future religious reformers, particularly the next generation of young, pietistic, Congregational clerics, would come to see the doctrine of disinterested benevolence as a unique contribution of the New Divinity movement.[49] For these religious reformers Hopkins furnished not only a dynamic theological doctrine but a role model as well. The American Revolution, the Newport slave trade, and the slave system itself presented Hopkins with opportunities to demonstrate his disinterested love of Being in general and to call for the reform of American society.

With the publication of his *Inquiry concerning the Nature of True Holiness* in 1773, Hopkins had contributed three radical theological doctrines to the New Divinity movement in a period of less than fifteen years: sin as an advantage to the universe, the greater vileness of the awakened as opposed to the unawakened sinner, and true virtue as self-effacing disinterested benevolence. Theologically, the next ten years were unproductive. The Revolution disrupted his ministry in Newport. More importantly, it stimulated him to develop and apply the social and political implications of the New Divinity.

chapter eight

TRUE VIRTUE AND SOCIAL REFORM:
Slavery and the Revolution

HOPKINS'S repudiation of the new morality and the self-love ethical theories upon which it was based originated in his rural upbringing and twenty-five year pastorate in the back-country. It was intensified by his experience of the worldly society and commercial economy of Newport, with its mercantile involvement in the slave trade and the production of rum which was used to secure human cargo on the coast of Africa. To the rustic theologian, committed to a simple and even ascetic socio-religious tradition, Newport appeared a symbol of what America was in danger of becoming — a society comprised of avaricious, self-centered individuals.

Moreover, the behavior of Newport slave merchants underlined the importance of distinguishing secondary virtue from true virtue. In terms of conventional social morality the respectable slave traders, most of whom were practicing Christians, seemed to be virtuous men. Measured against the yardstick of disinterested benevolence, however, their virtue fell far short of love to Being in general. Hopkins linked his attack on Newport's slave traders and the social order they represented with the Revolutionary struggle against Great Britain. To evangelicals like Hopkins, the Revolution held out the promise that the visionary goal of the mid-century revival — the moral renovation of American society — would finally be fulfilled. As they saw it, resistance to Great Britain offered the American people a new opportunity to rededicate themselves to true virtue and to the spirit and millennial expectation that had led Edwards to proclaim that God's latter day glory would most likely begin in America. And now the evangelical social perspective received reinforcement from secular calls for an American commitment to Spartan, republican virtue and the public good.[1] Indeed, in both rural and commercial areas of New England the republican ideology of the Revolution, with its emphasis on public virtue and simplicity, heightened the conflict between traditional social theory and contemporary behavior and fired evangelical hopes for radical social reform.

Translated into the secular language of the Revolution, Hopkins's doctrine of disinterested benevolence became self-denying public affection, while love of Being in general became synonymous with a commitment to the public good. In politicizing his theology, Hopkins made the antislavery cause the nexus between religious and secular idealism, between the Awakening and the Revolution, between the millennium and the virtuous republic.

Prior to his settling in Newport in 1770, Hopkins had not publicly or privately expressed any disapproval of or moral uneasiness with the slave trade or slavery. Both his theological mentor, Edwards, and his close friend, Bellamy, owned slaves. Furthermore, for several years of Hopkins's residence at Great Barrington a black female servant lived in his household.[2] The transformation of the theologian into a dedicated antislavery reformer occurred between 1770 and 1773, the same years in which he developed his doctrine of disinterested benevolence.[3] But Hopkins's new-found antislavery identity was not simply a logical deduction from his theology. It evolved from his earliest experiences in Newport. For the first time in his life the backcountry minister confronted the grim reality of the slave trade. Chained Africans were sometimes unloaded in Newport and sold to the highest bidder right before Hopkins's eyes. Undoubtedly Hopkins heard stories of the horrors of this traffic in human flesh — accounts of suffering and wholesale death from disease while crossing the Atlantic and gruesome tales of slave insurrections at sea necessitating the mass slaughter of the valuable human freight.[4] Also contributing to Hopkins's moral awakening to slavery was the fact that he came to see the slave trade as a major economic prop of the acquisitive commercial society of Newport. As a result, his antislavery stand became part of a larger pattern of social protest.

Finally, Hopkins's conversion to antislavery in the early 1770's was influenced by an emerging body of opinion in the years preceding independence that slavery was at worst a sin and at best a policy inconsistent with the American struggle for liberty against Great Britain.

Perhaps as early as 1771 Hopkins preached to his congregation on the iniquity of the slave trade. By 1773 he denounced the slave system itself. The circumstances surrounding these early sermons would be romanticized by nineteenth-century abolitionists and admirers of Hopkins, creating a heroic myth of a disinterested minister "rising up before his slaveholding congregation, and demanding, 'in the Name of the Highest, the deliverance of the captive, and the opening of prison doors to them that were bound.' "[5] While there were slaveowners in Hopkins's church, the vast majority of his parishioners were not wealthy enough to possess such a fashionable luxury. Of those who did own slaves, few held more than one.[6] Newport's major slaveowners and slave traders did not belong to Hopkins's church; rather they were members of Ezra Stiles's Second Church or of the seaport's non-Congregational churches. In relation to his own parishioners, Hopkins was risking little by preaching against slavery and the slave trade.

Furthermore, by the time Hopkins became an outspoken antislavery reformer many other voices were being raised against slavery. Jonathan Edwards, Jr., for example, published several anonymous antislavery articles in New Haven papers in the fall of 1773.[7] The following year Levi Hart, Hopkins's friend and theological follower, delivered an important sermon in Connecticut — published in 1775 — that attacked slavery as a moral evil and political inconsistency. "What have the unhappy Africans committed against the inhabitants of the British colonies and islands in the West Indies," Hart asked, "to authorize *us* to seize them, or bribe them to seize one another, and transport them a thousand leagues into a strange land, and enslave them for life?"[8] In the same year that Hart spoke these words, the Rhode Island General Assembly enacted a law henceforth freeing all slaves imported into the colony. While the law did not deal with the involvement of Rhode Islanders in the slave trade outside of the colony, the actions of the First Continental Congress did. The delegates to this assembly agreed in 1774 to prohibit the slave trade and called for boycotts of any merchants who defied the order.[9]

The importance of Hopkins's antislavery stand, then, does not stem from a heroic solitariness. Rather, it originates in the comprehensiveness of his arguments against the slave trade and slavery, their derivation from New Divinity theology and social criticism, and their linkage to the republican political thought of the Revolution. In 1776 Hopkins published *A Dialogue Concerning the Slavery of the Africans* . . ., the first of his two major antislavery essays, dedicating the work to the Continental Congress. He reminded the delegates that the American cause and the question of slavery were at bottom moral problems, not simply political issues. Hopkins sought reassurance that the 1774 resolution to prohibit the slave trade issued "not merely from political reasons; but from a conviction of the unrighteousness and cruelty of that trade and a regard to justice and benevolence. . . ." He prayed that the members of the Congress were "deeply sensible of the inconsistence of promoting the slavery of the Africans, at the same time we are asserting our own civil liberty, at the risk of our fortunes and lives."[10]

For Hopkins the slavery issue furnished an ethical test not only of the general moral purity of the struggle against Britain but of the virtue of individual revolutionaries as well. As a result of his emphasis on disinterested action as the distinguishing sign of conversion, antislavery and anti-imperial activism emerged as visible indications of spiritual regeneration and true virtue in Hopkins's thought during the Revolution. Since disinterested benevolence required opposition to slavery and the slave trade and not simply to the policies of Britain, Hopkins suggested, the slavery issue allowed one to separate Revolutionary hypocrites from authentic republicans wholeheartedly committed to true virtue and the public good. In short, support of the antislavery cause became a form of benevolence and a sign of conversion, which demonstrated whether American Whigs were motivated by true virtue, that is, by disinterested love of Being in general.

The classic problem of the Great Awakening and of the theological debate over the nature of true virtue — the attempt to discern genuine religious affections — was redefined by Hopkins in terms of the political issues of the Revolution.[11] In opposing oppression, whether at the hands of slave traders, slaveowners, or

British officials, a person could gain assurance that he was regenerate and was fulfilling the demands of disinterested benevolence. In Hopkins's view, all conduct short of allegiance to these twin goals had its foundation in anti-Christian, and antirepublican, selfishness. Thus in his *Dialogue*, he urged the Continental Congress to establish a virtuous political course, encourage the moral regeneration of America, and ensure the success of the Revolution by "bring [ing] about a total abolition of slavery in such a manner as shall greatly promote the happiness of those oppressed strangers, and [the] best interest of the public."[12]

When Hopkins came to the problem of the method of abolishing slavery, his *Dialogue* demonstrated his firm opposition to public policies based on self-interest. He maintained that the economic loss involved in freeing slaves should not be seen as a barrier to the abolition of slavery, because disinterested benevolence and the public good required a sacrifice of self-interest. He informed slaveowners that their Africans should not only be set free but that they "should also be supplied liberally out of your store, agreeable to divine command."[13] Hopkins concluded his discussion of the economics of abolition with a corporate analysis of the importance of regulating human selfishness:

> How common it is for men who hire others to complain that the laborers do not earn the wages they give, and that they are constantly losing all the labor they hire. And if it were left wholly to him who hires what wages he should give the laborer, and he was accountable to none, how soon his hire would be reduced to little or nothing. The lordly, selfish employer would soon find out that his laborers hardly earned the food he was obliged to find them.[14]

Similarly, the abolition of slavery could not be left to the workings of self-interest.

Hopkins saw the degradation of both enslaved and free blacks as rooted in prejudice. He insisted that arguments in favor of the natural inferiority of the African race could not be legitimately used by true Christians as excuses for holding blacks in bondage or for permitting them to live in a state of freedom but inequality. Social equality would become a reality for blacks when everyone saw them as true Christians did—as part of Being in general, "by nature and by right, on a level with our brethren and children, and . . . our neighbors."[15]

In his *Dialogue* Hopkins went on to join the chorus of covenant theologians who saw British oppression as a providential punishment for American sins. He argued that the enslavement of the African race stood first among American transgressions of divine law. "And I take leave here to observe," Hopkins warned in his antislavery jeremiad, "that if the slavery in which we hold the blacks is wrong, it is a very great and public sin; and therefore a sin which God is now testifying against in the calamities he has brought against us." Slavery must be abolished, he prophesied, "before we can reasonably expect deliverance or even sincerely ask for it."[16]

Taking the role of a proslavery spokesman in his *Dialogue*, Hopkins asked: Had not the American cause already experienced considerable success without the eradication of slavery? By prohibiting the slave trade two years earlier, Hopkins responded (as an antislavery reformer), the American people had demonstrated a "partial reformation" of their selfish behavior, and this accounted for God's Revolutionary blessings. What God demanded, however, and what the Revolution offered an opportunity for, was a "thorough reformation" of all "public sins."[17] The social transformation that the Awakening had failed to accomplish would, Hopkins hoped, be achieved by the Revolution. For several years he had seen the promise of radical moral reformation held out by resistance to Britain. "The struggle is like to prove fatal to tea drinking in America, which will save much needless expense," he had written to Reverend John Erskine in Scotland in 1774. "And there is a hopeful prospect of its putting an end to many other extravagances, unless accommodation should take place soon."[18] With the mode of life of Newport's wealthy merchant class undoubtedly in mind, Hopkins challenged the American people not only to abolish slavery but also to reform all their selfish, extravagant behavior. By concentrating on the evil of slavery he did "not mean to exclude other public, crying sins found among us, such as impiety and profaneness — formality and indifference in the service and cause of Christ and his religion — and the various ways of open opposition to it — intemperance and prodigality and other instances of unrighteousness, &c ." Slavery and all the public sins of America were "the fruits of a most criminal, contracted selfishness."[19]

In Hopkins's eyes few Americans were as guilty of indulgence and luxury as Newport's wealthy merchant class. He saw the pious women of the First Church's praying society as exemplary Christians whose simple mode of life contrasted sharply with the social behavior of Newport's commercial aristocracy. In a memorial to one of the leaders of the women's group Hopkins castigated "the gay, rich and great of this world, who are strangers to real piety, who delight in show and parade, to glitter in costly array, and shine at balls and assemblies. . . ." If such people only knew the "real worth and excellence" of true virtue and "how mean, foolish and despicable they appear in the sight of the Savior and all his true friends," they would reform their lives and turn away from "the diversions of the theatre, stage or card table, reading romances, or idle senseless chat."[20]

Since slave owning, slave trading, and the other modes of behavior which he saw as sinful were so common in Newport, Hopkins came to believe that the British occupation of Newport was God's visitation of a special affliction upon the seaport's residents commensurate with the gravity of their evil ways and with the radical reformation needed to establish disinterested benevolence among such hardened wrongdoers. Shortly after the publication of his *Dialogue* in 1776 Hopkins left Newport to escape a British onslaught. Throughout 1775 the King's warships had crowded Newport harbor, threatening the destruction of the seaport. From time to time, the British released hatred of the defiant Americans by directing cannon balls to shore or by firing upon privateers in Narragansett Bay. In the fall of 1775 American soldiers were dispatched to Newport to prevent British confiscation of livestock to feed their troops. A mass exodus of apprehensive Newporters soon followed; Stiles fled the seaport early in 1776, and Hopkins became a refugee when the British Army occupied the city toward the close of the year.[21]

For the next three years he supported his family by filling vacant pulpits in Massachusetts and Connecticut. In the meantime war brought destruction to Newport. The British army finally ended its occupation of the seaport in October 1779. A month later Hopkins visited the city and found it devastated. Hundreds of buildings had been leveled, and all that remained of once fashionable homes were charred ruins. Hopkins's parsonage and meeting house were heavily damaged. The British had used the meeting house as a hospital and barracks, and Hopkins found pews torn apart, windows broken, the church bell missing and his pulpit destroyed. The parsonage of the rival Second Church was completely ruined, and its meeting house was heavily damaged. "I have not yet found more than four or five families of your congregation," Hopkins informed Stiles, now installed as President of Yale. "They with those of mine are rather low spirited, and without courage, which I suppose to be in a great measure the effect of their being so long under taskmasters, and their present poverty." During the war more than half of Newport's population had fled for safety into the countryside, and few people had returned, Hopkins reported to Stiles, because of fear that the British might sail into port again.[22]

Hopkins left the seaport after his brief visit in November 1779 and did not return until the following spring. Along with many other Newporters Hopkins shared poverty in the present and the prospect of an uncertain future. The destitute and diminished membership of the First Church was unable to provide him with a salary or pay to have the meeting house repaired. Hopkins was forced to hold services in a Baptist meeting house. Furthermore, the members of the Second Church, who did not have a pastor and whose house of worship was in need of extensive repair, were confronted with the unpleasant necessity of worshipping under Hopkins.[23] Toward the middle of 1780, the disgruntled parishioners of the Second Church proposed to unite with the members of Hopkins's society, if the latter would agree to dismiss their pastor and call a new minister. The members of the Second Church "are resolved not to hear me," Hopkins wrote to Stephen West, "as they dislike my doctrines in general; and especially my opposition to the slavery of the Africans."[24] The plan of union proved unacceptable to the First Church, however, and eventually Stiles's former parishioners obtained the services of their own minister.

Hopkins's depleted society recovered slowly, though never completely, from the effects of the war. With the financial help of other churches under New Divinity men the members of the First Church managed to repair their meeting house. But they were never again able to pay their pastor a fixed annual salary. When Hopkins received a call to settle over a church in Middleborough, Massachusetts, near the end of 1780, his supporters, anxious not to lose him, managed to raise money for his maintenance. Yet for the rest of his life, he had to rely on weekly contributions and private benefactions in lieu of a regular salary.[25] Consequently, he was often on the verge of poverty.

While the First Congregational Church and the city of Newport would never return to their pre-war status, the slave trade and slavery in America survived the war with only relatively minor setbacks. By 1784 six northern states had taken legal action against slavery, four of them passing gradual emancipation laws, which took several decades to abolish slavery completely.[26] The Rhode Island General Assembly approved such gradual emancipation legislation in 1784. However, the law was unsatisfactory to Hopkins and other members of the state's antislavery movement who continued to work for more effective legislation.

Even before the official end of the war in 1783, merchants in Newport and other parts of Rhode Island had resumed their involvement in the slave trade.[27] In December of that year many of the state's Quakers, under the leadership of Providence's Moses Brown, petitioned the General Assembly to abolish slavery and to prohibit Rhode Islanders from trafficking in slaves. In response a committee of deputies designed a bill requiring the manumission of all slaves born after March 1, 1784, and recommending that they be Christianized and educated. The legislation also provided for the gradual emancipation of many blacks who were presently enslaved. Males were to be freed at the age of twenty-one and females at eighteen. Masters who freed slaves at a younger age were obliged to prevent them from becoming public charges. The bill reasserted the 1774 resolution of the Continental Congress prohibiting the slave trade and stipulated that the owners of all Rhode Island vessels sailing for Africa post a bond of £1,000 as a guarantee against their involvement in the evil traffic.[28]

The Assembly overwhelmingly defeated the bill early in 1784, and in its place passed a milder, amended version. The new bill endorsed the plan for gradual abolition of slavery but overlooked the earlier proposals for imposing fines on violators. Furthermore, the amended bill did not prohibit Rhode Islanders from participating in the slave trade outside the state.[29]

By and large Hopkins remained on the periphery of this first major antislavery confrontation in the Rhode Island General Assembly. He relied on Moses Brown to keep him apprised of the progress of the antislavery cause in the Assembly. His brother, the wealthy and influential John Brown, Moses informed Hopkins on March 3, "was days in opposition" to the original bill and was instrumental in securing its defeat. Moses was not disheartened, however, and he hoped to raise a groundswell of public indignation over the continuation of the "Unnatural and Unchristian practice of [slave] trading." To assist in achieving this objective he urged Hopkins to make a public statement protesting the ineffective action of the General Assembly.[30]

Hopkins responded in a long letter that had nothing but praise for Moses and the Quakers who were zealously attempting to obtain justice for the enslaved Africans. In Hopkins's view Brown, like the pious ladies of the First Church, personified disinterested benevolence. Indeed, the conversion of the Quaker-merchant from a trafficker in human flesh to a vigorous foe of the slave trade and slavery undoubtedly gave Hopkins hope that similar reformations would be realized. Moreover, the Revolutionary moral struggle of disinterested benevolence against selfishness seemed to be typified for Hopkins in the conflict between Moses and his brother John. While Moses had reformed his self-interested, unChristian behavior, John remained in a pre-Revolutionary moral state, opposing the antislavery legislation inspired by his brother and continuing his commercial involvement in the slave trade. Revolutionaries like John were hypocrites, Hopkins suggested in his letter to Moses, who, in failing to complete a thorough moral reformation of America, were provoking God to visit further afflictions on the new nation. Exaggerating the role of the slave trade in the history of Newport, Hopkins informed Moses: "I have dared publically to declare that this town is the most guilty respecting the slave trade, of any on the continent, as it has been, in a great measure, built up by the blood of the poor Africans; and the only way to escape the effects of Divine displeasure is to be sensible of the sin, repent and reform."[31]

In addition to his antislavery sermons, Hopkins encouraged his church to take ecclesiastical action against members who were guilty of owning or trading slaves. As early as 1781 he and the church members pressured a deacon to guarantee the future freedom of his young, black servant-girl. In March 1784 the First Church voted "that the slave trade and the slavery of the Africans, as it has taken place among us, is a gross violation of the righteousness and benevolence which are so much inculcated in the gospel; and therefore we will not tolerate it in this church."[32] Like his sermons against slavery in the early 1770's, Hopkins's preaching did not heroically challenge a slaveholding congregation when he urged the passage of this antislavery resolution. After the war only a small number of Hopkins's parishioners owned slaves. These individuals were obliged to provide for the future, not the immediate, freedom of their slaves. While significant, such action was neither radical—especially in light of Hopkins's doctrine of disinterested benevolence—nor unique to the First Church. Following the example of the Quakers, some evangelical churches began in the mid-1780's to prohibit their members from owning or trading slaves. In December 1784, for example, the Baltimore Conference of the Methodist Episcopal Church agreed that excommunication would be the penalty for members who failed to comply with state antislavery laws. Other denominations in various states took similar action. Nevertheless, after a burst of idealism, Protestant leaders withdrew hastily from the antislavery cause. Only a year after its passage, the antislavery rule of the Methodist Church was abandoned. Protestant denominations pursued a cautious policy of placing the slavery issue in the hands of individual churches on the local level.[33] Hopkins's church continued to adhere to its antislavery resolution of 1784.

At the same time that his church adopted an official position on slavery, Hopkins became more involved in the Rhode Island antislavery movement. In response to Moses Brown's suggestion that he issue a public statement against the deficient antislavery legislation that the Rhode Island General Assembly had passed in March 1784, Hopkins drafted a long letter to the editor of the *Newport Mercury*. In spite of personal threats for publishing earlier antislavery material submitted by Hopkins, the printer agreed to insert the letter in the May 1, 1784, edition of the paper. Hopkins's letter attacked the legal and political arguments the deputies had used to explain their failure to prohibit Rhode Islanders from engaging in the slave trade outside the state. The deputies claimed that this aspect of the slave trade was carried on at sea or in other states and was beyond the jurisdiction of the Assembly. They also argued that it was inappropriate for Rhode Island to take further action on the slave trade since Congress was considering an anti-slave trade petition from the Quakers. Hopkins brushed aside legalities and political considerations and stressed that the issue was a moral one. He praised the Assembly for making a start in the right direction by its recent passage of the bill to abolish slavery gradually in Rhode Island. But the legislation did not go far enough, and he feared that Rhode Islanders were missing the best opportunity "to wash our hands, as far as possible, from the blood that otherwise must be found on them and prevent impending wrath [from] bursting on our heads."[34]

From 1784 until the ratification of the Federal Constitution with its clause protecting the slave trade for twenty years, few Americans, perhaps not even the indefatigable Moses Brown, exceeded Hopkins in the amount of time and energy devoted to the antislavery cause. Hopkins did not confine his efforts to Rhode Island. Increasingly in the 1780's local groups of antislavery reformers in the northeast communicated with one another, passed articles, correspondence, and local information from hand to hand, and forged a supportive antislavery network and common consciousness which cut through regional and religious differences. By the close of the decade, Hopkins's contributions to this antislavery movement had won him recognition as a reformer comparable to the repute he had already achieved as a theologian.

In 1785 the newly formed New York Abolition Society (one of only two such societies then in existence in America) reprinted Hopkins's antislavery *Dialogue*, written nearly ten years earlier. The Society used two thousand published copies in a campaign to end the slave trade in New York. The *Dialogue* was distributed to all the members of Congress and to all the legislators of New York. For the next several years the Society's correspondence committee informed Hopkins of the progress of their efforts and sought information on antislavery activities in New England.[35]

During these years Hopkins repeatedly urged fellow ministers in Connecticut, Massachusetts, and Rhode Island to organize the clergy into a united front against the slave trade. Early in 1786 Moses Brown informed him that the dissenting clergy and a number of Quakers in England had begun to unite and launch efforts to end slavery in the British colonies and outlaw the slave trade. "I could wish the influence of the American clergy were more United and Engaged in this Business," Brown wrote.[36] Less than a month later Hopkins began working to unify the clergy against the slave trade. "Would it not be worth while," he suggested to

Levi Hart in Connecticut, "to attempt to get the convention of Clergy in Boston, the general Association in Connecticut, and the Synods of New York and Philadelphia to remonstrate against it to Congress or [in] some other way to bear testimony against it."[37] Hart in the eastern section of the state and Jonathan Edwards, Jr., in New Haven became Hopkins's allies in promoting such a plan in Connecticut. Several months later he reported to Moses Brown that the clergy in Boston had taken a public stand against the slave trade, and he hoped that the clergy in every state would openly protest the oppression of the blacks; "I am attempting to promote this," he notified Brown.[38] In 1787 he labored, with little apparent success, to organize first the ministers of Newport and then all the clergy of Rhode Island to petition the Assembly to suppress the slave trade.[39]

While keeping his hand in several state antislavery efforts, Hopkins began writing a new essay calling once again for a radical reformation of American behavior. The work was intended for publication in the *Newport Herald*, but Hopkins reported to Moses Brown that the printer had decided against publishing it because many of his subscribers were involved in the slave trade. Therefore Hopkins sought Brown's help in getting his piece published in Providence.[40]

The essay — signed "Crito" — appeared in two installments in the October 6 and 13, 1787, editions of the *Providence Gazette and Country Journal*; it was Hopkins's second major antislavery work.[41] Hopkins drafted the essay while the Constitutional Convention was still in session in Philadelphia. Although he did not dedicate the work to the Convention, his message was clearly directed toward the members of that body who had completed their deliberations by the time the essay appeared. "Crito" hoped that the delegates would devise a constitution giving the national government the power to prohibit American citizens from participating in the slave trade. The persistence of the unChristian trade and of slavery itself, he maintained, confirmed the hypocrisy of the Revolutionary commitment to Being in general and disinterested benevolence. The American people continued to be guilty of "a national sin, and a sin of the first magnitude — a sin which righteous Heaven has never suffered to pass unpunished in this world."[42]

America's national guilt was compounded, however, by the

hypocritical piety and opportunistic reforms of the Revolutionary years. Consequently, divine wrath was now aroused to an unprecedented degree. In fact, "Crito" insisted, the social and political disorder of the 1780's was clearly divine punishment for the failure of Americans to reform their selfish ways. Indeed, the continuing oppression of blacks stood as the main sign that the Revolution had failed to reform thoroughly all of America's indulgent, self-centered behavior and to reconstruct the social order on the basis of love to Being in general. The Revolutionary commitment to simplicity and frugality had been abandoned, "Crito" pointed out, and Americans were spending their money "for foreign luxuries or unnecessaries, and those things which might have been manufactured among ourselves." Instead of a society held together by disinterested benevolence, America in the 1780's was afflicted with "diversions and contentions" that appeared "to be hastening to universal confusion and anarchy." For "Crito" nothing less than the moral redemption of the Revolution and the salvation of America lay in the hands of the delegates to the Constitutional Convention. By suppressing the slave trade the Convention could rekindle Revolutionary idealism and dedication to disinterested benevolence and begin anew America's sweeping reformation. If the delegates failed to complete their moral task, greater providential scourges would descend upon America.[43]

Hopkins's essay was distributed widely. He sent it to Levi Hart, who persuaded newspapers in Norwich and Hartford to publish it free of charge. The New York Abolition Society used the work in a new petition effort to end the slave trade in that state.[44] Shortly after the essay's publication in Providence, Moses Brown had fifty copies printed and distributed to the members of the Rhode Island General Assembly who were then considering a new law against the slave trade.[45]

Hopkins's work was published just as the states began to debate the new constitution, which prevented Congressional interference with the slave trade until 1808, a provision that deeply disappointed many antislavery reformers. For Hopkins, official protection of the slave trade furnished final verification that the Revolutionaries had retreated from the lofty moral perspective of 1776. It also made clear to him that the new republic would be based on faulty moral foundations — on self-love rather than disinterested benevolence. "How does it appear in the sight of heaven, and of all good men, well informed," he wrote to Levi Hart, "that *these states*, who have been fighting for liberty, and consider themselves as the highest and most noble example of zeal for it, cannot agree in any political constitution, unless it indulge and authorize them to enslave their fellow men." Such a policy, he warned, would "bring a curse so that we cannot prosper."[46]

Nevertheless, Hopkins reluctantly endorsed the Constitution, because he feared that if it were "not adopted by the States as it now stands, we shall have none, and nothing but anarchy and confusion can be expected."[47] But even ratification, he confided to Levi Hart, would not allay his fears for America's future. The new Congress, he predicted, would be controlled by "unclean spirits" who "will turn the members of that august body into devils."[48] Although Hopkins, like so many New England clerics, became a supporter of the Federalist Party, his doctrine of disinterested benevolence, and the social and political thought that flowed from it, allowed at best only a lukewarm, skeptical endorsement of the new government.

Although the campaign to suppress the slave trade on a national level continued, the ratification of the Constitution placed an almost insurmountable legal obstacle in its way. Still, the new government was not empowered to prohibit action by individual states against the traffic. Hopkins's disappointment with the results of the Philadelphia Convention was partially offset in the fall of 1787 when the Rhode Island General Assembly approved a strong bill outlawing the slave trade. The deputies barred Rhode Island citizens and residents from engaging in the evil traffic. Violators would be punished by fines of £100 for every slave transported and £1,000 for each ship involved in the illegal trade.[49]

Soon Hopkins shifted his attention to Connecticut, where Rhode Island slavers were secretly carrying on their trading activities. He attempted to impress Levi Hart and Jonathan Edwards, Jr., with the urgency of prosecuting their earlier plan to organize a clerical protest against the slave trade in Connecticut as the first step in a campaign to achieve the legal suppression of the abominable traffic in that state. In the fall of 1788 the clergy of Connecticut united and created a committee, which included Edwards, to draft a petition requesting that the General Assembly follow the example of Rhode Island and outlaw the slave trade.[50]

Rhode Island citizens continued to traffic in slaves in Connecticut, however, and some were bold enough to defy the anti-slave trade law right at home. Rhode Island officials failed to enforce the law adequately and punish violators. Thus, Moses Brown and Hopkins agreed in the fall of 1788 that the time had arrived for the establishment of an abolition society in the state.[51] For a number of years both antislavery reformers had been corresponding with the two existing abolition societies in Philadelphia and New York. Indeed, Hopkins had worked so closely with these two groups of reformers that both societies conferred honorary membership on him in 1788.[52] Prior to that time Hopkins and Brown had discussed the prospect of establishing a local abolition society. When Hopkins had first heard of the formation of the New York Society in 1785 he had written to Brown expressing the hope that "similar societies will be formed in other states." Was "it not worthwhile to try one in this State?" he had asked Brown.[53] By 1788 an abolition society appeared to be a necessity to ensure compliance with Rhode Island's anti-slave trade law and to look after the welfare of the state's free blacks.

In February 1789 Rhode Island's antislavery reformers met and established the Providence Society for the Abolition of the Slave Trade. The following month Hopkins wrote to Moses Brown and conveyed his displeasure with the title of the new organization, which he found "too confined." He recommended that the name of the society "be extended to the whole state." Furthermore, he suggested, neither in its title nor in its activities should the new society "be confined to the Abolition of the Slave Trade. It ought to promote the freedom of those now in slavery, and to assist those who are free, as far as may be, to the enjoyment of the privileges of freemen and the comforts of life."[54] In spite of his objections and early refusal to sign the constitution of the organization unless the changes he proposed were made, Hopkins joined the new Providence-based society shortly after its formation.

With the appearance of the abolition society, some Rhode Island merchants geared up pro-slave trade presses for a concerted attack on the organization. John Brown, under the pseudonym "A Citizen," conducted a lengthy public campaign against the society in Providence newspapers.[55] In Newport, opposition was so intense, Hopkins reported to Moses Brown, that he saw no prospect of establishing a corresponding committee of the Society in the seaport: "No committee formed in this town would be able to do much; and if there should be any prosecutions, they must be carried on in Providence."[56] Hopkins demanded that the Society seek the punishment of those who had violated the anti-slave trading law prior to the establishment of the organization and not simply work for the prosecution of subsequent offenders.

By now Hopkins had grown accustomed to the opposition of segments of the Newport community to his antislavery efforts. In the 1780's local slave traders sometimes expressed more hostility toward Hopkins than did his theological enemies. The recollections of several contemporaries suggest that, in the words of one Newport resident, Hopkins's "ultra-Calvinism was taken advantage of by the slave traders . . . and he was grossly calumniated and his sermons and speeches were wickedly perverted." As a youth in the late eighteenth century, this Newporter heard such stories about Hopkins that he "was afraid of him as I should be of some monster."[57] Theologically and temperamentally, Hopkins was prepared to accept the consequences of advocating an unpopular cause, especially in a community like Newport, which, he believed, had a corrupt social order characterized by acquisitive, egoistic values and behavior. He was seemingly driven to challenge this social order. His doctrine of disinterested benevolence extended outward, embracing the Revolution, social protest, and reform. It also had an inward thrust, compelling him constantly to strive for a sacrificial, Christ-like purity in his heart. In championing the antislavery cause in Newport, Hopkins was attempting to satisfy his psychological needs as well as the ethical demands of disinterested benevolence.

chapter nine

THE CONVERSION
OF AFRICA:
Foreign Missions and
Black Colonization

HOPKINS believed that the ethical obligations of disinterested benevolence could not be fulfilled in merely a local, or even a national, context. Love of Being in general entailed universal benevolence. Hence, Hopkins had displayed an early interest in foreign missions. In the late 1780's and the 1790's, when prejudice against blacks appeared to be intensifying and when New England officials seemed reluctant to enforce state laws against the slave trade, Hopkins renewed a long-deferred desire to establish a mission colony of American blacks in Africa. During these years, which witnessed the start of the Second Great Awakening, Hopkins's self-effacing doctrine of disinterested benevolence merged with a revitalized millennial expectation to provide the New Divinity movement with a theological rationale for missionary work. As Leonard Woods, Hopkinsian Professor of Theology at Andover Seminary, put it in 1812 at the ordination of America's first foreign missionaries, with true virtue "reigning in his heart, the fervent, devoted Christian presents himself a living sacrifice unto God, and counts it a privilege to do and to suffer anything for the advancement of His cause." Disinterested benevolence, Woods continued, allowed "the sacrifice of property and pleasure; stripes, imprisonment, and death lose their terrors, and become more attractive, than any earthly good."[1]

Hopkins not only developed an interpretation of Christian social ethics that encouraged a missionary universal benevolence;

142

he continued in Newport the active engagement in missionary work that he had demonstrated in western New England. During the more than thirty years he preached in the seaport, Hopkins made repeated attempts to send free blacks to Africa to establish a mission. As a result of these efforts, Hopkins extended his network of antislavery acquaintances to include reformers in Britain, Scotland, and Africa. He also disclosed the evangelical implications of his theology and furnished a practical as well as a theoretical legacy to the foreign missionary and African colonization movements in New England.

Hopkins's thirty years of planning for an African mission began soon after his ordination in Newport in 1770. Among the black members of the First Church were two pious slaves whom he saw as potential African missionaries. John Quamine, one of the prospective missionaries, was a native of Guinea who had been brought from his homeland in a Newport merchant's ship and sold into slavery in the seaport around 1755. After being converted to Christianity, he experienced rebirth and in 1765 was admitted to the First Church. Similarly, Quamine's friend, Bristol Yamma, had been captured in Africa, transported to Newport, and eventually became a member of the First Church. Hopkins reported that this second native of Guinea was "more than common engaged in religion; and remarkably steady, discerning and judicious with respect to the nature of true religion, and the most important doctrines of the gospel. . . ."[2] In addition to their personal piety, both of these natives of Africa were suited for missionary work, Hopkins reasoned, because they retained their native language.

Hopkins discussed the African mission with the would-be missionaries who enthusiastically endorsed the subject. Indeed, Quamine had previously contemplated such a mission, he later informed Ezra Stiles. "He tells me," Stiles noted, "that ever since he tasted the Grace of the Lord Jesus, he conceived a Thought and Earnest Desire or Wish that his Relations and Country men in Africa might also come to a knowledge of, and taste the same blessings."[3]

In early 1771 Hopkins drafted a proposal for an African mission. He circulated the manuscript among fellow New Divinity ministers, many of whom encouraged his efforts.[4] It was not until the spring of 1773, however, that Hopkins began to seek public support for his proposal. In April of that year he divulged his plan to the influential Ezra Stiles. Justifiably, Stiles was skeptical of Hopkins's visionary hopes for the Christianization of Africa, which, the New Divinity minister argued, was a crucial step in the direction of the Christianization of the world. The more pragmatic pastor of Newport's Second Church deferred making a decision to aid the mission. He informed Hopkins that his proposed mission would require at least "30 or 40 proper and well instructed negroes. . . ." Even then, he cautioned, the chances that the project would succeed were slim.[5]

With Stiles's support Hopkins had hoped to begin soliciting funds from New England churches to purchase the freedom of the prospective missionaries. Stiles's reservations and indecision delayed such a course of action. Late in the spring of 1773, however, what Hopkins undoubtedly interpreted as the intervening hand of Divine Providence helped remove one of the major obstacles to the mission. Earlier in the year, Quamine and Yamma had jointly purchased a ticket in one of the innumerable public or private lotteries that helped finance so many eighteenth-century projects. The ticket won a prize of three hundred dollars for the Africans which enabled them to secure their freedom. Quamine's master agreed to free him for his one hundred fifty dollar share of the lottery prize and thirty more dollars which he would have to pay from money earned after manumission. On these terms Quamine gained his freedom immediately; but Yamma's master refused to set him free. Undaunted, Hopkins proceeded with arrangements for training the two missionaries while he attempted to persuade Yamma's master to grant him his freedom. In the summer of 1773, Yamma finally became a free man. His master consented to free him for two hundred dollars. Hopkins provided the fifty dollars that were needed to bring the slave's lottery share up to the required amount. This was done on the condition that Hopkins would be reimbursed by Yamma's labor or by charitable donations to the African mission.[6]

Stiles now gave a lukewarm endorsement to the project. Nothing had occurred to remove his misgivings about Hopkins's quixotic scheme; nevertheless, in August 1773 Stiles signed his name to a circular describing the proposed mission and soliciting contributions to make it a reality. From an unmistakably Hopkinsian perspective, the circular informed the public that Quamine and Yamma "are not only *willing*, but are *very desirous* to quit all worldly prospects, and risk their lives in attempting to open a door for the propagation of Christianity among their poor, ignorant, perishing heathen brethren." Hopkins tied the mission to the antislavery movement and the millennium. Contributions in support of the evangelization of Africa, the circular pointed out, should be made as partial compensation for the injustices committed against blacks in America. Moreover, all those Christians praying for the establishment of the kingdom of God on earth should "liberally contribute to forward this attempt to send the glorious gospel of the blessed God to all the nations who now worship false gods, and dwell in the habitations of cruelty, and the land of the shadow of death."[7]

Even though the influential Stiles publicly approved of the missionary project, liberal and moderate Calvinists were reluctant to assist any endeavor in which Hopkins played such an important role. Perhaps Charles Chauncy summed up the feelings of many opponents of the New Divinity when he protested, as Stiles reported, "that the Negroes had better continue in Paganism than embrace Mr. H[opkins's] scheme, which he judges far more blasphemous."[8]

In contrast to Chauncy's opposition and Stiles's half-hearted endorsement of the African mission, many Consistent Calvinists enthusiastically supported Hopkins's proposal. Shortly after issuing the circular publicizing the plan for the mission, Hopkins began to contact New Divinity ministers and churches to raise funds to educate and outfit the missionaries. The women's praying society of the First Church, Hopkinsians in Boston, and the ministers of Berkshire County quickly contributed money and moral support for the mission. Levi Hart spearheaded a drive in Connecticut to publicize the plan and raise money.[9]

In addition, Hopkins and Stiles sent their circular to ministers up and down the Atlantic Coast and across the ocean to Europe. Hopkins wrote to the Reverend John Erskine of the Society for Promoting Christian Knowledge in Scotland, hoping that this organization would lend its assistance to the mission. The Society responded in 1774, warmly endorsing the plan and contributing £30 towards its expenses.[10] Hopkins also sent a letter to Philip Quaque, a black missionary of the Society for the Propagation of the Gospel in Foreign Parts stationed in Guinea, requesting information on the prospect of establishing a mission in the area. Quaque's reply was sharply critical of the proposal. Guinea had been torn and impoverished by the slave trade, the Anglican missionary reported, and it was unlikely that such a mission as Hopkins proposed would have much chance of succeeding. Unless the missionaries went under the sponsorship of the S.P.G., they would most likely be "lured into debauchery" or die from disease.[11]

Hopkins brushed aside the criticisms and suggestions of Quaque. He received encouragement from the black poet Phillis Wheatley who had become deeply interested in the African mission. She agreed with Hopkins that the mission "was the beginning of that happy period foretold by the Prophets, when all shall know the Lord from the least to the greatest." "Let us not be discouraged," she wrote Hopkins in May 1774, "but still hope that God will bring about his great work, though Philip [Quaque] may not be the instrument in the divine hand to perform this work of wonder, turning the Africans from dark to light."[12]

Even before Hopkins received these encouraging words from Miss Wheatley, he had dismissed the criticisms of Quaque and proceeded with the plans for the African mission. He and Stiles began instructing Quamine and Yamma in the fall of 1773, and the following summer the two Africans were sent to Levi Hart for further schooling. From Hart's parsonage in Preston, Connecticut, the two missionaries journeyed to Princeton College for more detailed instruction. President John Witherspoon reported their progress at the college in a letter to Hopkins in February 1775: "Bristol Yamma has received the money you sent him. He and his companion behave very well. They are becoming pretty good in reading and writing & likewise have a pretty good Notion of the Principles of the Christian faith."[13]

The outbreak of military hostilities between Great Britain and the American colonies in 1775 hindered further planning for the mission. Its supporters found it difficult to communicate with one another or to generate sufficient interest in and financial backing for the project. Nevertheless, in the spring of 1776 Hopkins and Stiles issued a second circular which described the progress of the mission since 1773 and which requested additional contributions toward its fulfillment. They reported that two more Newport blacks had expressed a desire to join the mission. Money was now needed to support and educate these two new missionaries as well as to finance the voyage of Quamine and Yamma. Although the mission was only a small beginning, the circular expressed the hope that the endeavor would "issue in something very great, and open the way to the happiness and salvation of multitudes; yea, of many nations, who are now in the most miserable state, ready to perish in the darkness of heathenism." The circular concluded by urging the American people to see the connection between the African mission and the Revolution. Zeal in promoting the mission — like zeal in abolishing slavery and the slave trade and in bringing about a moral reformation of American society — would be rewarded by God with success against Great Britain, so that the proposed mission did not interfere with the Revolutionary cause, but on the contrary advanced it.[14]

Hopkins's New Divinity and his millennial expectation encouraged him to see the interrelatedness of the African mission, social reform, and the Revolution. In *Sin . . . an advantage to the Universe* he had argued that God would use evil, suffering, and sin as means for the promotion of His kingdom on earth. British oppression of the colonists was an evil which in 1776 appeared to be producing moral progress. Were not Americans espousing an inspiring dedication to the public good and practicing the virtues of thrift and simplicity? Had not the Continental Congress prohibited the slave trade, firing the hopes of those who sought the abolition of slavery? In short, was not the evil of British tyranny working as a means of good — a means of establishing the kingdom of God in America?

The millennium would begin in America, Hopkins believed, but it would cover the world. Thus slavery, like British oppression, was a means for good — a sin which God would turn into an instrument for the spread of Christianity around the world. From the Revolution to the end of his life Hopkins clung to the view that, as he affirmed in 1793, slavery "will not only have an end, but is designed by the Most High to be the means of introducing the gospel among the nations in Africa." In the Providential plan, converted ex-slaves were to be instruments for the Christianization of Africa. Such individuals, Hopkins wrote, "will by our assistance return to Africa and spread the light of the gospel in that now dark part of the world; and propagate those arts and that science, which shall recover them from their ignorance and barbarity which now prevail, to be civilized, Christian and happy people. . . ."[15] In the absence of meaningful support for the mission after 1776, Hopkins's millennial vision sustained his commitment to the African plan.

The circular of 1776 produced only a meager financial response. Even if the war ended, insufficient money was on hand to enable Quamine and Yamma to sail for Guinea. Instead, the missionaries returned to Newport to support themselves until another opportunity arose to launch their holy voyage. The circular of 1776 marked the end of Stiles's involvement in the proposed mission. The prospects of the mission suffered another setback when Quamine was killed aboard a privateer during the Revolutionary War.[16] Still undiscouraged, Hopkins resumed his efforts on behalf of the mission in 1784. In an unpublished manuscript that was similar to the circulars of 1773 and 1776, Hopkins expressed "hope that some way will be opened to bring the design to effect, and that the money which has been spent on it will not be in vain." Three of the four original missionaries were alive and eager to embark for Africa, he reported.[17]

By 1784 Hopkins had renewed his desire to Christianize Africa, but he did so in a way that compromised his commitment to social justice for American blacks. Increasingly in the 1780's he talked of colonizing free blacks in Africa. This new emphasis in his antislavery thought was a response to the realization that most whites were far from ready to view Africans as part of Being in general. As a result of the war and emancipation legislation, the free black population of America grew significantly in the 1780's. But the growth of free black communities only intensified white racial prejudice. Ultimately, Hopkins believed, God would see to it that blacks achieved social justice in America. In the meantime, however, free blacks were victimized by racial prejudice, and their resettlement in Africa, he concluded, was an interim solution to the problem of protecting their welfare. Furthermore, repatriated American blacks could bring the gospel and "civilization" to that continent.

In a letter to Moses Brown in April 1784, Hopkins described his new proposal and attempted to convince the Quaker reformer that African colonization should be an integral part of the antislavery crusade. Instead of the black missionaries returning to their homeland by themselves, as Hopkins and Stiles had earlier planned, they would be accompanied by a colony of emancipated slaves. Such a project was obviously more ambitious and costly than the pre-war proposal. In addition to buying a ship, hiring a captain and crew, and securing a cargo to be sold in Africa, Hopkins wrote to Brown, "a number [of blacks] who shall be thought best qualified for this business, must first be sent to Africa, to treat with some of the nations there and request of them lands, proper and sufficient for them and as many as shall go with them." The colony, Hopkins impressed upon Brown, would produce manifold benefits: "Such a settlement would not only be for the benefit of those who shall return to their native country, but it would be the most likely and powerful means of putting a stop to the slave trade, as well as of increasing Christian knowledge among the heathen." Clearly, such a large-scale plan would be doomed without the support of the Quakers, who in the 1780's were in the forefront of antislavery agitation. Thus Hopkins sought the influential Brown's approval, realizing the importance of securing the moral and financial backing of the Quakers. "I communicate these hints of a plan to you," he wrote, "that I may know how far you approve of it, and whether you think it practicable. And if you do, whether you, in conjunction with some of your able friends, would advance anything considerable to promote such a design."[18]

Brown was a dedicated antislavery reformer, but he was also a businessman who was far more practical-minded than the visionary Hopkins. Brown raised several objections to Hopkins's proposal. In the first place, he questioned, was Hopkins not aware of the Quaker "principle in respect to spreading the Gospel that it requires a special call and qualification? Should these appear in any blacks I hope we should not be wanting to incourage [sic] and assist them in that work." Until individual blacks experienced a call to preach the gospel, "or some christian state be drawn to patronice [sic] such an attempt" as Hopkins proposed, Brown would not consider supporting African colonization. He wished to concentrate on abolishing the slave trade, and he did not want involvement in Hopkins's fanciful proposal to interfere with more practical reform efforts. "At present," he wrote Hopkins, "it seems my business to suppress the pernisious [sic] trade from this state [Rhode Island] particularly."[19]

For the next several years Hopkins joined Brown and other

antislavery reformers in crusades close to home. He found little opportunity to promote African colonization. Indeed, few Americans during the mid-1780's thought seriously about colonizing blacks in Africa. To be sure, in March 1787 Hopkins was visited by William Thornton, a naturalized American citizen and native of the Virgin Islands, who in the late 1780's traveled about New England attempting to drum up black and white support for his own colonization scheme. Hopkins thought that Thornton was "too flighty and unsteady to be at the head of an affair in which he is very zealous. . . ." But he sent Thornton to Moses Brown with a letter conveying his continued hope for an African mission.[20] As Thornton would soon discover, however, the beginning of significant interest in the repatriation of American blacks was at least a decade away.

What rekindled Hopkins's hope for the African project in the late 1780's, and what would eventually spur the interest of less idealistic supporters of colonizing efforts in the 1790's, was the establishment of a British-sponsored colony of blacks in Africa in 1787. In February of that year four hundred colonists sailed from England to Sierra Leone.[21] For the next two years Hopkins waited impatiently for information on the progress of the settlement. During this period in America efforts to secure justice for the African race were being met with opposition at every turn. The Constitutional protection of the slave trade for twenty years, the open defiance of state laws against the traffic, and the specter of racial prejudice intensified Hopkins's commitment to African colonization.

At the beginning of 1789 Hopkins began anew to lay the groundwork for the African settlement. In 1788 the Reverend John Erskine had suggested that Hopkins and other supporters of the mission proposal appeal once again to the Scottish Society for Propagating Christian Knowledge for assistance in establishing an African colony. He predicted that the Society would probably make a significant financial contribution to the undertaking.[22] A group of Newport blacks was prepared to return to Africa, Hopkins reported to Erskine in 1789, but no steps had been taken toward obtaining a vessel to transport them or securing land on which they could settle. Hopkins now hoped that the Newporters would be able to join the recently established Sierra Leone Colony.

"If it should be found that they may," he wrote to Erskine, "the way would be opened to prosecute our plan, and then we should, doubtless, apply to your society for assistance, not doubting of their readiness to grant [it]."[23]

The basis of Hopkins's new optimism for the success of his African colony plan was undoubtedly Granville Sharp's invitation to American blacks to join the Sierra Leone experiment. Sometime after the formation of the colony, Sharp, a prominent British antislavery reformer and one of the prime movers behind Sierra Leone, notified the abolition societies in New York and Philadelphia that American blacks would be welcomed at the settlement.[24] From Philadelphia and New York the offer was most likely communicated to Hopkins and other antislavery reformers in New England.

On January 16, 1789, two days after he had written to Erskine in Scotland, Hopkins addressed a long letter to Sharp. After introducing himself and recounting his antislavery activities since his earliest days in Newport, Hopkins came to the purpose of his letter. Although many blacks were free in New England, he informed Sharp, "their circumstances are, in many respects, unhappy, while they live here among the whites; the latter looking down upon them, and being disposed to treat them as underlings, and denying them the advantages of education and employment, &c., which tends to depress their minds and prevent their obtaining a comfortable living, &c." Hopkins claimed that he knew many free blacks who wished to return to Africa. A number of these ex-slaves were deeply religious, he advised Sharp, and they desired to form their own church and lead all who were willing to go back to their homeland. Hopkins assured Sharp that the blacks from Newport and other parts of Rhode Island who would join the Sierra Leone Colony were "educated and habituated to industry and labor, either on lands, or as mechanics and are hereby prepared to bring forward such a settlement, better than any other blacks, I believe, that can be found." Since no one in America seemed to have more than hearsay information on the structure and progress of the Colony, Hopkins asked Sharp to supply details on the social, economic, religious, and political life of the settlement. Finally, Hopkins wished to know if the American colonists would be given "encouragement and assistance" in acquiring land in Sierra Leone.[25]

By the time Hopkins received Sharp's reply, nearly another year had gone by with still no actual progress made toward launching the mission colony from America. Sharp notified Hopkins that many of the whites who had been sent to aid the settlement had become involved in the slave trade. Nevertheless, the colony of approximately two hundred blacks appeared to be "very well united" and adhering to the "Regulations" governing its operation. He believed that the settlers would agree "to receive and accommodate all new comers with equal lots of land, *gratis*, until they amount at least to six hundred householders. . . ." Therefore, Sharp suggested, there was ample room for Hopkins's mission colony of Rhode Island blacks. The conditions of Sharp's offer were simple enough: "whatever people from America will engage to submit to the terms of the Regulations and the English government . . . will be admitted to free lots . . . provided that *they go all at one time*, and show this letter, or a copy of it, to the Governor and Assembly of Settlers in the Province of Freedom."[26]

Not since before the war had prospects looked so bright for the African mission. But much work needed to be done to take advantage of Sharp's invitation. Now nearly seventy years old and in declining health, Hopkins was in no position to assume full responsibility for raising the money, securing the necessities, and seeing to all the numerous details that such an ambitious project demanded. The only alternative was to appeal to abolition societies for help in organizing the colony. Hopkins sought to persuade existing antislavery organizations to function as missionary societies, protecting the rights and welfare of free blacks and working for the colonization of those who wished to return to Africa. For the next several years after he received Sharp's offer, Hopkins endeavored to convince his antislavery coworkers of the importance and feasibility of African colonization.

Hopkins concentrated his initial efforts on the Connecticut Abolition Society for reasons which he explained to Levi Hart in June of 1791. "The African Societies in Pennsylvania, New York and this State [Rhode Island]," he wrote, "are composed of so many Quakers, who make the most active, ruling part; and they, for some reason or other, are not disposed to promote such a design [as African colonization]." Thus Hopkins saw "no encouragement to apply to them for assistance." Instead he hoped that "if the society in Connecticut should take the lead in promoting such a design, perhaps they [the other abolition societies] might fall in afterwards and join to carry it on."[27]

Hopkins urged Hart to assume the leadership of the effort to organize a colony of free American blacks. "And you must plan, advise and prosecute," he exhorted Hart. "I am too old to do much." To begin the transfer of leadership, Hopkins recommended that Hart seek the Connecticut Abolition Society's approval of the colonization proposal and enlist the aid of its members in raising funds for the project. He further suggested that through the Connecticut Society, Hart should strive for official state approval of an African mission collection in all the churches of Connecticut.[28]

Two years later, in May 1793, while Hart continued to struggle, with little apparent success, to unite Connecticut's antislavery forces behind the African plan, Hopkins appeared before the Providence Abolition Society to deliver a long discourse which explained the benefits of colonization schemes like his own. Perhaps the Society had agreed to hear the aged theologian simply out of courtesy and respect for his persistent dedication to the antislavery cause, for Moses Brown and other Quaker members of the Society remained reluctant to support colonization efforts. For his part, Hopkins most likely saw the opportunity to speak to the Society as a final attempt to persuade men he knew were benevolently inclined to endorse his two-decade-old proposal.

Hopkins began by reminding his audience that Christ commanded all Christians — not simply the Apostles and future ministers of His word — to spread the Gospel. Christ obliged all of his followers, Hopkins argued, "in all proper ways, according to their ability, stations, and opportunities, to promote this benevolent design, and exert themselves for the furtherance of the gospel, that, if possible, all may hear, and share in the happy effects of it." Disinterested missionaries were urgently needed in Africa to redress the evil image of Christianity that nominally religious slave traders had been presenting to the heathen.[29]

Hopkins's theological justification for African colonization borrowed heavily from his *Treatise on the Millennium* which was published in 1793. Slavery and the slave trade, he insisted, should be viewed from a millennial perspective. They were part of the sixth vial of history which the Book of Revelation had warned would be the darkest time for true Christians. But the sixth vial was about to run its course, and it would soon be followed by the seventh vial — the period in which the kingdom of God would begin to be established on earth. "In the prospect of this," Hopkins maintained, "we may rejoice in the midst of the darkness and evils which now surround us, and think ourselves happy, if we may be, in any way, the active instruments of hastening on this desirable predicted event."[30] African colonization offered an opportunity for evangelical activism which would accelerate the progress of the millennium.

When Hopkins published this *Discourse* later in 1793 he added an appendix which contained arguments in favor of African colonization that were designed to appeal to a wider audience than one consisting solely of antislavery reformers. If readers were not moved by his grand millennial expectation, they were presented with a more practical reason to support Hopkins's African project — racial prejudice against blacks. Millennial considerations aside, responsible people should work for the repatriation of free blacks, Hopkins argued, because "whites are so habituated, by education and custom, to look upon the blacks as an inferior class of beings." As a result of this prejudice, blacks in America were "sunk so low by their situation, and the treatment they receive among us, that they never can be raised to an equality with the whites and enjoy all the liberty and rights to which they have a just claim."[31]

Finally, Hopkins pointed out, a colony of American blacks in Africa would promote commerce and further the prosperity and temporal well-being of both countries. Therefore, "even self-ishness will be pleased with such a plan as this, and excite to exertion to carry it into effect, when the advantages of it to the public and to individuals are well considered and realized."[32] For the first time in his career as a reformer and theologian, Hopkins seemed to compromise with the new egocentric social morality. Perhaps this was simply a measure of his desperation to establish the African mission colony. Perhaps it was a reflection of a new element of "realism" that emerged in his social thought in the 1790's. The direction of Hopkins's thinking after 1793 is difficult to assess. The *Discourse* was the last critical work that he wrote. Furthermore, his correspondence declined sharply in the 1790's, and was even more curtailed after he suffered a paralyzing stroke in early 1799.

Hopkins's *Discourse* foreshadowed the arguments of nineteenth-century advocates of African colonization, a fact that has led one recent historian of that movement to single out Hopkins as the American "father of African colonization."[33] However useful and persuasive Hopkins's wide-ranging arguments on behalf of the African mission may have been to nineteenth-century colonizationists, they did not convince the Providence Abolition Society to support the endeavor in the 1790's. In May 1794, a year after Hopkins delivered his *Discourse*, the Society was still debating the merits of his proposal. Hopkins was now convinced, he wrote to Levi Hart, that the members would take no action: "The friends are always backward in promoting such settlement, and are the most active members, and nothing can be done without them."[34]

Nevertheless, a group of Providence blacks, after consulting with and winning the support of the African colonizationists in Newport, applied to the authorities of Sierra Leone for permission to settle in that colony. Zachary Macaulay, the acting governor of Sierra Leone, wrote to Hopkins and expressed a willingness to receive no more than twelve families, provided "they present satisfactory testimonials of their moral character, signed by you and another clergyman, and by the President of the [Providence] Abolition Society." These recommendations, Macaulay noted, were designed to prevent more of the internal troubles that had recently plagued Sierra Leone.[35]

Hopkins refused to recommend the Providence blacks. He questioned the character of the leader of the Providence group and conveyed his reservations to Macaulay. In the meantime, French soldiers destroyed Sierra Leone, and by the time the colony began to reestablish itself in 1796, Hopkins, now seventy-five years old, undoubtedly concluded that the American blacks would not sail for Africa during his lifetime.[36] Indeed, the time when a group of Rhode Island blacks, led by two of the original missionaries whom Hopkins had recruited, would make their way back to Africa was yet three decades away. Finally in 1826, a colony of thirty blacks sailed for Africa under the leadership of Newport Gardner and Salmar Nubia.[37]

But Hopkins's efforts in support of African colonization produced more immediate results. In the first place, his doctrine of disinterested benevolence and his millennial expectation in general, and their application to the mission colony scheme in particular, fostered a missionary spirit within the New Divinity movement. Samuel J. Mills, Jr., for example, the son of a New Divinity minister in Torringford, Connecticut, and a leader of America's first group of foreign missionaries, expressed a Hopkinsian "long[ing] to have the time arrive, when the gospel shall be preached to the poor *Africans*, and likewise to all nations."[38] At Andover Seminary, Mills's alma mater, there developed a strong commitment to African colonization as a means of spreading the gospel.[39]

Second, in addition to demonstrating the practical, evangelical implications of his theology, the mission colony plan taught Hopkins and his followers a valuable lesson. The African mission was aborted in Hopkins's lifetime largely because he could not persuade existing antislavery societies to accept either the theological importance or the practicality of his African project. Hopkins and his New Divinity followers came to realize in the mid-1790's that as long as their missionary commitment failed to be institutionalized, evangelical proposals like the African mission would be unproductive. Consequently, in the late 1790's and early 1800's the New Divinity men emerged as leaders of the efforts to create specialized missionary societies in New England.

In Connecticut, for instance, Levi Hart was among those chosen by the General Association of ministers to draw up a proposal for the establishment of a missionary society in the state. At the General Association's meeting in 1798, four ministers, three of whom were New Divinity men (Hart, Jonathan Edwards, Jr., and Nathan Strong) were appointed to draft a constitution for the missionary society. New Divinity men were influential not only in the Society but in its unofficial journal, *The Connecticut Evangelical Magazine*, begun in 1800.[40]

In Massachusetts in 1799, a group of Hopkinsians from a New Divinity association of ministers formed around 1780 in the southeastern section of the state established the Massachusetts Missionary Society. The new organization was designed "to diffuse the knowledge of the Gospel among the *heathen*, as well as other people in remote parts of our country, where Christ is seldom or never preached."[41] The inner circle of Hopkins's followers (namely, his brother Daniel of Salem, Nathanael Emmons of Franklin, Samuel Niles of Abington, David Sanford of Medway, and Samuel Spring of Newburyport), controlled the society and its official journal, *The Massachusetts Missionary Magazine*. The Hopkinsian members of the Massachusetts Missionary Society were prominent among the founders of Andover Theological Seminary. Established in 1808, Andover was the theological seedbed of America's first foreign missionary efforts and the recruitment and training center for the young men who were to carry the gospel abroad.

In spite of his poor health, Hopkins was determined in the late 1790's to establish a missionary society in Rhode Island. As late as 1799 he continued to express the hope that the African mission would become a reality.[42] Two years later he helped form the Missionary Society of Rhode Island and was installed as the new organization's first president. The purpose of the new society, its constitution outlined, was "to promote the gospel in any part of the State where there may be opportunity for it and to assist Africans in coming to a knowledge of the truth in any way which may consist with our means and advantages."[43]

The New Divinity movement monopolized neither the theological justifications nor the evangelical efforts which led to the rise of the missionary movement in America. Indeed, the American foreign missionary movement was but one phase of a larger transatlantic missionary movement of the late 1790's and early decades of the nineteenth century. Zachary Macaulay reported to Hopkins in 1796, for example, his amazement at the proliferation of missionary efforts in England. Returning from Sierra Leone to England for a brief visit, Macaulay "had the satisfaction of seeing a mission undertaken by the Baptists to India and another to Africa, one undertaken by the Wesleyan Methodists to the interior of the same country, and one put in a fair way of being undertaken by the Moravians." In addition, he informed Hopkins, the Pedo-Baptists had established a missionary society which would begin its evangelizing in the South Sea Islands.[44]

In approximately two decades America would experience a similar upsurge of missionary interest and activity. American efforts were stimulated by British example and drew on a common stock of theological ideas. In 1799 Hopkins admitted to British clergyman Andrew Fuller that "all the missionary societies lately formed in America owe their rise to those formed in England, and their extraordinary exertions." But, Hopkins hastened to add, the existing American societies were largely founded by New Divinity men: "There are five of these societies now in New York, Connecticut, and Massachusetts States, the leaders in all [of] which, except one, (if that is to be excepted) are Edwardeans."[45] In short, the New Divinity men laid special theological claim to missionary efforts. Hopkins's theology and its application in the plan to Christianize Africa did not in themselves constitute the only legacy upon which missionary-minded clerics could draw. But Hopkins did provide a theological and practical heritage which ensured that his followers would be in the forefront of the missionary movement in America, and that they would stress, as he did, the evangelical benefits of African colonization.

chapter ten

THE NEW
DIVINITY CODIFIED

POVERTY and personal tragedy characterized the private life of Hopkins in the 1780's and early 1790's—the years in which he was most active as a reformer. Reflecting on this period in his autobiography, Hopkins reported that "frequently if a dollar extraordinary had been called for it would have rendered me a bankrupt." Hopkins accepted his plight with equanimity. "I have been saved from anxiety about living," he claimed, "and have had a thousand times less care and trouble about the world, than if I had a great abundance, and had been in high life, attended with servants, equippage, much company and high living."[1] Such a statement cannot be dismissed as a rationalization of his circumstances, for he repeatedly displayed a temperamental disposition toward and an intellectual commitment to a simple mode of life. This led him on occasion to strike what sounded like a note of spiritual pride, as when he remarked that although he was surrounded by the worldly attractions of Newport, he had not been tempted into "seeking *great things* in the world" but had remained "unconnected with the great and the rich in the world, and [with] gay, unprofitable company. . . ."[2]

Hopkins's New Divinity helped reconcile him not only to the poverty of the post-war years but also to the personal tragedies of this period. Between 1786 and 1792 his three daughters and one of his sons died. (His four surviving sons lived far from Newport—two at Great Barrington and two others in New York and Maryland.) In 1793 his wife, who had suffered from consumption for years, died at Great Barrington where she had sought the dry air of the Berkshire hills. Grief-stricken but resigned to accept the will of God, Hopkins did not become morose or prone to self-pity in the face of these losses.[3]

In addition to the deaths in his family, Hopkins also saw many of his friends and longtime supporters in the First Church pass from this world in the 1780's and 1790's. Despite the onset of old age and his increasing isolation, Hopkins did not betray a sense of intense loneliness in his correspondence during this period. Yet within a year of his wife's death, he had chosen a new companion with whom he would live out his last years. In 1794 the seventy-three year old theologian married a school teacher and member of the First Church who was eighteen years his junior.

Work had always provided Hopkins with the greatest pleasure in life, and this was never more true than in the Newport years of poverty and loss. Throughout his career in the ministry Hopkins endeavored to be both a David Brainerd and a Jonathan Edwards. More than any other follower of Edwards, he attempted to combine the evangelical and exegetical demands of the New Divinity movement. Such a commitment required sixteen-hour work days, a schedule that Hopkins and other New Divinity men were introduced to in the schools of the prophets. During his years in Newport, Hopkins's day usually began at four o'clock in the morning. Seated at the desk in his parsonage study, with the daily bustle of the seaport yet to begin, Hopkins drafted an antislavery essay, organized a Sunday sermon, or pored over Scripture as he refined the arguments of a theological work. After several hours of intense study he was ready for breakfast, which was often followed by a walk in the neighborhood or a visit to a parishioner. Returning to his parsonage by mid-morning, Hopkins continued reading and writing through late afternoon, frequently until the dinner hour at six. The early evening offered a time for correspondence with fellow New Divinity ministers and with supporters of the antislavery movement or the African colonization plan. Before retiring at ten o'clock, Hopkins conducted an hour of family prayer.[4]

The 1780's and early 1790's were particularly work-filled years for Hopkins. The Revolutionary War had brought a temporary halt to New England's paper war of theology. After the publication of *True Holiness* in 1773, Hopkins did not publish another theological work until 1783. In the 1780's theological controversy returned to New England and brought with it a new period of prosperity for the printers of the region. While he labored to abolish slavery and the slave trade and to promote the colonization of American blacks, Hopkins renewed his efforts to explain and defend the New Divinity. Indeed, during his most active years as a reformer he completed his magnum opus, a comprehensive, eleven-hundred page codification of the New Divinity entitled a *System of Doctrines contained in Divine Revelation*.[5] With the publication of his work in 1793, the Hopkinsian version of Consistent Calvinism became the starting point for the theological training of the next generation of New Divinity men. Furthermore, to the *System of Doctrines* Hopkins appended *A Treatise on the Millennium*, which altered Edwards's millennialism in the direction of social utopianism.

The significance of Hopkins's *System of Doctrines* in the history of New England theology was correctly pointed out by Frank H. Foster more than seventy years ago.[6] The work was the first indigenous American system of Calvinist theology. An earlier system, *A Compleat Body of Divinity* published by Samuel Willard in 1726, had failed to move New England Calvinism beyond the Westminster Confession.[7] Hopkins's *System*, like the New Divinity in general, drew on but extended traditional Reformed thought. For ten years, beginning in 1782, he labored to codify the neo-Edwardsian theology of the New Divinity movement. His *System* thus became the cornerstone of *the* New England theology.[8]

"It has been a laborious work to me," Hopkins observed a few years after the publication of the *System*, "which I consider the greatest public service that I have done."[9] Apparently his New Divinity friends agreed; they circulated proposals for printing the *System*, and twelve hundred advance subscriptions were obtained. Hopkins sold the copyright to the Boston firm of Thomas and Andrews for nine hundred dollars, which eased his poverty in the last years of his life. Although this was a modest financial reward, Hopkins was unaccustomed to worldly success, and he assured his followers — and himself — in his autobiography that he had worked disinterestedly on the *System*: "I had no expectation of getting a penny by the publication [of it] when I began and while I was preparing it for press, nor had the least view or thought of it."[10]

Unlike his earlier theological publications, Hopkins's *System* was not a work of polemical divinity. It was a two-volume tome of systematic theology that sought to explain the doctrinal "chain, or consistent scheme of truth, which runs through the whole of the Bible." Using a popular eighteenth-century metaphor, Hopkins pointed out that each Scriptural doctrine was "as much a part of the whole, as is each link of a chain, so that no one can be broken or taken out without spoiling or at least injuring the chain."[11] Beginning with the nature of the Deity and the creation of the world and ending with the millennium, Hopkins proceeded link by doctrinal link to reconstruct God's theological chain and thus to help his New Divinity followers rise above the religious confusion of New England's ongoing paper war and secure their faith in a comprehensive scheme of divine truth.

Hopkins admitted that his *System* would not fasten each link of the Biblical chain of truth as firmly as possible, since a complete understanding of Scripture would have to await the millennium. As history moved closer to that glorious time, God would gradually shed further light on the Bible. Divines would appear who would promote the progressive unfolding of Scriptual truth. Edwards and the members of the New Divinity movement were such individuals, Hopkins suggested. But their theological accomplishments would be eclipsed by subsequent divines residing nearer the dawn of the millennial age when "many things which are now overlooked and disregarded . . . and those things which now appear intricate and unintelligible will then appear plain and clearly." At that sacred time, Hopkins conceded, his *System* would be judged "imperfect and inconsiderable compared with that superior light, with which the church will then be blessed."[12]

Thus the *System* was simply a record of the theological progress that Calvinist divines had made toward absolute Scriptural truth. Like the New Divinity, the work was a synthesis of strict Reformed theology, Edwardsianism, and Consistent Calvinist improvements on these traditions. In spite of its length and comprehensiveness, the *System* advanced little that had not already been discussed in New England's theological paper war. Indeed, Hopkins's portrayal of the millennium as a social utopia in an appended treatise was the most novel section of his massive work.

Though short on originality, the *System* did at least elaborate on the "improvements" of other New Divinity theologians and furnish their movement with a doctrinal encyclopedia. Hopkins's

System borrowed more heavily from Joseph Bellamy than any other of Jonathan Edwards's "improvers." Not only did Hopkins's *Treatise on the Millennium* build upon Bellamy's work on the same subject published in 1758, but the *System* also elevated the Pope of Litchfield County's views on the atonement to the level of New Divinity orthodoxy. In the process Hopkins further developed the theologically liberal side of the New Divinity, forging a doctrinal chain of hyper-Calvinist and liberal Calvinist links.

The emphasis that both Bellamy and Hopkins placed on the benevolence of the Deity led them to modify the traditional Calvinist understanding of Christ's atonement. That standard interpretation, whose essential elements were reaffirmed by Jonathan Edwards, stressed the sovereignty of God. Christ's death glorified the sovereignty of God; by vicariously suffering for the sins of mankind, Christ paid the vindictive death that a sovereign, wrathful Deity required before He offered salvation to sinners. As a result of Christ's mediatorial work in placating His offended Father, a limited portion of mankind would attain eternal salvation. [13]

Bellamy challenged this interpretation of Christ's sacrifice with the notion of a general atonement based upon the moral government of a benevolent Deity. Both Bellamy and Hopkins absorbed the Great Awakening's hyper-Calvinist emphasis on the sovereignty of God, but in the decades after the revival they both attempted — with considerable intellectual difficulty at times — to reconcile this position with a liberal Calvinist understanding of God's benevolence to mankind. [14] God was a benevolent Moral Governor, Bellamy argued, not a wrathful Father "influenced, activated and governed by a groundless, arbitrary self will." God was so benevolent "that there is no act of kindness or grace so great, but that he can find in his heart to do it. . . ." [15] Only the claims of moral justice and order circumscribed God's benevolence. For example, God could not offer salvation to sinners without first satisfying the requirements of the divine law which Adam and his posterity had transgressed. A punishment had to be exacted to preserve the moral order of God's government. Christ's sacrificial death was a moral necessity. It was not a reflection of the sovereign wrath of God but an act which upheld his moral law, thereby enabling the benevolent Governor to offer salvation to man. "Thus," Bellamy concluded, "the whole mediatorial scheme is designed, and in its own nature adopted, to do honor to the divine law."[16]

While he was introducing the moral government theory into New England theology in the 1750's, Bellamy also began to alter the traditional Calvinist doctrine of a limited atonement. Christ's death, Bellamy wrote in *True Religion Delineated*, honored God's moral law, just "as the perfect obedience of Adam, and of all his race, would have done; the rights of the Godhead are as much asserted and maintained." As a result, the benevolent Moral Governor of the universe could now "pardon the whole world . . . , consistently with his honor."[17] In a sermon on the millennium published in 1758, Bellamy used population statistics to suggest that the atonement would be far from limited. Along with many other eighteenth-century thinkers, Bellamy was impressed with the rapid growth of population in Europe and America. He assumed that the rate of increase would continue unabated until the millennium, and he provided a chart which divulged that the bulk of the world's population was yet to be born. All of this was designed by God so that the greatest part of the world's population would witness the gradual establishment of the millennium on earth and attain salvation. Even if all of mankind living prior to the realization of the millennium suffered damnation, Bellamy granted for the sake of argument, the growth of the population during the one thousand years of the millennium would still ensure a general atonement. "That is, above 17,000 would be saved, to one lost; which was the point to be proved: Therefore nothing hinders, but that the greatest part of mankind may yet be saved, if God so pleases."[18]

The New Divinity men did not develop Bellamy's modifications of the accepted view of the atonement until the 1780's. In the preceding decades, liberal Calvinists had adopted the moral government theory of the atonement.[19] More importantly, liberals began to argue for universal salvation, a controversial position that reopened the paper war in the 1780's and that encouraged the New Divinity men to develop their own interpretation of the moral government theory of the atonement and to argue for a general, though not universal, atonement.

Since well before the Revolution several liberal Calvinist ministers, most notably Charles Chauncy, had privately expressed confidence in universal salvation. In the early 1770's an itinerating

English preacher, John Murray, landed in New England and began to preach a version of universal redemption at odds with the views of the liberals. Murray argued that Christ died for all the sins of mankind and that sinners would no longer suffer punishment. Chauncy became alarmed that such views of universal salvation were "*an encouragement to Libertinism*" and "criminal excesses!"[20] To counter the influence of Murrayism, Chauncy and other Arminians joined to publicize their own theory of universal salvation. In 1782 Chauncy and John Clarke of Boston's First Church published an anonymous pamphlet, entitled *Salvation for All Men*, and in two additional works published in 1783 and 1784 Chauncy further explained the liberal Calvinist understanding of universal salvation. Chauncy carefully distinguished his own position from the universalism of Murray. God was certainly a benevolent deity, but this did not mean, as Murray argued, that He would not condemn sinners to hell. On the other hand, Chauncy maintained, Calvinists were wrong in assuming that such punishment was for eternity, whether as a way of demonstrating God's absolute sovereignty or of preserving his moral government. For Chauncy, eternal damnation was irreconcilable with God's benevolence. Hell was only a providential means of reforming sinners — the greater the sinner the longer the punishment. All sinners would eventually repent and attain salvation.[21]

The universalism of Chauncy and Murray provoked an outburst of pamphlet warfare in the 1780's. Hopkins was among the first to raise his pen in defense of evangelical Calvinism. In 1783 he published *An Inquiry Concerning the Future State of those who die in their Sins* which drew on the work of Bellamy to answer the proponents of universal salvation. The preservation of the moral order of God's government, Hopkins argued, required the eternal damnation of sinners: "In the everlasting punishment of the wicked the infinite dignity and worthiness of God, and the excellence of his law and government, are expressed and asserted in a very advantageous and striking manner; and this is one important end and design of this punishment." But since God was a benevolent governor, the consequences of Christ's atonement would be far from limited. Scripture, according to Hopkins's reading, did not support the idea "that but few, or a very small part of mankind, will be saved." Rather it gave Christians "reason to believe that many more of the human race will be happy than miserable."[22]

Stephen West, Jonathan Edwards, Jr., Nathanael Emmons, and other New Divinity men followed up Hopkins's work with tracts of their own that attacked universal salvation and enlarged upon Bellamy's interpretation of the atonement. Consequently, the moral government understanding of the atonement came to be associated with the New Divinity movement, especially after Hopkins's *System of Doctrines* synthesized many of the common elements in the various Consistent Calvinist tracts and placed his imprimatur on both the moral government and general atonement theories that Bellamy had advanced in the 1750's. Through Christ, Hopkins wrote in the *System*, mankind was "saved, consistent with the divine character, with truth, infinite rectitude, wisdom and goodness, and so as not to set aside and dishonor but support and maintain the divine law and government." In terms similar to Bellamy's Hopkins went on to uphold a general atonement in which "many more will be saved, than lost, perhaps some thousands to one." Such a prospect, Hopkins concluded in a missionary vein, made "the offer of salvation [available] to all, without exception. . . . The direction and command is to preach the gospel to all nations, to every creature."[23]

The moral governor and general atonement theories that the New Divinity men did so much to develop and popularize in late eighteenth-century New England were among the more enduring theological contributions of the movement. They enabled nineteenth-century theologians and laymen to steer a middle course between what many perceived as a democratically unappealing Calvinist belief in an arbitrary deity and a limited atonement on the one hand, and a too sanguine Unitarian view of a loving deity and a universal atonement on the other.[24]

Liberalizations of both Reformed theology and Edwardsianism, such as the moral government and general atonement theories, existed side by side in Hopkins's *System* with hyper-Calvinist interpretations. The controversial tenets of Hopkinsianism were reaffirmed in the work.[25] In addition, the *System* incorporated the high Calvinist views of Jonathan Edwards on such questions as original sin. Hopkins's discussion of this doctrine was so Calvinistic, for instance, that the younger Edwards, in spite of his endorsement of the *System* in general, objected in a letter to Hopkins that he had gone "too far into the idea that Adam's sin is the sin of all posterity and that they consent to that sin. . . ." Mankind,

Edwards wrote, does "no more consent to that sin than they do to the sin of Joseph's brethren or any other sin."[26]

Hopkins's *System* clearly discloses that the New Divinity was an amalgam of hyper-Calvinist and liberal Calvinist doctrines. The New Divinity originated in Edwardsianism and in the reassertion of the pristine doctrines of Calvinism that the Great Awakening encouraged. Yet in the decades after the revival, New England Calvinism began to flow in a liberal, humanistic direction. The New Divinity movement, as Hopkins's *System* reveals, was influenced by this intellectual current. But the New Divinity men were not inundated by its moralizing waters. Hopkins's interpretations of the benevolence of the Deity and of a general atonement, for example, liberalized Edwardsianism and foreshadowed the diluted Calvinism of the nineteenth century. However, his low opinion of the moral ability of natural man harked back to seventeenth-century strict predestinarian Calvinism.

Hopkins's *Treatise on the Millennium* embodies the same kind of progressive and retrogressive theological perspectives that may be found in his *System*. He fell heir to the millennialism of Jonathan Edwards, but, as with other aspects of his theological heritage, Hopkins's *Treatise* altered his benefactor's ideas on the kingdom of God.

The Great Awakening revived pessimistic Calvinist doctrines; yet it also encouraged an optimistic millennial expectation. Such a millennial outlook was adopted and promoted by Jonathan Edwards. Influenced by the work of an English divine, Moses Lowman, Edwards formulated a post-millennial eschatology which held that the kingdom of God would soon begin to be gradually established on earth and that Christ's second return would follow the millennium.[27] This position is often contrasted with premillennialism — the culturally pessimistic view that there would be no steady moral progress in history and that the kingdom would only become a reality after Christ's second return.

As early as 1739, in a series of well-known sermons, which were published by his followers in 1786 under the title *A History of the Work of Redemption*,[28] Edwards outlined his post-millennial understanding of history. In 1747 he published *A Humble Attempt to Promote Explicit Agreement and Visible Union of God's People in Extraordinary Prayer . . . Pursuant to Scripture Promises and*

Prophecies Concerning the Last Times, a work in which he explained the reasons for his belief that the beginning of the kingdom of God was imminent. With the waning of the revival Edwards urged Christians to join in a Concert of Prayer — weekly and quarterly meetings at which believers would pray for a new out-pouring of God's grace and for the arrival of the millennium. To offset the pessimism that followed the decline of the revival and to encourage Christians to participate in the Concert of Prayer, Edwards stressed that the fall of Antichrist, which had been oc-curring gradually since the Reformation, was far advanced. The darkest time for the church of God — the spiritual midnight of popery prior to the Reformation — had passed into history. Ed-wards proclaimed his confidence that "the beginning of that glo-rious work of God's Spirit, which, in the progress and issue of it, will overthrow Antichrist, and introduce the glory of the latter days, is not very far off."[29]

There is little question that the Awakening and Edwards's eschatology helped shift the millennial thinking of many New England Calvinists in an optimistic direction. But to assert a rel-atively rapid transformation from a pessimistic pre-millennial to an optimistic post-millennial outlook, with Edwards's thought and the Great Awakening as the watersheds, is in fact too simple an account of the millennialism of seventeenth- and eighteenth-century New England. The contrast between pessimistic and opti-mistic millennialism smacks of other facile generalizations about Puritan thought that do not do justice to its complexity — the trans-formation from piety to moralism or from an unconditional to a contractual covenant in theology, for example. Calvinist theolo-gians took intellectual delight in exploring the paradoxical nature of human existence. The paradoxical emphasis of their thought was never more evident than in their understanding of prophetic history.

Millennialism in New England after the Awakening displays a significant degree of continuity with pre-revival millennialism. Both prior to and after the Awakening the millennial perspective of Puritan New England was a compound of pessimism and op-timism. Patterned after the model of individual conversion, in which a believer endeavored to reconcile spiritual hope and de-spair, the Puritan view of the redemption of the world combined providential favors and judgments — hope and despair.[30] History was the record of providential afflictions and blessings from which God's kingdom would emerge. This perspective has recently been called the "afflictive model of progress."[31] Good would not gradually triumph over evil; rather, even though the kingdom of God would make progress in the world, Christians would see an ongoing, bitter struggle between the forces of light and the forces of darkness until the millennium was established. Indeed, as the world drew closer to the millennium afflictions would increase as Satan intensified his efforts to defeat the coming kingdom.

The idea of moral progress through affliction furnished Calvinist ministers with a way of reconciling a millennial expectation with discouraging social realities—a way of urging hope and optimism in the face of historical events that promoted social despair and pessimism. For this reason, while Edwards deemphasized the afflictive model of progress, his prophetic history did not abandon it entirely. He argued that the darkest time for the kingdom of God had passed into history, but he also believed that prior to the establishment of the millennium "there would probably be many sore conflicts and terrible convulsions, and many changes, revivings and intermissions, and returns of dark clouds and threatening appearances."[32] In the *Humble Attempt* he informed Christians "that there is yet remaining a mighty conflict between the church and her enemies, the most violent struggle of Satan and his adherents, in opposition to true religion, and the most general commotion that ever was in the world. . . ." Then in the same breath Edwards expressed an optimistic millennial expectation that "Satan and Antichrist shall not get the victory, nor greatly prevail; but on the contrary be entirely conquered and utterly overthrown, in this great battle."[33] Such a position suggests that Edwards's prophetic history and the experience of the Awakening upon which he based his optimistic millennialism produced not a radical "new departure in eschatology" but a change of emphasis within traditional New England Calvinist thought.[34]

Hopkins inherited both Edwards's optimistic post-millennial expectation and the traditional afflictive model of progress. In his *Treatise on the Millennium* Hopkins stressed the idea of progress through affliction more than Edwards did in his millennial writings. Thus Hopkins's prophetic history was more pessimistic than his teacher's; his gloomy assessment of American society during the period in which he wrote his *Treatise* influenced his millennial outlook.

The social and political conflicts of the 1780's and early 1790's had a sobering effect on Hopkins's millennial expectation—an expectation that had been aroused earlier by the Great Awakening, by the American victory in the French and Indian War, and by the Revolutionary struggle against the British. Instead of regenerating the behavior of the American people, the Revolution, in Hopkins's view, seemed only to have temporarily arrested their selfishness, materialism, and contention. In 1792 he reported that the moral state of Newport was "growing worse and worse, of which all are sensible; And there is no prospect of an alteration for the better. . . ." The seaport, indeed all America, Hopkins wrote to Levi Hart, appeared "like a falling stone, the descent [of which] increases in velocity as it falls."[35]

The *Treatise on the Millennium* reflected this pessimistic assessment of American society; yet at the same time it carried a message of hope. Hopkins warned Christians that conditions in America would grow worse before they would get better, and he anticipated objections to his pessimistic prophesy: "It will probably be suggested that the representation of such a dark scene and evil time . . . is matter of great discouragement, and tends to damp the spirits and hopes of Christians, and discourage them from attempting to promote [the millennium]." Hopkins's intent, however, was not to sow despair but to inspire hope in the coming kingdom—"to support, comfort and encourage Christians, in the present dark appearance of things respecting the interest of Christ and his church." He urged Christians to have "faith, patience, and perseverance in Obedience to Christ; putting on the hope of salvation as a helmet."[36] To assure Christians that affliction would bring moral progress and that the continued reign of Antichrist was part of the millennial plan, Hopkins reaffirmed his position — formulated in the dark moments of the 1750's—that sin and suffering were moral advantages to the universe. The kingdom of God would "be enjoyed to a higher degree, and be more pleasant and glorious . . . than if it had not been preceded by a dreadful night of darkness, confusion and evil, by the wickedness of men, and the power and agency of Satan."[37]

The world, Hopkins argued, was presently living under the sixth vial of history, and mankind was experiencing the dreaded curses that the Bible had foretold, and that Edwards had agreed, would precede the establishment of the millennium. But this two-hundred-year period had been running since the seventeenth century, Hopkins pointed out, and it was fast approaching its last days. Although the sixth vial would run into part of the nineteenth century, Christians were not to despair, for Scripture forecast that toward the close of this age "the power of antichrist is to be greatly weakened, and the way prepared for his utter overthrow. . . ." The nineteenth century would witness the beginning of the seventh vial of history — the final epoch before the millennium — during which the kingdom of God would begin to be established "gradually, by different, successive great and remarkable events." Look beyond the dark times of the present, Hopkins urged his readers, for "the end of the reign of antichrist draws near."[38]

Still, the traditional idea of progress through affliction persisted as a key element in Hopkins's post-millennialism, tempering the optimism of his prophetic history. During the period of the seventh vial, the kingdom of Satan and the papal beast would be progressively defeated. While antichrist was falling, Hopkins prophesied, "there will doubtless be remarkable revivals of religion, in many places, . . . and there will be advances made in the purity of doctrines, and . . . the churches will be formed into a greater union with each other." But wickedness and irreligion would also increase, for as the kingdom advanced, Satan would redouble his efforts to defeat it. The millennium would come into existence only after "a series of divine judgments that will be inflicted under the seventh vial."[39]

Christians currently living in the latter years of the sixth vial and those who would live under the seventh vial could not remain passive as the providential drama leading to the millennium unfolded. Evangelical activism was an essential element in the work of redemption. Christians must "prepare the way" for the kingdom and "promote its coming in proper time." The church militant must be kept alive, "thousands must be converted, and there must be a succession of professing and real christians down to that day" when the millennium would arrive.[40]

Hopkins did not leave to the imagination of his readers the nature of the millennial social order that would begin to emerge from the gradual defeat of Antichrist. He portrayed the coming kingdom as a social utopia, a significant improvement on the millennialism of Edwards. Like most post-millennial expositors, Edwards was far more interested in reconciling Biblical prophecy and human history than in depicting the millennial state that would evolve in the world. Both the *History of the Work of Redemption* and the *Humble Attempt* pay scant attention to the nature of the coming kingdom of Christ. The former work virtually ignores this subject, while the latter concentrates on explaining or modifying the ideas of Moses Lowman and on describing how many of the Biblical prophecies of events that were to precede the millennium have already been fulfilled. In the few pages in the *Humble Attempt* where Edwards does deal directly with the coming kingdom he uses vague generalities to describe it. He writes, for example, that the millennium will be

> A time wherein the world shall be delivered from that multitude of sore calamities that before had prevailed (Ezek. xlvii.20), and there shall be a universal blessing of God upon mankind, in soul and body, in all concerns, and all manner of tokens of God's presence and favor, and God *shall rejoice over them as a bridegroom rejoiceth over his bride and the mountains shall as it were drop down new wine, and the hills shall flow with milk*, Joel iii.18.[41]

Thus, although Edwards located the kingdom within history, his brief descriptions of the millennial state were of a piece with his interpretation of Being in general — they were a glimpse of a spiritual existence, of a moral state, considerably removed from social reality.

Hopkins's *Treatise on the Millennium* combined his own prophetic exposition of history with a detailed account of the nature of the coming kingdom. Not only divine truth and the life of the church but the material life of the human race would flourish during the millennium: "the art of husbandry will be greatly advanced, and men will have skill to cultivate and manure the earth, in a much better manner and more easy, than ever before; so that the same land will then produce much more than it does now, twenty, thirty, sixty, and perhaps an hundred fold more." Beneficial uses would be found even for the numerous rocks and boulders that were the bane of New England farmers.[42]

Technological progress would accompany agricultural advances, and "all the necessary and convenient articles of life, such as all utensils, clothing, buildings, &c. will be formed and made in a better manner, and with much less labor than they now are." Printing, an indispensable means of spreading the divine truth that would shine during the millennium, would advance and "make it possible for hundreds of thousands of copies of a book to be cast off by one impression." In short, the coming kingdom would be a time of religious and material prosperity—a time in which all knowledge would "promote the spiritual and eternal good of men, or their convenience and comfort in this life."[43]

It would be an age of abundance but also of true virtue— virtue distinguished by "great prudence and economy" in the use of worldly objects. The social evils that Hopkins had railed against for years would be thoroughly reformed. "The intemperance, excess, extravagance and waste, in food, raiment, and the use of the things of this life which were before practiced will be discarded and cease, in that day." Disinterested benevolence toward Being in general would finally lead to universal peace, as Christians expressed "general cordial friendship" and "mutual love" of one another.[44]

Hopkins's description of the coming kingdom resembles the social utopian post-millennialism of the nineteenth century. "The millennium was more than a belief to him," the rationalist William Ellery Channing wrote of Hopkins in 1840. "It had the freshness of visible things. He was at home in it. His book on the subject has an air of reality, as if written from observation."[45] More importantly, perhaps, the prophetic history of Hopkins's *Treatise on the Millennium*, and of his earlier *Sin . . . an advantage to the Universe*, had a clear social purpose, a purpose common to much eighteenth-century eschatology; namely, to foster hope and evangelical action in times of providential judgment and affliction.[46]

Hopkins's *System of Doctrines* and the appended *Treatise on the Millennium* played a major role in the transmission of the theology of the New Divinity's founding fathers to the next generation of Consistent Calvinist theologians, missionaries, and revivalists. Ministerial candidates found a complete body of divinity in the *System* which covered all the theological problems that would be raised at licensing time. The work provided answers to the theological questions that Hopkins, Bellamy, and others had been circulating throughout the New Divinity movement for nearly forty years. For this reason, the *System* became indispensable reading in the schools of the prophets and at Andover Theological Seminary.[47]

At New England colleges sympathetic to the New Divinity the *System* attained a similar vogue. Hopkins's work became standard reading at Yale, and Ebenezer Fitch, New Divinity president of Williams, established the *System* as that college's theological text because, Stephen West informed Hopkins, "he thought it much exceeded any thing of the kind he had seen." Eventually the lay members of the Board of Trustees, which included members of the Williams family (the clan that had opposed Edwards in Northampton and Stockbridge), removed the work from the curriculum. The clerical members of the Board protested this decision but to no avail. Nevertheless, the ministerial aspirants in the student body at Williams continued to read Hopkins's work.[48]

Since the publication of the *System* was a financial success, as early as 1794 Hopkins and his publisher were considering the preparation of a second edition. Hopkins began to make arrangements with New Divinity ministers to aid him in revising and correcting the work.[49] The second edition, however, was not issued until 1811. In that year, Nathanael Emmons wrote that the New Divinity followers of Hopkins "suppose that this eminent divine not only illustrated and confirmed the main doctrines of Calvinism, but brought the whole system to a greater degree of consistency and perfection, than any who had gone before him." The *System of Doctrines* was the clearest statement of the New Divinity, Emmons suggested, because it included not simply Hopkins's original "improvements" but a complete body of divinity which he had fashioned from the unsystematized theological advances of the entire first generation of Consistent Calvinists. Now, Emmons maintained, a second generation of New Divinity men "only profess the same design of still further perfecting the same system" that Hopkins had handed down to them.[50] Hopkins had finally replaced his mentor as the theologian whose work other New Divinity men strove to improve.

chapter eleven

THE SECOND GREAT AWAKENING

IN the early 1780's ministers in many parts of New England witnessed a renewed interest in religion and increases in conversions. These local "harvests" of souls marked the start of the Second Great Awakening in New England — a major religious movement that would extend well into the nineteenth century and that would come to be characterized not only by revivalism but also by religious reform organizations. These reform agencies comprised a "benevolent empire" whose function it was to make the new republic a truly Christian nation and to prepare the way for the coming kingdom of God.

Historians have tended to belittle the role of the New Divinity movement in the Second Great Awakening. While recognizing the influence of Hopkins's doctrine of disinterested benevolence on religious reformers — especially the members of the American Board of Commissioners for Foreign Missions, one of the institutions of the benevolent empire — historians have argued that the New Divinity men committed metaphysical suicide in an age of vital piety. According to this view, years of theological sifting yielded, by the time of the Second Great Awakening, a highly refined intellectual product which met neither the emotional needs nor the doctrinal inclinations of the Congregational laity. By over-intellectualizing the piety of the mid-century revival and by discussing theological controversies and abstruse metaphysics in their pulpits, the New Divinity men supposedly undermined the experimental religion of the First Great Awakening from which their movement had grown.[1]

Central to this interpretation is a caricature of the New Divinity men as preachers. Not content to spin metaphysical cobwebs in their studies, they carried hairsplitting analyses into their pulpits. They became arid scholastics — throwbacks to the Puritan divines of old. Severe and aloof as preachers, these detached and anachronistic intellectuals read ponderous discourses to congregations who needed, to repeat Jonathan Edwards's words, not to have their heads stored but to have their hearts touched.

In reality, however, the New Divinity men recognized and endeavored to maintain a distinction between the work of the study and the work of the pulpit, between the purpose of the written word and the purpose of the spoken word. Far from divorcing their movement from the experimental religion of the First Great Awakening, the first generation of New Divinity men handed down to their theological offspring both a revivalistic commitment and a record of evangelical success. Furthermore, the stature of the New Divinity movement advanced hand in hand with the progress of the Second Great Awakening in New England. Indeed, the high-water mark of the movement was not reached until the early 1820's. By this time several of the institutions of the benevolent empire were well established, and New Divinity men were fully involved in organized reform efforts.

One reason for the New Divinity movement's vitality in a revivalistic era was that Edwards's disciples, adhering to the position he had taken during and after the First Great Awakening, viewed the written discourse as the primary forum for pursuing theological analysis and for advancing doctrinal knowledge. The sermon, in contrast, had a more evangelical objective; its purpose was not simply to instruct the minds of Christians but, more importantly, to encourage a desire for grace and a dedication to benevolence in their hearts. In his *Life of Edwards* Hopkins emphasized that the eminent theologian's sermons were "instructive, plain, entertaining, and profitable" because they were not "dry speculations." Edwards's widely recognized skill as a preacher, Hopkins believed, "was very much the effect of his great acquaintance with his own heart, his inward sense, and high exercise of true experimental religion." As a consequence, Edwards's sermons "lay truth before the mind, so as not only to convince the judgment, but to touch the heart and conscience."[2] Edwards's approach to preaching reflects a larger pattern of popular, extemporaneous discourse which the First Great Awakening encouraged. Harry S. Stout has recently argued that within American religion—indeed, within early American culture as a whole—the revival marked a shift away from the printed word and a formal approach to persuasion toward a more popular mode of communication: "The revivalists sought to transcend both the rational manner of polite liberal preaching and the plain style of orthodox preaching in order to speak directly to the people-at-large."[3]

Like Edwards, most New Divinity men recognized the importance of the popular, extemporaneous mode of preaching which the Awakening promoted. Some New Divinity men found it difficult making the transition from the study to the pulpit. One may find examples of Consistent Calvinists discussing abstract polemical divinity in the pulpit and of a few even reading written texts that were more suitable for publication. But, like Edwards, most New Divinity men reserved formal theological analysis and doctrinal polemics for published works, which were directed at fellow ministers and a few highly educated members of the laity, and which produced the religious "paper war" of late eighteenth-century New England. Thus Jonathan Edwards, Jr., in an unpublished manuscript entitled "Miscellaneous Observations on Preaching," which contained advice that he passed along to young men studying for the ministry, recommended that ministers "avoid an argumentative strain of preaching" and deliver their sermons with "zeal and devotion."[4] In *The Christian Minister*, an ordination sermon delivered in 1771, New Divinity minister Levi Hart insisted that preachers should not fill their discourses with "the noisy din of controversy . . . or with the learned unmeaning lumber of the schools."[5] Similarly, New Divinity ministers such as Joseph Bellamy and Nathanael Emmons, who opened their parsonages to numerous clerical aspirants, urged students to adopt an Edwardsian mode of preaching which eschewed pulpit metaphysics in favor of sermons that were "intelligible to . . . hearers of every age and capacity."[6]

Moreover, in Bellamy the New Divinity movement claimed a preacher whose eloquence in the pulpit and whose success as a revivalist were more than a match for Edwards. Bellamy was one of the outstanding preachers in mid-eighteenth-century New England. When he left his study and entered the pulpit, Bellamy left behind the world of metaphysical speculation and would, Rev. Benjamin Trumbull reported, "from the native vigor of his soul, produce the most commanding strokes of eloquence, making his audience come alive."[7] In the view of Rev. Thomas Robbins, Bellamy was "to be reckoned among the sons of thunder." Virtually all accounts of Bellamy's preaching agree with Robbins's assessment that he spoke "with a prodigious voice, a vivid imagination, great flow of language, and a deep sense of the importance of his message. . . ." Thus, Bellamy "rarely failed to secure an earnest attention" from his audience.[8]

Within the New Divinity movement Bellamy represented a major link between the First and Second Great Awakenings. As a result of his popularity as a preacher, Bellamy continued to intinerate long after the mid-century revival. Furthermore, his evangelical style of preaching furnished a model for the numerous students he trained for the ministry. Many of these students led local revivals in the Second Great Awakening. Bellamy lived until 1790 and was able to answer the invitations of his former students in the early 1780's and participate in the first phase of the Second Great Awakening. In 1780, for example, New Divinity minister Chandler Robbins of Plymouth, Massachusetts, informed Bellamy that a revival was in progress in the churches of the Old Colony. "I never Saw Such a Season before, in Regard to Religion as in most of the Towns around us," Robbins reported as he urged his former teacher to come preach to the awakened people of the area. Not only Robbins's congregation but churches under New Divinity ministers in Abington and Middleboro were sharing in this local revival.[9]

By the mid-1780's the revival had spread from the old Plymouth Colony area northward toward New Hampshire and westward toward central Massachusetts. In a succession of small agricultural towns — communities like Rowley, Byfield, Medway, and Franklin — the revival swept through churches under New Divinity preachers. In Franklin 70 people were converted under Nathanael Emmons's preaching in 1785. Emmons experienced two more revivals in 1794 and in the years 1808 and 1809.[10]

In western Massachusetts and Connecticut, New Divinity men were also at the center of the Awakening's emotional whirlwind. Stephen West, the Hopkinsian minister of Stockbridge, for instance, led local revivals in the early 1780's and late 1790's.[11] West was a productive theologian who in addition to his work on the atonement published an important essay on free will. Yet he did not preach in an abstract or argumentative manner, according to the Reverend Chester Dewey, one of West's students: "A Hopkinsian would understand the bearing of some of his language as leading to that system, but the common hearers would recognize nothing beyond a general view of the Gospel plan of salvation. I have heard him say that many things in religion and philosophy, he never preached, because the direct object of his ministry should be to lead sinners to God and salvation."[12]

Nathan Strong of Hartford was another successful New Divinity revivalist. Indeed, after Bellamy's death in 1790, Strong was recognized as the most dynamic preacher in the New Divinity movement. His Hartford parish experienced revivals in 1794, 1798—1799, 1808, and 1815.[13] While not as successful as Strong, other Connecticut New Divinity men, such as Jonathan Edwards, Jr., of Colebrook and Charles Backus of Somers, led local revivals during this period. The reports of these revivals contained in *The Connecticut Evangelical Magazine* clearly disclose the widespread participation of the New Divinity men in the Second Great Awakening in their home state.[14]

In a letter to the Reverend John Ryland in England in 1799, Hopkins glowingly and quite accurately described the involvement of the New Divinity men in the new spiritual awakening. "A remarkable revival of religion has lately taken place in New England and part of New York State," he wrote, "it is said in more than 100 towns, mostly if not wholly under the preachers of Edwardean divinity."[15] But the progress of the revival and the reports of New Divinity evangelical successes did not only give Hopkins a new sense of hope for America; the surrounding activity also left him with a feeling of personal failure, for his Newport parishioners were unaffected by the Awakening. In fact, except for a few occasions in the early 1740's when he was an itinerating minister and when the First Great Awakening was at its height, Hopkins experienced little success as an evangelical preacher.

Writing in his autobiography in 1800, Hopkins commented on his failure as a revivalist. He described the "doubt and discouragement" he felt because his preaching had not been a means "of awakening and converting sinners." He had entered the ministry, he recalled, in the middle of the First Great Awakening, "when many were awakened, and thought to be converted, and many ministers were successful in this, and had great revivals in their congregations; but no such thing has appeared under my preaching, though some individuals have sometimes appeared in some degree awakened."[16]

Historians have seized upon Hopkins's failure at revivalism as evidence that the New Divinity movement undermined the Edwardsian evangelicalism of the First Great Awakening. Hopkins, it is argued, read ponderous theological sermons to his parishioners and attempted to store their heads instead of touching their hearts. From his conspicuous failure as a revivalistic preacher, historians have extrapolated a larger evangelical failure of the New Divinity movement.[17] A careful analysis of Hopkins's case, however, leads to conclusions which contradict the conventional wisdom.

Hopkins's lack of success as an evangelical preacher did not stem from his reading metaphysical discourses in the pulpit. At the beginning of his clerical career he did rely on a written text, but Jonathan Edwards advised Hopkins and other New Divinity men to deliver sermons in an extemporaneous manner.[18] Edwards wrote out all of his sermons but committed the major points of the text to memory. Consequently, Hopkins pointed out in his *Life of Edwards*, "if some thoughts were suggested while he was speaking, which did not occur when writing, and appeared to him pertinent, he would deliver them; and that with as great propriety and fluency, and oftener with greater pathos, and attended with a more sensible good effect on his hearers, than all he had wrote."[19]

Edwards's extemporaneous style of preaching became a model for the New Divinity men. As early as 1743 Hopkins was preaching in an Edwardsian manner. Frequently in the 1740's and 1750's his diary records his pleasure in "preaching without notes." In his autobiography he remarked, "I have not been confined to my notes in preaching, except for a short time, when I first began. . . ."[20] Indeed, Hopkins adopted an even more extemporaneous style of preaching than Edwards, because he eventually abandoned his teacher's practice of writing out sermons in advance. Instead of drafting entire sermons, Hopkins merely outlined the major points to be covered and reviewed his brief notes before entering the pulpit.[21]

Simply adopting an extemporaneous style, however, did not make Hopkins an effective preacher, for, unlike Edwards, Bellamy, and other New Divinity men, he did not possess the characteristics of a good public speaker. The basic reason for Hopkins's failure as a revivalist was not a penchant for pulpit metaphysics but his serious deficiency as a public speaker. "I am troubled with a sort of tone, which I cannot get rid of,"[22] he complained in his diary at the age of twenty-two, when as a newly ordained New Light minister he was aspiring to be a revivalist. Throughout his ministry a deep, nasal monotone hampered Hopkins's effectiveness as a preacher. He anguished over his preaching and struggled for years, with little apparent success, to improve his delivery. "My preaching has always appeared to me as poor, low and miserable, compared with what it ought to be . . . ," he noted in his autobiography.[23] Old age seems to have aggravated Hopkins's shortcomings as a public speaker. William Ellery Channing, who observed Hopkins preaching in Newport in the 1780's and 1790's, recollected that the theologian's voice "was most untunable." His preaching "approached a cracked bell, more nearly than anything to which I can compare it," Channing reported.[24]

Near the close of his clerical career, as reports of the new revival of religion were transmitted to Newport, Hopkins became burdened with a sense of personal failure. Precisely because a commitment to revivalism was such a central element of the New Divinity ministry and because so many Consistent Calvinists were successful evangelical preachers, Hopkins believed that he was a failure in this important aspect of the Lord's work. "I should expect that a good minister of Christ would be succeeded in this respect [revivalism]," he commented in 1800, "especially when others around him were successful — more than I have appeared to be."[25]

The growth of the New Divinity movement among the Congregational clergy seemed to parallel the progress of the Second Great Awakening in New England. In 1792 fifty-eight ministers in Connecticut identified themselves as New Divinity men. This group represented more than one third of all the Congregational ministers in Connecticut in 1792.[26] In that same year, the Consistent Calvinists claimed to have the allegiance of all new clerical candidates in Connecticut, a boast that was largely substantiated by Ezra Stiles's complaint from the presidency of Yale at this time that when Connecticut churches attempted to fill vacant pulpits they could find "no other ministers" but New Divinity men.[27] The popularity of Consistent Calvinism with aspirants to the Congregational ministry in Connecticut would continue to grow well into the nineteenth century. Already by the early 1790's the New Divinity men were no longer confined to the western area of the state. In 1792 Litchfield County, with twenty New Divinity men in pastorates, remained the stronghold of the movement. But New London County in the eastern part of the state claimed thirteen New Divinity pastors, followed by Middlesex County with nine and Windham County with eight.[28]

In Massachusetts the New Divinity men made inroads upon Harvard territory in the late eighteenth century. From Berkshire County the movement expanded into central and eastern Massachusetts. By the time the Second Great Awakening's transforming power began to be felt in New England, New Divinity men were serving numerous small town churches in an arc outside the Boston area extending from the old Plymouth Colony to the New Hampshire border. Ezra Stiles noted in his diary in 1781, "New Divinity preachers collect some large Congregations in some parts [such] as Taunton, Middleboro, [and] Abington."[29] William Bentley, another theological foe of the movement and the liberal Calvinist minister of Salem, surveyed the ecclesiastical terrain of inland Massachusetts in 1790 and concluded alarmingly that he was surrounded "by men called Hopkintonians." Not only in his own Essex County but "In Middlesex County bordering upon us these enthusiasts abound," Bentley recorded in his diary.[30] The establishment of the predominantly Hopkinsian Andover Seminary furnished the New Divinity movement with an institutional center, which also proved to be a fertile recruiting ground. In 1808, the same year in which Andover opened, Bentley estimated that there were one hundred and seventy Hopkinsian ministers in Massachusetts alone.[31]

The New Divinity also spread into the northern New England backcountry in the late eighteenth and early nineteenth centuries. The movement followed Connecticut settlers northward up the Connecticut River Valley into Vermont, for example. "Vermont abounds with the New Divinity," a disturbed Ezra Stiles noted in his diary in 1792.[32] The observations of such New Divinity foes as Stiles and Bentley lend support to Hopkins's assessment of the state of the movement in the 1790's. Hopkins claimed, in

1795, that the New Divinity was "fast increasing" and that Consistent Calvinist doctrines appeared "to be coming more and more into credit, and are better understood, and the odium which was cast on them and those who preached them is greatly subsided."[33] Four years later Hopkins sent Reverend John Ryland in England an even brighter report on the progress of the New Divinity. "Edwardean sentiments are spreading among divines and others in New England," he wrote in 1799, "and bid well to take the lead in divinity and silence all opposition."[34]

To be sure, Hopkins's hopes were exaggerated; the surge of the New Divinity, far from silencing all criticism of the movement, stimulated new sources of opposition. So many young men who were attracted to the Congregational ministry in the late eighteenth and early nineteenth centuries became advocates of the New Divinity that, as Ezra Stiles pointed out, growing numbers of churches were faced with the alternative that earlier had only confronted backwoods churches — accept a Consistent Calvinist minister or none at all. Thus, some New Divinity men found themselves embroiled in disputes with churches that had grown accustomed to a milder brand of Calvinism.[35]

Still, Consistent Calvinist ministers were far more popular with or acceptable to New England Congregationalists during the Second Great Awakening than has generally been recognized. By portraying the New Divinity men as scholastics who preached abstruse doctrines from the pulpit, historians have exaggerated the extent to which the movement alienated the laity. As Edwardsians, the New Divinity men understood the evangelical function of the spoken word. Furthermore, they preached their hyper-Calvinist doctrines not as part of a novel metaphysical system but as extensions of or as emphases within the evangelical Calvinism of the First Great Awakening. The term New Divinity, after all, was an invention of Hopkins's opponents. It is significant that there was little objection to Hopkins's probationary preaching in Newport, until his clerical foes wrenched from context one of the doctrinal positions he had taken in a *written work*.

Among the Congregational laity, the New Divinity movement benefited from the religious mood that the Second Great Awakening fostered. The New England phase of the Awakening continues to be viewed as an evangelical campaign contrived and promoted by ministers who democratized Calvinism with a doctrine of moral ability and who used the reform agencies of the benevolent empire as instruments of social control to replace the crumbling state-established church system.[36] Such an interpretation may be true for the last stage of the Awakening — for a period beginning after 1820 and coinciding with the rise of both Jacksonian Democracy and the so-called "new revivalistic measures" of Charles Grandison Finney — during which Lyman Beecher and Nathaniel Taylor popularized a moderate evangelical brand of Calvinism. But at least in the New England backcountry, the Awakening appears to have originated not with theocratically motivated clergy but in a post-Revolutionary crisis of religious legitimation among the laity, a conflict between established normative values and new modes of behavior unleashed by the Revolution. On the one hand, the republican ideology of the Revolution, with its call for the creation of a Christian Sparta, its emphasis on public virtue and the public good, and its criticism of extravagance, luxury, and self-interest, revitalized New England's corporate social ethic. On the other hand, however, the Revolution promoted economic and demographic changes and encouraged challenges to authority which violated traditional social norms. The local revivals which comprise the Second Great Awakening in New England need to be viewed in the context of the conflict between a revitalized corporate social ethic and post-Revolutionary modes of behavior.[37]

Indeed, one of the major institutional consequences of these revivals — the proliferation of moral societies across New England — was a Congregational response to what was perceived as a social crisis. The creation of these local societies was a reaction to changing social behavior that church leaders attributed to a drastic decline in personal morality and public virtue. Consisting of ministers and prominent members of the laity, moral societies attempted to promote reform on the local level by encouraging conversions and by supporting the regulation of "vices" such as Sabbath-breaking, gambling, and the use of alcohol and profanity. By 1810 moral societies were a common part of New England town life, especially in the New Divinity stronghold of Connecticut, where a statewide organization, The Connecticut Society for the Reformation of Morals and Suppression of Vice, was established in 1812.[38]

The Second Great Awakening not only continued the Revolution's revitalization of traditional New England social values, a process reflected in the moral society movement; but it also appears to have stimulated, particularly in the backcountry, a renewed lay interest in and willingness to accept the kind of conservative Calvinist doctrines preached by the New Divinity men. One resident of rural New England, David Morrill, a doctor in Epsom, New Hampshire, left a suggestive account in his autobiography of how conversion in the Second Great Awakening led him to adopt New Divinity views. After experiencing his spiritual rebirth in 1799, Morrill found his minister's preaching wanting:

> . . . it was too smooth and Arminian, but the Bible did not become completely clear. I had been attending the Free Will Baptists and now inquired into their points and found they did not accord with the Scripture nor with the sentiments of the most pious divines. . . . I now began to embrace Calvinistic doctrines, as the most agreeable to the Bible and sound reason. I obtained Dr. Hopkins's system of Divinity, which I read with great comfort and benefit. I most heartily embraced all the doctrines discussed in his system, I became fully satisfied with their truths and importance and have never doubted their correctness to the present time, 1836. . . .[39]

Similarly, New Divinity ministers reported in *The Connecticut Evangelical Magazine* how local revivals in their parishes during the Second Great Awakening encouraged an acceptance of hyper-Calvinist doctrines. Samuel Mills, the New Divinity minister of Torringford, Connecticut, for instance, reported that a revival in his church in 1798 promoted a new recognition of "the duties of unconditional submission and disinterested affection." Mills found many people readily expressing the Hopkinsian idea that a Christian ought to be willing to be damned for the glory of God.[40] In short, the ecclesiastical history of the New Divinity movement during the Second Great Awakening refutes the idea that, as Edmund S. Morgan put it, few Consistent Calvinists "could retain a popular following [since] most of the time their congregations found them simply dull."[41]

On the clerical level, the New Divinity's increasing appeal to aspirants for the Congregational ministry in the late eighteenth and early nineteenth centuries derived in part from the movement's intellectual challenge. Ezra Stiles conceded that the New Divinity attracted many of the brightest Yale graduates.[42] For such young men the New Divinity's intellectual challenge was not limited to mastering the thought of the movement's theological triumvirate of Edwards, Hopkins, and Bellamy; it included a personal commitment to advancing Scriptural knowledge. From the presidency of Yale, Stiles complained that the New Divinity men "all want to be Luthers."[43]

In addition to the intellectual attraction of Consistent Calvinism, the dedication of the New Divinity men to theological instruction ensured that their movement would win the allegiance of a significant portion of the rising generation of ministers. In Connecticut, schools of the prophets run by such men as Joseph Bellamy, Nathan Strong, John Smalley, and Levi Hart established a tradition of New Divinity dominance over post-graduate theological education that went virtually unchallenged in the state until the formation of the Yale Divinity School in 1822.[44] In Massachusetts the efforts of Nathanael Emmons, Stephen West, and others introduced the New Divinity to clerical aspirants, and Andover Seminary supplied a steady flow of recruits to the movement in the early nineteenth century.

Finally, for many pious but not metaphysically inclined ministerial candidates, the New Divinity's lofty social ethics were more appealing than its intellectual challenge. The New Divinity's animus against selfishness and its emphasis on disinterested benevolence furnished a theological framework which encouraged the kind of reaffirmation of New England's corporate social values that was embodied in the moral society movement. Such a reaffirmation may have been particularly appealing to many pietistic young men from rural New England who were converted in the local revivals of the Second Great Awakening and who, like the Andover missionaries, adopted the New Divinity and became engaged in reform efforts.

As the Second Great Awakening led to the establishment of reform organizations and churches in new settlements, it created an increasing demand for ministers. But Congregational authorities found that they could only meet this demand by vigorous efforts to recruit young men for the ministry. In the first place, many of the new clerical openings were of the sort that would tend not to attract professionally ambitious youth. The numerous clerical vacancies in the new settlements of northern New England, for example, promised a future of low pay, high insecurity, and missionary hardships. Furthermore, for college graduates from socially established backgrounds, the declining appeal of the ministry as a profession — a development that was well-advanced by the middle of the eighteenth century — was not reversed by the Second Great Awakening. In the post-revolutionary decades such young men continued to find careers in business, politics, law, and medicine more rewarding than the ministry; and many who still sought clerical careers summarily dismissed the small settlements of the backcountry and fixed their sights on Boston, New Haven, Hartford, Providence, and other growing urban centers in New England.[45]

As a consequence, the Second Great Awakening, like the First, attracted significant numbers of young men from modest and poor backgrounds into the Congregational ministry. Congregational authorities established societies to finance the education of such young men who were converted in the local revivals of the Second Great Awakening and who aspired to the ministry. New Divinity men played a major role in these efforts, which led to the founding of the American Education Society, one of the institutions of the benevolent empire, in 1815.

In 1804, Vermont Consistent Calvinist William Jackson formed one of the first charitable societies in New England "to aid pious and needy young men in acquiring education for the work of the gospel ministry."[46] Within a short time, local education societies were organized across the region. At the same time ministerial associations began providing financial aid to clerical aspirants of limited means. In 1809, for example, the New Divinity-controlled Litchfield County North Association assumed the task "of aiding pious, indigent young Men, in obtaining education, for the work of the Gospel Ministry."[47] Four years later Yale established a Benevolent Society to provide financial assistance to needy individuals in its student body. This action was followed by the formation in New Haven of the Charitable Society for the Education of Pious Young Men for the Ministry of the Gospel, which provided funds for needy students, and the Female Education Society, which supplied such students with clothes and other necessities.[48]

In Massachusetts similar local education societies began operation during the Second Great Awakening, and much of the New England effort to finance the preparation of young men of limited means for the ministry came to be concentrated at Andover Theological Seminary. The founding of the Seminary, which was financed largely by two wealthy laymen from Daniel Hopkins's Salem church and Samuel Spring's Newburyport church, established not only a conservative theological bastion against the doctrinal liberalism of eastern Massachusetts, but it also created an educational refuge for ministerial aspirants of limited means. The school did not charge tuition, and it even provided funds to relieve indigent students from expenses for room and board. Enrollment soared beyond the expectations of the school's authorities. The average number of students in a class increased from fifty during the early years to over one hundred by the end of Andover's first decade of operation.[49] Both the school's faculty and the Samaritan Female Society of Andover and Vicinity periodically reported on the limited financial resources of the ministerial candidates. The Female Society noted in 1817 how its members were "frequently called to witness among the students, and especially the indigent (of which last description there are in both seminaries [Andover and Phillips Academy] more than a hundred individuals) various and affecting cases of sickness and distress. . . ." A year later the Andover faculty recommended to the school's trustees that library fines be dropped because so many students were unable to pay them.[50]

Andover authorities were already involved in a broad effort to finance the education of clerical aspirants from modest and poor families. In 1815 the leaders of the Seminary joined with other Congregational officials to establish the American Society for Educating Youth for the Gospel Ministry (later its name was changed to the American Education Society). Working from its headquarters in Andover, the Society formed branches and auxiliaries which attempted to organize and expand the local charitable efforts that had been in operation for over a decade. The number of charity students that the Society aided quickly climbed into the hundreds, and within approximately two decades it rose to over a thousand.[51] Only through such efforts were increasing numbers of young men, including many who became New Divinity ministers, able to enter the Congregational ministry during the Second Great Awakening.

The charitable institutions of New England contributed to ongoing changes in the social composition of the Congregational ministry, changes that had been in evidence as early as the First Great Awakening.[52] Thus some clerics, especially those from socially established backgrounds, doubtless agreed with John G. Palfrey, the prominent Massachusetts Unitarian, who decried "the claims of what are called Education Societies, societies which finding a young man at the plough or in the workshop dispose to change his calling for that of a minister, take him up, and carry him at little or no present expense to himself, through all the steps of his preparation for that office. . . ." A New England youth "in the humbler walks of industry," Palfrey pointed out, often viewed the Congregational ministry as an opportunity of bettering "his condition." And when the road to the ministry was paved with the beneficence of charitable societies, "the temptation cannot but be strong and the minds of such subjected to a powerful bias to suppose themselves directed to this employment by a religious motive, when, if they examined more clearly, they might find it only a worldly calculation."[53]

Palfrey's disdain for revivalism made it difficult for him as a rationalist to understand how conversion could engender in pietistic young men from the "humbler walks" of New England life an idealistic commitment to disinterested benevolence. Many of the professional opportunities that these young men were recruited to fill required just such a commitment. Nevertheless, Palfrey's social criticism of recruits to the Congregational ministry resembles earlier attacks on the "upstart," "Farmer Metaphysicians" of the New Divinity movement who were "struggling to rise," and it suggests how the social makeup of the Congregational clergy continued to change in the Second Great Awakening.

The involvement of the New Divinity men in the benevolent empire was not restricted to the American Education Society and the American Board of Commissioners for Foreign Missions; it extended to other reform organizations that were an outgrowth of the Second Great Awakening.[54] Samuel Hopkins, whose theology made such a major contribution to the emergence of a commitment to reform within the New Divinity movement, did not live to see the formation of the benevolent empire, or the founding of Andover Seminary, or the establishment of a theological magazine bearing his name.[55] Hopkins continued to preach and write in Newport until 1803, but during the last years of his life he spoke and wrote only with difficulty. In January 1799, in his seventy-eighth year, he suffered a stroke which partially paralyzed the right side of his body, affecting his ability to write and considerably slurring his speech. He accepted the stroke "as a warning [from God] to be ready for death."[56]

After several months of convalescence, Hopkins returned to the pulpit in the spring of 1799. Each Sunday, Newport Gardner, a former slave, a prospective African missionary, and at the time the sexton of the First Church, would walk or ride in a one-horse chaise with Hopkins from the parsonage to the meeting house and help the theologian mount the steps to his pulpit. Once an imposing man standing over six feet tall and weighing in excess of two hundred pounds, Hopkins was now an aged, frail figure who struggled through the services under the watchful eye of the black sexton, who sat a few feet behind the pulpit always prepared to aid the infirm minister.[57]

Hopkins preached for nearly four years after suffering his paralytic stroke. The end came slowly and painfully toward the close of 1803. After a second stroke early in October, Hopkins's vital organs began to fail. He was never again able to eat solid food, and by mid-December his emaciated body signaled the imminence of death. The final throes began on December 18, when, according to the report of a follower who was at his bedside, Hopkins's "bodily distress was beyond description." After three days of suffering, his life expired, "without a sigh or groan," on December 20.[58] His funeral was held in Newport three days later. The vitality of the New Divinity movement during the next two decades revealed that his life and labor had not been in vain.

THE MAN AND
THE MOVEMENT

HOPKINS was a failure as a revivalist and far less prominent and successful as a theological teacher than other New Divinity men. While he instructed individual students, he never established his own school of the prophets. It was as a theologian and reformer, rather than as a revivalist and teacher, that Hopkins made his major contributions to the New Divinity movement.

As a result of his efforts to develop the theological implications of the First Great Awakening and to improve upon the thought of Jonathan Edwards, Hopkins contributed three original doctrinal interpretations to the New Divinity: God's willing sin into existence as an advantage to the universe; the greater vileness, in God's eyes, of the awakened as opposed to the unawakened sinner; and the nature of true virtue as consisting in radical disinterested benevolence toward Being in general. Although rational Calvinists singled out these views for derision and labeled them "new divinity," Hopkins's novel interpretations were merely extensions of the hyper-Calvinist covenant theology of the First Great Awakening. His position on the moral state of the awakened sinner, for example, was an attempt to underline the unconditional nature of rebirth. Hopkins's other two novel interpretations were not simply abstract theological formulations; they were responses to major social and intellectual problems in mid-eighteenth-century New England. His view of sin as an advantage to the universe was intended to convey the sense of God's sovereignty that the Awakening stimulated; it was also an attempt to counter the social pessimism of the 1750's and to encourage the millennial expectation of evangelical Calvinists. With his interpretation of true virtue as radical disinterested benevolence, Hopkins reaffirmed traditional

New England communal social values against an emergent individualistic social ethic. By placing the New Divinity in the larger social and intellectual context in which it was formulated, we can begin to understand how the movement grew in popularity in the decades between the First and Second Great Awakenings.

In addition to his original doctrinal interpretations, Hopkins made another important theological contribution to the New Divinity movement. He produced a system of divinity in a massive work that synthesized Edwards's theology and the New Divinity improvements upon Edwardsianism. Hopkins's *System of Doctrines* remains the most complete statement of *the* New England theology.

The major tension in Hopkins's theology stems from his efforts to reconcile the sovereignty and benevolence of the Deity. Unlike Jonathan Edwards, Hopkins was unable to resolve this problem without liberalizing his Calvinist theology. At different times Hopkins's writings stress either God's absolute sovereignty or His disinterested benevolence toward mankind. Ultimately Hopkins embraced a liberal Calvinist view of God as a benevolent moral governor, an interpretation that led him to accept the theory of a general atonement.

Although he liberalized major aspects of Edwardsianism and although a commitment to Christian social ethics was the central element in his definition of true virtue, Hopkins stopped far short of transforming Calvinist piety into Christian moralism. While advocating a liberal Calvinist view of the Deity, Hopkins clung to a hyper-Calvinist understanding of man. For this reason another "new divinity" was needed to move New England Calvinism further down the road to Christian moralism. During the last stage of the Second Great Awakening—from the mid-1820's through the 1830's—the New Haven Theology that was being developed by Nathaniel Taylor, Professor of Theology at the Yale Divinity School, became increasingly influential within the Congregational churches of New England. Building upon the moderate evangelical Calvinism of his teacher, Timothy Dwight, Taylor used the Scottish common sense philosophy to develop a system of divinity that reconciled self-love, or self-interest, with Christian ethics and that stressed the moral ability of natural man to save himself.[1] Such positions were heretical to the Hopkinsians; thus once again a New Divinity precipitated a paper war of theology and sharp divisions among the Congregational clergy. This time the future did not belong to the Hopkinsians. By the mid-1830's the moderate evangelical Calvinism of men like Taylor and Lyman Beecher had become the dominant theological school within New England Congregationalism. Perhaps this theological shift from Hopkinsianism to Taylorism symbolized New England's larger intellectual adjustment to the contemporary social values of Jacksonian America.[2]

Hopkins's reputation as a reformer survived the demise of the New Divinity movement. In the 1840's and 1850's abolitionists in New England recalled (often romantically, to be sure) Hopkins's early and persistent efforts against the slave trade and slavery. In 1847, for example, Quaker poet and abolitionist John Greenleaf Whittier published a vignette of Hopkins that memorialized the theologian as a reformer. "Let those who prefer to contemplate the narrow sectarian rather than the universal man," Whittier wrote, "dwell upon his controversial works and extol the ingenuity and logical acumen with which he defended his own dogmas and assailed those of others." Whittier preferred to remember and honor Hopkins "not as the founder of a new sect, but as the friend of all mankind — the generous defender of the poor and the oppressed."[3] Similarly, Harriet Beecher Stowe, in her historical novel *The Minister's Wooing* (1859), hailed Hopkins as an antislavery reformer. "The only mistake made by the good man," she observed, "was that of supposing that the elaboration of theology was preaching the gospel. The gospel he was preaching constantly, by his pure unworldly living . . . and by the grand humanity, outrunning his age, in which he protested against the then admitted system of slavery and the slave trade."[4] In the midst of this "rediscovery" of Hopkins by New England abolitionists, all of the theologian's major antislavery writings were reissued in a volume entitled *Timely Articles on Slavery by the Reverend Samuel Hopkins*.

Thus it was as a reformer that Hopkins's influence on antebellum American Protestantism endured beyond the life of the New Divinity movement. In spite of a limited, often paternalistic, vision of reform that prevented him from understanding more fully than he did the needs and rights of Indians or from recognizing earlier than he did the plight of blacks in America, Hopkins bequeathed a religious legacy to subsequent nineteenth-century activists who crusaded against slavery and other social sins in America.

NOTES

PROLOGUE

[1]See E. Brooks Holifield, *The Covenant Sealed: The Development of Puritan Sacramental Theology in Old and New England, 1570–1720* (New Haven, 1974), ch. 7, esp. p. 224. As Holifield points out, the arguments used by New England sacramental theologians derived from post-Reformation European thought.

[2]Clifford Shipton, "The New England Clergy in the 'Glacial Age,'" *Publications of the Colonial Society of Massachusetts*, 32 (1937), 56; John Bumsted, "The Pilgrims' Progress: An Ecclesiastical History of Southeastern Massachusetts" (Ph.D. diss., Brown University, 1965); Paul R. Lucas, *Valley of Discord: Church and Society Along the Connecticut River, 1636–1725* (Hanover, N.H., 1976); Gerald Goodwin, "The Myth of 'Arminian Calvinism' in Eighteenth-Century New England," *New England Quarterly*, 41 (1968), 213–217.

[3]Jonathan Edwards, "Some Thoughts on the Revival of Religion in New England," *Works*, 4 vols. (New York, 1843), III, 306–307. All citations, except where noted, are from this reprint of the Worcester edition.

[4]This description of New Light parties has drawn on Richard L. Bushman, *From Puritan to Yankee: Character and the Social Order in Connecticut, 1690–1765* (Cambridge, Mass., 1967), pp. 259–260.

[5]*Works*, I, 79–80; also see Conrad Wright, *The Beginnings of Unitarianism in America* (Boston, 1955), chs. 2, 3.

[6]Samuel Hopkins, *Twenty-one Sermons on a Variety of Interesting Subjects Sentimental and Practical* (Salem, 1803), p. 377.

[7]William Hart, *A Letter to the Reverend Samuel Hopkins . . .* (New London, 1770), p. 13.

[8]William G. McLoughlin, *Isaac Backus and the American Pietistic Tradition* (Boston, 1967), pp. 184–186.

[9]Stephen West, ed., *Sketches of the Life of the Late Rev. Samuel Hopkins, D.D., Pastor of the First Congregational Church in Newport, Written by Himself; Interspersed With Notes Extracted From His Private Diary* (Hartford, 1805), p. 102.

[10]*The Diary of William Bentley*, 4 vols. (Salem, 1905–1914), IV, 302.

[11]Frank H. Foster, *A Genetic History of New England Theology* (Chicago, 1907), pp. 1–3.

[12]The classical statement of this view is Joseph Haroutunian, *Piety versus Moralism: The Passing of the New England Theology* (New York, 1935). For the historiography on the New Divinity, see the bibliographical essay below, and Joseph A. Conforti, "Samuel Hopkins and the New Divinity: Theology, Ethics, and Social Reform in Eighteenth-Century New England," *William and Mary Quarterly*, 34 (1977), 573.

[13]See "Ezra Stiles versus the New Divinity Men," *American Quarterly*, 18 (1965), 248–258.

[14]On this conflict see Jack Greene, "Search for Identity: An Interpretation of the Meaning of Selected Patterns of Social Response in Eighteenth-Century America," *Journal of Social History*, 3 (1970), esp. 191–205.

CHAPTER ONE

[1]See Birdsall, "Ezra Stiles versus the New Divinity Men," pp. 248–252, and Edmund S. Morgan, *The Gentle Puritan: A Life of Ezra Stiles, 1727–1795* (New Haven, 1962).

[2]*The Diary of William Bentley, D.D.*, 4 vols. (Salem, 1905–1914), IV, 303; III, 465; II, 139.

[3]William Hart, *Brief Remarks on a number of false Propositions and dangerous Errors which are spreading in the Country* . . . (New Haven, 1769), pp. 17, 24–25.

[4]*The Diary of William Bentley*, I, 161, 243, 275.

[5]Quoted in Glen P. Anderson, "Joseph Bellamy: The Man and His Work" (Ph.D. diss., Boston University, 1971), p. 466. For similar social criticism of Samuel Hopkins see William Ellery Channing to E.A. Park, Feb. 14, 1840, Yale MSS., Sterling Memorial Library, Yale University; and William Patten, *Reminiscences of the Late Samuel Hopkins, D.D. of Newport, R.I., illustrative of his character and doctrines, with incidental subjects: from an intimacy with him of twenty-one years, while Pastor of a sister church in said town* (Providence, 1843), pp. 55–56, 130. Patten reported (p. 56) that while Hopkins was a minister in Great Barrington, Massachusetts, he was seriously considered for a professorship of divinity at Princeton. But a representative of the college who was sent to interview Hopkins felt he was unfit for the position because of "the country style in which Mr. H. lived and the correspondence of his manners to such a state."

[6]This is the term used by Daniel H. Calhoun in *Professional Lives in America: Structure and Aspiration, 1750–1850* (Cambridge, Mass., 1965), p. 157, to describe social strains in the Congregational ministry in the mid-nineteenth century. A sense of "social distance" and of social rank within the New England clergy are evident in the eighteenth century as well. See J. William T. Youngs, *God's Messengers: Religious Leadership in Colonial New England, 1700–1750* (Baltimore, 1976), pp. 68–69.

[7]Youngs, *God's Messengers*, pp. 65–69; James W. Schmotter, "The Irony of Clerical Professionalism: New England's Congregational Ministers and the Great Awakening," *American Quarterly*, 31 (1979), 148–168. See also Donald M. Scott, *From Office to Profession: The New England Ministry, 1750–1850* (Philadelphia, 1978), ch. 1.

[8]See Alan Heimert, *Religion and the American Mind from the Great Awakening to the Revolution* (Cambridge, Mass., 1966), pp. 170–171; Greene, "Search for Identity," pp. 206–207; and Michael Zuckerman, "The Fabrication of Identity in Early America," *William and Mary Quarterly*, 34 (1977), 200.

[9]For a discussion of this problem see James W. Schmotter, "Ministerial Careers in Eighteenth-Century New England: The Social Context, 1700–1760," *Journal of Social History*, 9 (1975), 264, n. 5.

[10]Richard Warch, *School of the Prophets: Yale College, 1701–1740* (New Haven, 1973), p. 252.

[11]Schmotter, "Ministerial Careers in Eighteenth-Century New England," p. 251.

[12]This conclusion is reinforced by other studies. See, for example, P.M.G. Harris, "The Social Origins of American Leaders: The Demographic Foundations," *Perspectives in American History*, 3 (1969), 186–191.

[13]Ibid., pp. 249–255. The reasons for the declining attractiveness of the ministry in the eighteenth century are discussed in Chapter Five, below. David F. Allmendinger has documented important changes in the composition of New England college student bodies, changes beginning in the mid-eighteenth century which brought large numbers of rural youth of limited means to the region's colleges and which undoubtedly had an impact on the social structure of the ministry. See Allmendinger, "New England Students and the Revolution in Higher Education," *History of Education Quarterly*, 4 (1971), 381–389, and his *Paupers and Scholars: The Transformation of Student Life in Nineteenth-Century New England* (New York, 1975). Philip J. Greven, Jr., has found that in Andover, Massachusetts, in the middle of the eighteenth century, farming fathers were sending more of their sons to college instead of giving land as family land holdings shrunk after three generations of divisions and subdivions. See *Four Generations: Population, Land, and Family in Colonial Andover* (Ithaca, 1970), pp. 246–251.

[14]On the practice of social ranking see Franklin B. Dexter, "On Some Social Distinctions at Harvard and Yale before the Revolution," in *A Selection from the Miscellaneous Historical Papers of Fifty Years* (New Haven, 1918), pp. 203–222; Samuel E. Morison, "Precedence at Harvard in the Seventeenth Century," American Antiquarian Society, *Proceedings*, new ser., 42 (1932), 371–431; Clifford K. Shipton, "Ye Mystery of Ye Ages Solved, or, How Placing Worked at Colonial Harvard and Yale," *Harvard Alumni Bulletin*, 57 (1954), 258–263; Harris, "The Social Origins of American Leaders," p. 244.; and Warch, *School of the Prophets*, pp. 255–257.

[15]Schmotter, "Ministerial Careers in Eighteenth-Century New England," pp. 251–253.

[16]Harry S. Stout, "The Great Awakening in New England Reconsidered: The New England Clergy," *Journal of Social History*, 8 (1974), 27–28. As Stout points out, both Old Lights and New Lights recruited most heavily from the middle class. Sixteen percent of New Lights and 13.9 percent of the Old Lights had lower class origins.

[17]Ibid., pp. 24, 27–28.

[18]Ibid., pp. 33–36.

[19]This group of fifty-six New Divinity men was composed from a number of sources. Conrad Wright, in *The Beginnings of Unitarianism in America* (Boston, 1955), pp. 288–291, identified twenty-one New Divinity men, although one of these individuals, Timothy Dwight, has weak credentials as a Consistent Calvinist. See Stephen E. Berk, *Calvinism versus Democracy: Timothy Dwight and the Origins of Evangelical Orthodoxy* (Hamden, Conn., 1974). The correspondence of Hopkins and Joseph Bellamy and the diaries of Ezra Stiles and William Bentley name many New Divinity men. In addition theological persuasions of individual ministers have been identified or confirmed through the following: Franklin B. Dexter, *Biographical Sketches of the Graduates of Yale College with Annals of the College History*, 6 vols. (New York, 1885–1912); William B. Sprague, *Annals of the American Pulpit*, 9 vols. (New York, 1857–1869); and town histories. On the size of the New Divinity movement between the Awakening and the Revolution see the estimate of Stiles in Franklin B. Dexter, ed., *The Literary Diary of Ezra Stiles, D.D. LL.D.*, 3 vols. (New York, 1901), III, 363, and a similar estimate by Jonathan Edwards, Jr., reported in ibid., II, 227.

[20]The most famous incident of dissatisfaction with the system of social ranking involved Israel Williams, a Connecticut "River God," whose son was ranked fourteenth in a class of thirty-four at Harvard in 1747. Williams and other fathers of backcountry youth felt that college authorities discriminated against their sons. The Williams affair, the resentment of many backwoods farmers against the ranking system at Harvard and Yale, and the need to provide greater educational opportunities for rural youth all led to an abortive attempt to establish a new college in western New England in the middle of the eighteenth century. See Henry Lefavour, "The Proposed College in Hampshire County in 1762," Massachusetts Historical Society, *Proceedings*, 66 (1936–41), 53.

[21]Quoted in Dexter, "On Some Social Distinctions between Harvard and Yale," p. 218. For a sketch of Avery see Dexter, *Yale Biographies*, III, 305–310.

[22]On this typology of New England towns see Edward M. Cook, Jr., *The Fathers of the Towns: Leadership and Community Structure in Eighteenth-Century New England* (Baltimore, 1976), ch. 7. Cook's volume contains a wealth of information on the social and political structure of various New England communities as well as population data on numerous towns.

[23]Dexter, *Yale Biographies*, II, 53, 430.

[24]Quoted in Dexter, "On Some Social Distinctions between Harvard and Yale," p. 218.

[25]Edwards A. Park, *Memoir of the Life and Character of Samuel Hopkins, D.D.* (Boston, 1854), pp. 9–11.

[26]Henry Bronson, *History of Waterbury, Connecticut, with an Appendix of Biography, Genealogy, and Statistics* (Waterbury, 1858), chs. 1, 2; Joseph Anderson, *The Town and City of Waterbury, Connecticut, from the Aboriginal Period to the Year Eighteen Hundred and Ninety-Five*, 3 vols. (New Haven, 1896), I, 158–161.

[27]Katherine A. Prichard, ed., *Proprietors' Records of the Town of Water-*

bury, Connecticut, 1677 – 1761 (Waterbury, 1911), pp. 10 – 11; Bronson, *History of Waterbury*, pp. 113 – 124.

[28]Bronson, *History of Waterbury*, pp. 101 – 108, 566.

[29]Prichard, ed., *Proprietors' Records*, pp. 99 – 100.

[30]Bronson, *History of Waterbury*, p. 154.

[31]West, ed., *Sketches of the Life of Samuel Hopkins*, p. 24. Samuel was actually the second son born to his parents; the first died at birth.

[32]Ibid., pp. 24 – 25.

[33]Bronson, *History of Waterbury*, p. 566.

[34]West, ed., *Sketches of the Life of Samuel Hopkins*, pp. 24 – 25.

[35]For the Connecticut context see Bushman, *Puritan to Yankee*, and Lucas, *Valley of Discord*.

[36]Bronson, *History of Waterbury*, ch. 17; Anderson, *The Town and the City of Waterbury*, chs. 24 – 25.

[37]Bronson, *History of Waterbury*, pp. 569 – 571.

[38]See the tax lists reprinted in ibid., pp. 565 – 566, and in Anderson, *The Town and City of Waterbury*, pp. 303 – 309.

[39]Anderson, *The Town and City of Waterbury*, p. 309.

[40]West, ed., *Sketches of the Life of Samuel Hopkins*, p. 24.

[41]See Edmund S. Morgan, *The Puritan Family* (1944; rpt., New York, 1966), pp. 68 – 78.

[42]West, ed., *Sketches of the Life of Samuel Hopkins*, p. 27.

[43]Bronson, *History of Waterbury*, p. 154; Anderson, *The Town and City of Waterbury*, p. 359.

[44]West, ed., *Sketches of the Life of Samuel Hopkins*, pp. 52 – 53.

[45]Ibid., p. 27.

[46]Dexter, *Yale Biographies*, I, 661 – 663.

[47]Louis L. Tucker, *Puritan Protagonist: President Thomas Clap of Yale College* (Chapel Hill, 1962) offers an excellent analysis of life at Yale in the middle of the eighteenth century; see especially ch. 4. See also Warch, *School of the Prophets*, chs. 6, 10.

[48]West, ed., *Sketches of the Life of Samuel Hopkins*, p. 27.

[49]Tucker, *Puritan Protagonist*, pp. 77 – 80; Warch, *School of the Prophets*, chs. 8, 9.

CHAPTER TWO

[1]On the broad appeal of the Awakening see Edwin S. Gaustad, *The Great Awakening in New England* (New York, 1957), p. 142; and Bushman, *Puritan to Yankee*, p. 185. On the appeal of the revival to young men, see Cedric Cowing, "Sex and Preaching in the Great Awakening," *American Quarterly*, 20 (1968), 624 – 644; James Walsh, "The Great Awakening in Woodbury, Connecticut," *William and Mary Quarterly*, 28 (1971), 543 – 562; and Gerald Moran, "Conditions of Religious Conversion in the First Society of Norwich, Connecticut," *Journal of Social History*, 6 (1972), 336 – 337. On the relationship between socio-economic conditions and the response of young males to the revival, see John Bumsted, "Religion, Finance, and Democracy in Massachusetts: The Town of Norton as a Case Study," *Journal of American History*, 17

(1971), 817–831, and Patricia J. Tracy, *Jonathan Edwards, Pastor: Religion and Society in Eighteenth-Century Northampton* (New York, 1980), ch. 4. For a recent demographic overview of the revival, see J. M. Bumsted and John E. Van De Wettering, *What Must I Do to be Saved? The Great Awakening in Colonial America* (Hinsdale, Ill., 1976), ch. 7.

[2]See Joseph Kett, "Growing Up in Rural New England, 1800–1840," in Tamara K. Hareven, ed., *Anonymous Americans* (Englewood Cliffs, N.J., 1971), pp. 10–12, and Kett, "Adolescence and Youth in Nineteenth-Century America," in Theodore Kabb and Robert I. Rothberg, eds., *The Family in History* (New York, 1973), pp. 95–103.

[3]Quoted in Lois Banner, "Religion and Reform in the Early Republic: The Role of Youth," *American Quarterly*, 23 (1971), 682n.

[4]"Thoughts on the Revival in New England," *Works*, III, 387.

[5]*George Whitefield's Journals* (London, 1960), p. 462. On Whitefield see Luke Tyerman, *George Whitefield* (New York, 1877), and Stuart C. Henry, *George Whitefield* (Nashville, 1957).

[6]*George Whitefield's Journals*, p. 476.

[7]West, ed., *Sketches of the Life of Samuel Hopkins*, p. 30; Tucker, *Puritan Protagonist*, pp. 116–118.

[8]*George Whitefield's Journals*, p. 480.

[9]West, ed., *Sketches of the Life of Samuel Hopkins*, pp. 30–31.

[10]For an excellent description of the aftermath of Whitefield's weekend revival at Yale, see Tucker, *Puritan Protagonist*, pp. 117–128.

[11]This was a constant theme of Tennent and other New Lights. See Tennent, *The Danger of an Unconverted Ministry* in Alan Heimert and Perry Miller, eds. *The Great Awakening* (New York, 1967) p. 95. On Tennent's background and life, see Charles Maxson, *The Great Awakening in the Middle Colonies* (Chicago, 1920), ch. 3, and Sprague, *Annals*, III, 35–41.

[12]West, ed., *Sketches of the Life of Samuel Hopkins*, p. 37.

[13]Ibid., pp. 32–35.

[14]Ibid., p. 35.

[15]On Davenport's life, see Sprague, *Annals*, III, 80–92; for his activities at New Haven, see Tucker, *Puritan Protagonist*, pp. 125–128, and Morgan, *The Gentle Puritan*, pp. 31–33.

[16]Quoted in Dexter, *Yale Biographies*, I, 661.

[17]"Distinguishing Marks of a Work of the Spirit of God," *Works*, I, 526; Morgan, *The Gentle Puritan*, pp. 33–35, offers an excellent analysis of the circumstances surrounding the sermon.

[18]"Distinguishing Marks of a Work of the Spirit of God," p. 526.

[19]Ibid., pp. 540–544.

[20]Ibid., pp. 552–555.

[21]Ibid., p. 546.

[22]West, ed., *Sketches of the Life of Samuel Hopkins*, p. 38.

[23]Samuel Hopkins, *Life and Character of the Late Reverend, Learned and Pious Mr. Jonathan Edwards* (Northampton, 1764), p. 55.

[24]West, ed., *Sketches of the Life of Samuel Hopkins*, pp. 38–40.

[25]Ibid., p. 40; see also Hopkins, "A Short Sketch of Mrs. Edwards' Life and Character," in his *Life of Edwards*, esp. pp. 102–103.

[26]West, ed., *Sketches of the Life of Samuel Hopkins*, pp. 41–43.

[27]Ibid., p. 43.

[28]Ibid., pp. 44–45.

[29]Ibid., p. 44. See also Hopkins, *Journal*, June 12, 1743, Williams College Library, Williamstown, Mass.

[30]West, Ed., *Sketches of the Life of Samuel Hopkins*, pp. 45–46; Hopkins, *Journal*, December 5, 1742–May 29, 1743, Williams MSS.

[31]Hopkins, *Journal*, June 21, 1743, Williams MSS.

[32]Anderson, "Joseph Bellamy," pp. 132–133, 136–139.

[33]Edwards A. Park, *Memoir of Nathanael Emmons with Sketches of his friends and Pupils* (Boston, 1861), p. 32. On Emmons see also John T. Dahlquist, "Nathanael Emmons: His Life and Work" (Ph.D. diss., Boston Univ., 1963). For information on Smalley see C. L. Goodell, "John Smalley," *Congregational Quarterly*, 15 (July, 1873), 351–364.

[34]Gilbert Tennent, "The Danger of an Unconverted Ministry," Heimert and Miller eds., *The Great Awakening*, pp. 95, 98. See also Alan Heimert, *Religion and the American Mind from the Great Awakening to the Revolution*, (Cambridge, 1966), ch. 4.

[35]Youngs, *God's Messengers*, ch. 4, esp. p. 64.; Schmotter, "The Irony of Clerical Professionalism," pp. 148–158. On the worldliness of the Congregational ministry, see Shipton, "The New England Clergy in the 'Glacial Age,' " pp. 51–52; Ola Elizabeth Winslow, *Meetinghouse Hill, 1630–1783* (New York, 1952), pp. 218–219; and David Hall, *The Faithful Shepherd: A History of the New England Ministry in the Seventeenth Century* (Chapel Hill, 1972), pp. 182–183.

[36]Samuel Willard, *Brief Directions to a Young Scholar Designing the Ministry for the Study of Divinity* (Boston, 1735), p. iii.

[37]Later editions of Whitefield's *Journal* removed some of the revivalist's harsh criticism of New England's ministers and colleges. See *Whitefield's Journals*, p. 462n. The quote in the text and the full attack on Harvard and Yale may be found in the installment, *A Continuation of Reverend Mr. Whitefield's Journal* (Boston, 1741), p. 96.

[38]*George Whitefield's Journals*, p. 354. On the Log College which eventually became Princeton see Archibald Alexander, *Biographical Sketches of the Founder and Principal Alumni of the Log College* (Philadelphia, 1851).

[39]Tucker, *Puritan Protagonist*, pp. 129–135.

[40]See Richard Warch, "The Shepherd's Tent: Education and Enthusiasm in the Great Awakening," *American Quarterly*, 30 (1978), 177–198.

[41]Shipton, "The New England Clergy of the 'Glacial Age,' " pp. 48–49; Tucker, *Puritan Protagonist*, p. 266; Lawrence Cremin, *American Education: The Colonial Experience, 1607–1783* (New York, 1970, p. 554; Warch, *School of the Prophets*, p. 270. Also see above, p. 12.

[42]For a discussion of this new emphasis on grace, see Youngs, *God's Messengers*, pp. 131–134.

[43]A description of Bellamy's school with biographical sketches of his students is in Anderson, "Joseph Bellamy," pp. 371–444; see also Percy C. Eggleston, *A Man of Bethlehem, Joseph Bellamy, D.D. and his Divinity School* (New London, 1908). The best analysis of the schools is Mary L. Gambrell,

Ministerial Training in Eighteenth-Century New England (New York, 1957), chs. 6, 7; see also Samuel Simpson, "Early Ministerial Training in America," *Papers of the American Society of Church History*, 2nd ser., 2 (1910), 117–129; William Shewmaker, "The Training of the Protestant Ministry in the United States, Before the Establishment of Theological Seminaries," *Papers of the American Society of Church History*, 2nd ser., 6 (1921), 75–197; and Roland Bainton, *Yale and the Ministry* (New York, 1957), ch. 3.

[44]For information on Emmons's school and biographical sketches of his students, see Park, *Memoir of Emmons*, pp. 222–265. John Smalley, Stephen West, Levi Hart, Nathan Strong, and Ephraim Judson were some of the other early theological teachers.

[45]See Youngs, *God's Messengers*, pp. 17–24.

[46]Quoted in Anderson, "Joseph Bellamy," p. 695.

[47]Hopkins, *Life of Edwards*, pp. 54–55; see also Ola Elizabeth Winslow, *Jonathan Edwards, 1703–1758* (New York, 1940), p. 130.

[48]Hopkins, *Life of Edwards*, p. 54. The theoretical justification of Edwards's interpretation of the role of the ministry may be found in "The True Excellency of the Gospel Ministry," *Works*, III, 591–592. See also Tracy, *Jonathan Edwards, Pastor*, esp. pp. 193–194.

[49]Quoted in Park, *Memoir*, pp. 57–58.

[50]Bellamy to Hopkins, Jan. 30, 1756, Gratz MSS., Historical Society of Pennsylvania, Philadelphia.

[51]See Hopkins to Bellamy, June 9, 1756, Feb. 24, 1758, Joseph Bellamy Papers, Hartford Seminary Foundation Library, Hartford, Connecticut, and Bellamy to Hopkins, Aug. 14, 1756, Gratz MSS., Historical Society of Pennsylvania. See also a list of theological questions copied by one of Jonathan Edwards, Jr.'s students, Maltby Geltson, "A Systematic Collection of Questions and Answers in Divinity," MSS., Yale University Library.

[52]Hopkins to Bellamy, July 7, 1766, in Park, *Memoir of Hopkins*, p. 59n.

[53]Quoted in Park, *Memoir of Emmons*, pp. 217–218. New Divinity preaching is discussed in detail in Chapter Eleven.

[54]Increase Tarbox, ed., *The Diary of Thomas Robbins, D.D., 1796–1854*, 2 vols. (Boston, 1886), I, 68. Robbins's *Diary* offers a first-hand account of student life in the schools of the prophets.

[55]Ibid.

[56]For a brief description of some of these in-law relationships see Wright, *The Beginnings of Unitarianism*, pp. 267–268.

CHAPTER THREE

[1]Ephraim Judson, David Perry, Jacob Catlin, Job Swift, and Seth Swift, for example, all held pastorates in Berkshire County.

[2]A county by county breakdown of Connecticut ministers in 1792 may be found in Stiles, *Literary Diary*, III, 463–468. See also Arthur Goodenough, *The Clergy of Litchfield County* (Litchfield, 1901).

[3]Dorothy Deming, "Settlement of Litchfield County, Connecticut," Tercentenary Commission of History, *Publications* (New Haven, 1933); Lois Kimball Mathews, *The Expansion of New England* (Boston, 1909), pp. 78–81;

Charles S. Grant, *Democracy in the Connecticut Frontier Town of Kent* (New York, 1961), pp. 1—11; Joseph E. A. Smith, ed., *History of Berkshire County, Massachusetts*, 2 vols., (New York, 1885), II, ch. 1; Richard D. Birdsall, *Berkshire County: A Cultural History* (New Haven, 1959), pp. 17—21.

[4]Charles Taylor, *History of Great Barrington* (Great Barrington, 1882), pp. 77—143; Howard J. Conn, *The First Congregational Church of Great Barrington, 1743—1943, A History* (Great Barrington, 1943), pp. 2—13; Birdsall, *Berkshire County*, p. 21.

[5]Quoted in Taylor, *History of Great Barrington*, p. 81.

[6]West, ed., *Sketches of the Life of Samuel Hopkins*, p. 47.

[7]Taylor, *History of Great Barrington*, p. 82.

[8]Hopkins, *Journal*, Aug. 1, Dec. 11, 1743, Williams MSS.

[9]Ibid., Sept. 30, Nov. 23, 1743; Taylor, *History of Great Barrington*, pp. 91—93; J. W. Turner, *The Centennial Anniversary of the Congregational Church, Great Barrington* (Pittsfield, 1844), pp. 101—102.

[10]Hopkins, *Journal*, Dec. 14, 1743, Williams MSS.

[11]Ibid., Dec. 14, 23, 1743.

[12]The "Church Covenant" and "Confession of Faith" with the names of the original church members are in the Congregational Historical Society Library in Boston.

[13]Quoted in Park, *Memoir of Samuel Hopkins*, pp. 41—42. On the impact of the "Indian problem" and the war on Hopkins's ministry and the area in general, see Hopkins, *Journal*, Nov. 22—23, 1745, Williams MSS.; Hopkins, *Journal* 1754—1756, *passim*, Samuel Hopkins Papers, Andover—Newton Theological School; Hopkins to Bellamy, Aug. 11, Dec. 28, 1756, and July 1, 1757, Bellamy Papers, Hartford Seminary Foundation; Taylor, *History of Great Barrington*, pp. 135—143; Birdsall, *Berkshire County*, pp. 18—19; and Grant, *Democracy in the Connecticut Frontier Town of Kent*, pp. 6—9.

[14]For nearly six weeks Housatonic was unsafe and Hopkins lived in Canaan. Cf. Hopkins, *Journal*, Sept. 12, Oct. 23, 1754, Hopkins Papers, Andover—Newton Theological School.

[15]Ibid., *passim*.

[16]Ibid.; See also Hopkins, *Journal*, Aug. 3, 4, 1745, Williams MSS.

[17]*Works*, III, 587; Heimert, *Religion and the American Mind*, pp. 162—163.

[18]Heimert, *Religion and the American Mind*, p. 312.

[19]"The True Excellency of the Gospel Ministry," *Works*, III, 590; see also Edwards, "Christ the Example of Ministers," *Works*, III, 593—603; and Levi Hart, *A Christian Minister Described* (New Haven, 1787), p. 28.

[20]*Works*, I, 661, 668; Heimert, *Religion and the American Mind*, pp. 312—314.

[21]West, ed., *Sketches of the Life of Samuel Hopkins*, p. 44. West incorrectly dates this diary entry August 7, 1743. It was probably written by Hopkins on August 7, 1742, but this portion of the original diary has been lost.

[22]Hopkins, *Journal*, Dec. 24, 1743, Williams MSS.

[23]"Petition to George III for a Royal Charter for Queen's College," in LeFavour, "The Proposed College in Hampshire County," p. 78.

[24]On the Stockbridge mission, in addition to Samuel Hopkins, *Historical*

Memoirs Relating to the Housatonic Indians (Boston, 1755), see Electra F. Jones, *Stockbridge, Past and Present* (Springfield, 1854), pp. 41–167; and Sarah Cabot Sedgwick and Christina Sedgwick Marquand, *Stockbridge, 1739–1939, A Chronicle* (Springfield, 1939), pp. 1–125.

25West, ed., *Sketches of the Life of Samuel Hopkins*, p. 54.

26Edwards to Provincial Secretary Willard, May, 1754, quoted in Joseph E.A. Smith, *History of Pittsfield*, 2 vols. (Boston, 1869–76), I, 100.

27Quoted in ibid., I, 99n.

28Quoted in Perry Miller, *Jonathan Edwards* (New York, 1949), p. 265; see also Sedgwick and Marquand, *Stockbridge*, pp. 61–68.

29Smith, *History of Pittsfield*, I, 100–104.

30Hopkins to Andrew Eliot, March 30, 1767, misc. bound MSS., Massachusetts Historical Society, Boston.

31Hopkins to Andrew Eliot, Jan. 30, March 30, Aug. 25, Oct. 28, 1767, ibid.

32Hopkins to Andrew Eliot, Jan. 30, 1767, ibid.

33Hopkins to Andrew Eliot, March 30, 1767, ibid.

34Birdsall, *Berkshire County*, p. 40; Sedgwick and Marquand, *Stockbridge*, p. 91.

35Park, *Memoir of Hopkins*, p. 45. On Wheelock see James D. McCallum, *Eleazar Wheelock, Founder of Dartmouth College* (Hanover, N.H., 1939).

36See Hopkins to William Hyslop, July 17, 1761, Washburn Papers, Massachusetts Historical Society; Park, *Memoir of Samuel Hopkins*, pp. 44–45; Anderson, "Joseph Bellamy," pp. 641–643.

37Hawley's activities and contacts with Edwards, Hopkins, and Bellamy are detailed in the "Journal and Letters of Gideon Hawley," 4 vols., Congregational Library MSS. See also the sketch of the missionary in Sprague, *Annals of the American Pulpit*, I, 497–500.

38"Extracts of Letters from Samuel Hopkins relating to the Indians in the country of the Six Nations," in Gideon Hawley to Andrew Oliver, May 20, 1761, Hawley Papers, Massachusetts Historical Society; Hopkins to William Hyslop, July 17, 1761, Washburn Papers, Massachusetts Historical Society.

39Hopkins to Gideon Hawley, June 7, 1762, Thompson MSS., Hartford Seminary Foundation Library.

40David Swift, "Samuel Hopkins: Calvinist Social Concern in Eighteenth-Century New England," *Journal of Presbyterian History*, 47 (1969), 35–36.

41West, ed., *Sketches of the Life of Samuel Hopkins*, p. 53.

42Hopkins, *Journal*, Feb. 12, 1756, Hopkins Papers, Andover-Newton Theological School; Bellamy to Hopkins, Dec. 22, 1755, and Jan. 30, 1756, Gratz MSS., Historical Society of Pennsylvania.

43Hopkins to Bellamy, Jan. 19, 1758, Bellamy Papers, Hartford Seminary Foundation.

44Hopkins, *Life of Edwards*, p. 70.

45On Perry, Judson, and another New Divinity man, John Bacon, see Birdsall, *Berkshire County*, pp. 41–42.

[46]Robert Ferm, *Jonathan Edwards the Younger, 1745–1801* (Grand Rapids, 1976), pp. 148–150.

[47]Birdsall, *Berkshire County*, p. 21; Rising Lake Morrow, "Connecticut Influences in Western Massachusetts and Vermont," Connecticut Tercentenary Commission of History, *Publications* (New Haven, 1936), pp. 1–8. Both the clergy and laity in Connecticut tended to view their churches as being more orthodox than the Massachusetts establishment. This interpretation was reinforced by the establishment of the ecclesiastically liberal Brattle Street Church in Boston in 1699. Indeed, the founding of Yale College in 1701 was in part a response to what the Connecticut clergy saw as a movement toward liberalism on the part of Harvard and the Massachusetts establishment. See Warch, *School of the Prophets*, pp. 16–19.

[48]Albert Hopkins, "Historical Discourse," *Proceedings at the Centennial Commemoration of the Organization of the Berkshire Association of Ministers* (Boston, 1864), pp. 5–6; Birdsall, *Berkshire County*, pp. 53–54.

[49]Hopkins to Bellamy, March 18, 1766, Hopkins Papers, Andover-Newton Theological School. On the ecclesiastical history of the Connecticut River Valley, see Lucas, *Valley of Discord*.

CHAPTER FOUR

[1]Jedidiah Mills, *An Inquiry concerning the State of the Unregenerate under the Gospel* (New Haven, 1767), p. 121.

[2]Quoted in Morgan, *The Gentle Puritan*, p. 215.

[3]The works of Perry Miller, particularly *The New England Mind: The Seventeenth Century* (New York, 1939), and "The Marrow of Puritan Divinity," in *Errand into the Wilderness* (Cambridge, 1956), pp. 48–98, remain the starting point for an understanding of the covenant in New England Calvinist thought. However, Miller's work has been extensively criticized and modified. See Michael McGiffert, "American Puritan Studies in the 1960's," *William and Mary Quarterly*, 26 (1969), 36–67. My analysis of the covenant theology, and of New England Puritanism in general, has been influenced by post-Miller scholarship such as Norman Pettit, *The Heart Prepared: Grace and Conversion in Puritan Spiritual Life* (New Haven, 1966); Robert Middlekauff, *The Mathers: Three Generations of Puritan Intellectuals 1596–1728* (New York, 1971); James Jones, *The Shattered Synthesis: New England Theology before the Great Awakening* (New Haven, 1973); Ernest B. Lowrie, *The Shape of the Puritan Mind: The Thought of Samuel Willard* (New Haven, 1974); E. Brooks Holifield, *The Covenant Sealed: The Development of Puritan Sacramental Theology in Old and New England, 1570–1720* (New Haven, 1974); and Emory Elliott, *Power and the Pulpit in Puritan New England* (Princeton, 1975).

[4]These two covenant traditions are described in McGiffert, "Puritan Studies in the 1960's," pp. 49–50; see also Middlekauff, *The Mathers*, pp. 60–61; and Hall, *The Faithful Shepherd*, ch. 11.

[5]McGiffert, "Puritan Studies in the 1960's," p. 49. While not dealing with the two covenant traditions, James Jones suggests a similar interpretation of Puritan theology when he describes it as a synthesis of piety and moralism; see *The Shattered Synthesis*. He argues, however, that this synthesis began to

break down in the late seventeenth century and New England Calvinism became moralistic. Such an analysis is open to serious question.

⁶Quoted in Charles Akers, *Called unto Liberty: A Life of Jonathan Mayhew, 1720–1766* (Cambridge, Mass., 1964), p. 117.

⁷Ibid., pp. 119–120.

⁸Quoted in ibid., p. 121.

⁹See above, pp. 32–33.

¹⁰Stiles, *A Discourse on the Christian Union* (Boston, 1761), p. 53; Birdsall, "Ezra Stiles versus the New Divinity Men," pp. 249–250.

¹¹*A Discourse on the Christian Union*, pp. 51–52.

¹²Samuel Hopkins, *The True State and Character of the Unregenerate* . . . (New Haven, 1769), p. 173.

¹³Tucker, *Puritan Protagonist*, pp. 165–166. One such individual suspected of being an Arminian was James Noyes, pastor of New Haven's First Church where the Yale community worshipped. To remove the students and faculty from Noyes's influence, Clap separated from First Church in 1757 and organized a college church. See Tucker, *Puritan Protagonist*, ch. 8, and Ralph Gabriel, *Religion and Learning at Yale, the Church of Christ in the College and University, 1757–1957* (New Haven, 1958), chs. 1, 2.

¹⁴On the Wallingford controversy see Charles Davis, *History of Wallingford, Connecticut, from 1670 to the present time* (Meriden, Conn., 1870), ch. 9, and Benjamin Trumbull, *A Complete History of Connecticut, Civil and Ecclesiastical* . . . , 2 vols. (New London, 1898), II, 408–449.

¹⁵Bellamy to Thomas Foxcroft, Oct. 25, 1758, Houghton Library, Harvard University.

¹⁶*A Letter to a friend, occasioned by the unhappy controversy at Wallingford* (New Haven, 1760), p. 7.

¹⁷See, for example, Edward Eells, *Some Serious Remarks . . . relative to Mr. James Dana's call and settlement in Wallingford* . . . (New Haven, 1759).

¹⁸Bellamy, *A Letter to Scripturista* . . . (New Haven, 1760), pp. 15–20.

¹⁹*A Winter-Evening's Conversation* . . . (Boston, 1757), pp. 5–8, 24.

²⁰See Wright, *The Beginnings of Unitarianism*, pp. 83–90; and Haroutunian, *Piety versus Moralism*, ch. 2.

²¹For a precise statement of the implications of these problems for New Light millennialism at mid-century, see Nathan O. Hatch, "The Origins of Civil Millennialism in America: New England Clergymen, War with France, and the Revolution," *William and Mary Quarterly*, 32 (1975), 411–417.

²²*Sin, thro' Divine Interposition an advantage to the Universe* . . . (Boston, 1759), p. 22

²³Bellamy, *Four Sermons on the Wisdom of God in the Permission of Sin* (Boston, 1758), p. 28.

²⁴*Sin . . . an advantage to the Universe*, pp. 21, 48.

²⁵Ibid., p. 19.

²⁶Ibid., pp. 8, 14, 15.

²⁷Ibid., p. 30.

²⁸Ibid., p. 22.

²⁹Hopkins, *The True State and Character of the Unregenerate*, p. 1; see

also Hopkins, *An Inquiry concerning the promises of the Gospel* . . . (Boston, 1765), pp. ii–iii.

[30]Pettit, *The Heart Prepared*, esp. pp. 18–19, 120–121.

[31]Ibid., p. 19.

[32]*Striving to enter in at the strait gate* . . . , *And the Connexion of Salvation therewith Proved from the Holy Scriptures* (Boston, 1761), p. 21.

[33]Ibid., p. 6; Wright, *The Beginnings of Unitarianism*, pp. 118–126.

[34]*An Inquiry concerning the Promises of the Gospel*, p. 1.

[35]Ibid., p. 54.

[36]Ibid., p. 94.

[37]Williston Walker, *The Creeds and Platforms of Congregationalism* (New York, 1893), p. 384. On Mather's strict predestinarian views see Middle-kauff, *The Mathers*, pp. 234–237.

[38]*An Inquiry concerning the Promises of the Gospel*, pp. 124–125.

[39]Ibid., p. 127.

[40]*An Inquiry concerning the State of the Unregenerate*, pp. vi, 5.

[41]See *The True State and Character of the Unregenerate*, p. 6; and *Two Discourses* . . . (Boston, 1768), pp. 54–55.

[42]*Brief Remarks on a Number of False Propositions and Dangerous errors which are spreading in the Country* . . . (New London, 1769), p. iv.

[43](New Haven, 1769). In the 1770's Moses Hemmenway succeeded Hart in leading the Old Light critique of Hopkins's interpretation of the state of the unregenerate. See *A Vindication of the Power, Obligation and Encouragement of the Unregenerate to attend to the means of Grace* (Boston, 1772), and *Remarks on the Reverend Mr. Hopkins's Answer* . . . (Boston, 1774).

[44]This is not to say that Hopkinsianism and the New Divinity were theologically synonymous. The Edwardsian wing of the movement continued to follow more closely the thought of Bellamy. Nevertheless, by the late eighteenth century the Hopkinsians achieved clear dominance over the movement. For an interesting analysis of the two branches of the movement, which highly exaggerates the differences between them, see Berk, *Calvinism versus Democracy*, ch. 4.

[45]Hopkins to Bellamy, Jan. 19, 1758, Bellamy Papers, Hartford Seminary Foundation.

[46]West, ed., *Sketches of the Life of Samuel Hopkins*, p. 57; Hopkins to Gideon Hawley, Sept. 19, 1758, Thompson MSS., Hartford Seminary Foundation; Hopkins, *Life of Edwards*, pp. 87–89; Park, *Memoir of Hopkins*, p. 217.

[47]Hopkins to Bellamy, Jan. 4, 1764, Bellamy Papers, Hartford Seminary Foundation; West, ed., *Sketches of the Life of Samuel Hopkins*, pp. 57–58; Hopkins, *Life of Edwards*, pp. 87–89; Park, *Memoir of Hopkins*, p. 217.

[48]Cf. Leonard J. Trinterud, "The New England Contribution to Colonial American Presbyterianism," *Church History*, 18 (1948), 32–43; and his *The Forming of an American Tradition* (Philadelphia, 1949), pp. 212–213.

[49]Hopkins to Bellamy, March 16, 1767, in Park, *Memoir of Hopkins*, pp. 66–67; Trinterud, *The Forming of an American Tradition*, p. 213.

[50]See the Appendix: "The New Divinity Men."

[51]Hart, *Brief Remarks*, pp. iii–iv.

[52]James Caldwell to Joseph Bellamy, March 16, 1767, Bellamy Papers, Hartford Seminary Foundation.

[53]E. Bradford to Joseph Bellamy, April 18, 1772, ibid.

[54]James Caldwell to Joseph Bellamy, Dec. 29 , 1773, ibid.; Trinterud, *The Forming of an American Tradition*, pp. 223–225.

[55]Dexter, ed., *Extracts from the Itineraries and Other Miscellanies of Ezra Stiles*, p. 51.

[56]Edmund S. Morgan, "The American Revolution Considered as an Intellectual Movement," in Arthur M. Schlesinger, Jr., and Morton White, eds., *Paths of American Thought* (Boston, 1963), p. 19.

[57]*The True State and Character of the Unregenerate*, pp. 179–180.

[58]See chapters 7, 8, below.

CHAPTER FIVE

[1]Chauncy to Stiles, Nov. 14, 1769, in Dexter, ed., *Itineraries and Miscellanies of Ezra Stiles*, pp. 449–450; Birdsall, "Ezra Stiles versus the New Divinity Men," p. 249.

[2]Taylor, *History of Great Barrington*, ch. 2.

[3]Records, First Congregational Church of Great Barrington, Typescript, Cooke Collection, Berkshire Athenaeum, Pittsfield, Mass., pp. 190–200; Hopkins, *Journal*, March 28, 1756, Hopkins Papers, Andover-Newton Theological School; Howard J. Conn, *The First Congregational Church of Great Barrington, 1743–1943, A History* (Great Barrington, 1943), pp. 1–13.

[4]*Letters to the Reverend Samuel Hopkins . . .* (Sheffield, 1759), pp. 11, 15. Dewey published his letters in a fit of pique because in an anonymous pamphlet dealing with the controversy over original sin, *A Bold Push in a Letter to the Author of a Late Pamphlet, entitled FAIR PLAY, etc.* (Boston, 1758), Hopkins had published one of his own letters to his parishioner on sin.

[5]See, for example, Stiles, *Literary Diary*, I, 279–281.

[6]Church Records, Cooke Collection, Berkshire Athenaeum, p. 225.

[7]Quoted in Taylor, *History of Great Barrington*, p. 195; see also Church Records, Cooke Collection, Berkshire Anthenaeum, p. 226.

[8]Holifield, *The Covenant Sealed*, esp. ch. 7; Robert G. Pope, *The Halfway Covenant: Church Membership in Puritan New England* (Princeton, 1969).

[9]Edwards, "Inquiry Concerning Qualifications for Communion," and "Reply to the Rev. Solomon Williams," *Works*, I, 85–194 and 195–294, respectively. See also Tracy, *Jonathan Edwards, Pastor*, ch. 8.

[10]"Inquiry Concerning Qualifications for Communion," p. 191.

[11]Ibid., p. 169; see also Clarence C. Goen, *Revivalism and Separatism in New England, 1740–1800* (New Haven, 1962), pp. 160–164.

[12]Bellamy, "Dialogue on the Half-way Covenant," *Works*, 3 vols. (New York, 1812), I, 438–439.

[13]Ibid., p. 418.

[14]Ibid., pp. 394, 422, 424.

[15]Hopkins to Bellamy, May 9, 1769, Bellamy Papers, Hartford Seminary Foundation.

[16]Judson to Bellamy, July 21, 1769, ibid.

[17]Hopkins to Rev. [Samuel] Newell, Feb. 29, 1752, Hopkins Papers, Andover-Newton Theological School.

[18]Ibid.

[19]Taylor, *History of Great Barrington*, pp. 185–186.

[20]Ibid., p. 187.

[21]Records of the Town of Sheffield, Vol. I, March 11, 1760, Town Hall, Sheffield, Mass. On the development of parishes in the late seventeenth and early eighteenth centuries, see Bushman, *Puritan to Yankee*, pp. 62–71, and Cook, *The Fathers of the Towns*, pp. 131–135.

[22]Church Records, Cooke Collection, Berkshire Athenaeum; Taylor, *History of Great Barrington*, p. 163; Park, *Memoir of Hopkins*, p. 67.

[23]Quoted in Taylor, *History of Great Barrington*, p. 188.

[24]Ibid., p. 189.

[25]Great Barrington Town Records, 1762–1793, Town Hall, Great Barrington, Mass., pp. 12–13.

[26]Joseph Hooper, "The Protestant Episcopal Church in Berkshire," *Berkshire Historical and Scientific Society Collections*, No. 3 (Pittsfield, 1890), pp. 187–212; Taylor, *History of Great Barrington*, pp. 196–200; Park, *Memoir of Hopkins*, p. 68. Patten in *Reminiscences of Hopkins* (pp. 55–59) estimates that the number of unbaptized children in the town had grown to between 60 and 80, creating support for the calling of an Anglican clergyman.

[27]West. ed., *Sketches of the Life of Samuel Hopkins*, p. 49.

[28]Quoted in Taylor, *History of Great Barrington*, p. 189.

[29]Town Records, p. 32.

[30]Ibid., pp. 61, 67; Hopkins to Bellamy, May 4, 1768, Bellamy Papers, Hartford Seminary Foundation; Hopkins to Ebenezer Little, July 18, 1766, and Jan. 9, 1767, Congregational Historical Society MSS., Boston.

[31]See above, pp. 11–12.

[32]On these developments see Ola Elizabeth Winslow, *Meeting-House Hill* (New York, 1952), pp. 211–212; Shipton, "The New England Clergy," pp. 49–50; Bumsted, "The Pilgrim's Progress," pp. 63–70; Youngs, *God's Messengers*, pp. 102–108, and Schmotter, "Ministerial Careers in Eighteenth-Century New England," pp. 257–263.

[33]Quoted in Youngs, *God's Messengers*, p. 107.

[34]Hopkins to Bellamy, April 4, 1768, Webster MSS., Presbyterian Historical Society, Philadelphia.

[35]"The True Excellency of the Gospel Ministry," p. 452.

[36]Ibid., pp. 453–454; see also Edwards, "Christ the Example of Ministers," p. 469.

[37]Hopkins to Bellamy, March 16, 1766, Hopkins Papers, Andover-Newton Theological School.

[38]Hopkins to Bellamy, July 26, 1766, Yale MSS.

[39]Town Records, p. 67; Hopkins to Bellamy, May 4, 1768, Bellamy Papers, Hartford Seminary Foundation.

[40]Stiles, *Literary Diary*, I, 50n.; Park, *Memoir of Hopkins*, p. 70.

[41][An account of the Ecclesiastical Council at Great Barrington which dismissed Samuel Hopkins from the First Congregational Church], First Congregational Church, Newport, R.I., Papers, Newport Historical Society.

Another copy of this manuscript, in the handwriting of Joseph Bellamy, the scribe of the council, is in the Bellamy Papers at the Hartford Seminary Foundation.

[42]Ibid.

[43]See above, p. 48.

[44]Great Barrington Town Records, p. 107.

[45]Samuel Peters, *General History of Connecticut* (1781; rpt. Boston, 1877), pp. 254–256. Ingersoll was one of the leading politicians and opponents of Hopkins in the town.

[46]*Reminiscences of Samuel Hopkins*, pp. 44–45.

[47]West, ed., *Sketches of the Life of Hopkins*, pp. 49–50.

[48]Hamilton A. Hill, *History of the Old South Church Boston, 1669–1884*, 2 vols. (Cambridge, Mass., 1890), II, 158–159; Stiles, *Literary Diary*, I, 87.

[49]Quoted in Hill, *History of the Old South Church*, II, 168n.

[50]Quoted in ibid., pp. 160–161.

[51]Quoted in ibid., p. 165.

[52]*Plymouth Church Records*, 2 vols. (New York, 1920), I, 321–322.

[53]Chandler Robbins, *A Reply to Some Essays Lately Published by John Cotton, Esq.* . . . (Boston, 1773), p. 40; John Cotton, *The General Practices of the Churches of New England, Relating to Baptism, Vindicated* . . . (Boston, 1772), and *The General Practice* . . . *Further Vindicated* (Boston, 1773); *Plymouth Church Records*, I, 334–345; Robbins to Bellamy, January 28, 1771, Webster MSS., Presbyterian Historical Society.

[54]*Plymouth Church Records*, I, 339.

[55]Stiles, *Literary Diary*, III, 338; Mortimer Blake, *A Centurial History of the Mendon Association of Congregational Ministers* (Boston, 1853), p. 108.

[56]Dexter, *Yale Biographies*, III, 306–307; David Avery, *A Narrative of the Rise and Progress of the Difficulties which have issued in a Separation between the Minister and People of Bennington* (Bennington, 1783).

[57]Samuel Hopkins Emery, *The Ministry of Taunton with Incidental Notices of Other Professions*, 2 vols. (Boston, 1853), I, 116; Samuel Hopkins to Levi Hart, May 25, 1792, Gratz MSS., Historical Society of Pennsylvania. Two of Judson's sermons are reprinted in *The Ministry of Taunton* (pp. 46–113) and they bear a clear New Divinity stamp. See especially "A Sermon preached at the Ordination of the Rev. Jonathan Strong . . ., January 28, 1789," pp. 54–55.

[58]See *The History of Middlesex County, Massachusetts, with Biographical Sketches of Many of its Pioneers and Prominent Men*, compiled under the supervision of D. Hamilton Hand, 4 vols. (Philadelphia, 1890), III, 498.

[59]Schmotter, "Ministerial Careers in Eighteenth-Century New England," pp. 256–257, 266n., and "The Irony of Clerical Professionalism," p. 159; Scott, *From Office to Profession*, pp. 3–4; and Calhoun, *Professional Lives*, pp. 94–107.

[60]Stiles to William Williams, Aug. 15, 1793, *Literary Diary*, III, 505–506n.; ibid., 247; Birdsall, "Ezra Stiles versus the New Divinity Men," p. 249n.

[61]Two of these offers (those from Halifax, Nova Scotia, and Topsham, Maine) were from small, isolated churches, like those in western New England,

which welcomed the New Divinity. A third offer was from a small urban church in Newport. The largest and most prestigious church interested in Hopkins's services was in Salem. This prospect, however, was the least promising. See Hopkins's reservations about the Salem church in his letter to Bellamy, July 7, 1767, in Park, *Memoir of Hopkins*, p. 70n.

CHAPTER SIX

[1]West, ed., *Sketches of the Life of Samuel Hopkins*, p. 61.

[2]Ibid.; Hill, *History of the Old South Church*, II, 92, 98 – 99.

[3]Hopkins to Bellamy, May 9, 1769, Bellamy Papers, Hartford Seminary Foundation; West, ed., *Sketches of the Life of Samuel Hopkins*, pp. 61 – 62.

[4]West, ed., *Sketches of the Life of Samuel Hopkins*, p. 62.

[5]Ibid.

[6]Ibid., p. 63.

[7]Ibid.

[8]Carl Bridenbaugh, *Cities in Revolt* (New York, 1955), p. 136; Morgan, *The Gentle Puritan*, p. 192.

[9]Bruce M. Bigelow, "The Commerce of Rhode Island with the West Indies before the Revolution" (Ph.D. diss., Brown University, 1930); Bridenbaugh, *Cities in Revolt*, pp. 46 – 47, 74, 270. Recent studies of New England commerce in the eighteenth century demonstrate that the merchants of the region, including those of Newport, were not involved in an extensive triangular trade and that slave trading was only a relatively minor part of their commercial activities. See Gilman M. Ostrander, "The Making of the Triangular Trade Myth," *William and Mary Quarterly*, 30 (1973), 635 – 644, and Virginia Bever Platt, " 'And Don't Forget the Guinea Voyage': The Slave Trade of Aaron Lopez of Newport," ibid., 32 (1975), 601 – 618.

[10]Bridenbaugh, *Cities in Revolt*, pp. 166, 227, 368.

[11]Cf. Gladys Bolhouse, "Old Churches of Newport" (typescript, n.d., Redwood Library, Newport, R.I.).

[12]Patten, *Reminiscences of Samuel Hopkins*, pp. 91 – 98; Park, *Memoir of Hopkins*, p. 85; R. W. Wallace, *Sermons on Congregationalism in Newport* (Newport, 1895), pp. 33 – 34; Charles E. Hammett, Jr., "A Sketch of the History of the Congregational Churches of Newport, R.I., Compiled from the Records and Other Sources" (typescript, 1891, Newport Historical Society), p. 125.

[13]First Congregational Church, Newport, R.I., Records, Aug. 10, 1768 – Aug. 12, 1770, Newport Historical Society.

[14]First Congregational Church Records, 1743 – 1831, Newport Historical Society.

[15]*Literary Diary*, I, 20 – 21. For the terms of Hopkins's settlement see the First Congregational Church Records, Aug. 25, 1769.

[16]West, ed., *Sketches of the Life of Samuel Hopkins*, pp. 69 – 70; First Congregational Church Records, Feb. 26, 1770.

[17]Dexter, ed., *Itineraries and Miscellanies of Ezra Stiles*, p. 592.

[18]Ibid., pp. 445 – 450.

[19]*A Sermon of a New Kind*, pp. iii–iv.

[20]Whittelsey to Stiles, Feb. 26, 1770, in Isabel M. Calder, ed., *Letters and Papers of Ezra Stiles, President of Yale College, 1778–95, Presented to Yale University Library by Mrs. Edward S. Harkness* (New Haven, 1933), p. 25.

[21]*A Sermon of a New Kind*, p. 18.

[22]Gratz MSS., Historical Society of Pennsylvania. Much of the correspondence between Hopkins and Miss Anthony is at the Historical Society of Pennsylvania, and other letters to her and Sarah Osborn, the other leader of the society, are in the Samuel Hopkins Papers at the Andover-Newton Theological School. Cf. also Samuel Hopkins, *The Life and Character of Miss Susanna Anthony* (Worcester, 1796), and his *Memoirs of the Life of Mrs. Sarah Osborn* (Worcester, 1799).

[23]Letter of Nov. 28, 1769, Gratz MSS.

[24]*Literary Diary*, I, 44.

[25]Levi Hart to Joseph Bellamy, March 12, 1770, quoting Hopkins's letter, Bellamy Papers. See also Hopkins to Stephen West, Jan. 12, 1770, Hopkins Papers, Andover-Newton Theological School.

[26]Calder, ed., *Letters and Papers of Ezra Stiles*, p. 25; Morgan, *The Gentle Puritan*, pp. 172–175.

[27]*Literary Diary*, I, 37–38.

[28]Church Records, Feb. 26, March 12, 1770; West, ed., *Sketches of the Life of Samuel Hopkins*, pp. 70–71; Stiles, *Literary Diary*, I, 41–42.

[29]First Congregational Church, Marriages, Baptisms and Miscellaneous [Records], 1747–1826, March 18, 1770 (p. 99), Newport Historical Society.

[30]Quoted in Patten, *Reminiscences of Samuel Hopkins*, pp. 60–61.

[31]Journal entry, March 21, 1770, in West ed., *Sketches of the Life of Samuel Hopkins*, p. 72.

[32]Ibid., p. 71.

[33]First Congregational Church Committee Book, March 19, 1770, Newport Historical Society; West, ed., *Sketches of the Life of Hopkins*, p. 74; Hammett, "History of the Congregational Churches in Newport," p. 154. Hopkins's answer to the final call is in First Congregational Church Marriages, Baptisms, and Miscellaneous [Records], p. 100.

[34]*Literary Diary*, I, 43.

[35]Thompson MSS., Hartford Seminary Foundation.

[36]Hart to Joseph Bellamy, March 12, 1770, Bellamy Papers, ibid.

[37]*Animadversions on Mr. Hart's Late Dialogue; in a Letter to a Friend* (New London, 1770), pp. 9, 28.

[38]First Congregational Church Marriages, Baptisms, and Miscellaneous [Records], Aug. 3, 1770, Newport Historical Society; West, ed., *Sketches of the Life of Samuel Hopkins*, pp. 75–76; Hammett, "History of the Congregational Churches of Newport," p. 142. See also Samuel Hopkins, *Rare Observations or Some Remarks on Several Points Rarely Considered* (Providence, 1770), which provided a formal statement of his ecclesiastical views for his parishioners.

[39]Hammett, "History of the Congregational Churches in Newport," p. 151.

[40]Quoted in Park, *Memoir of Hopkins*, p. 85. Financial difficulties fol-

lowed Hopkins to Newport, however, and qualified his pre-Revolutionary success in the ministry. Salary arrears began to mount in 1774 because of a slump in the seaport's economy which resulted from the colonial response to British policies. By early 1776, Hopkins was owed well over £100 in back salary. See First Congregational Church Committee Book, Nov. 5, 1774, and Records, Oct. 30, 1775 and Feb. 6, 1776.

[41]William Hart, A Letter to the Reverend Samuel Hopkins . . . (New London, 1770), p. 11.

CHAPTER SEVEN

[1]Conrad Wright has labeled their synthesis of natural and revealed religion "supernatural rationalism." See The Beginnings of Unitarianism in America, p. 135. Also see Henry May, The Enlightenment in America (New York, 1976), esp. pp. 12, 57.

[2]Remarks on President Edwards's Dissertation concerning the Nature of True Virtue . . . (New Haven, 1771), pp. 9, 21, 41, 45–46.

[3]True Virtue, Works, II, 262. The concept of Being in general may be traced back to Edwards's early theological efforts. See, for example, his essay "Of Being," in Harvey Townsend, ed. The Philosophy of Jonathan Edwards from his Private Notebooks (Eugene, Ore., 1955), pp. 1–20. The best interpretation of the concept is in Douglas Elwood, The Philosophical Theology of Jonathan Edwards (New York, 1960), esp. pp. 22–23.

[4]True Virtue, Works, II, 261–266.

[5]Ibid., p. 261. Roland A. Delattre, Beauty and Sensibility in the Thought of Jonathan Edwards (New Haven, 1968), offers an excellent analysis of the role of aesthetics in Edwards's theology. See also Clyde A. Holbrook, The Ethics of Jonathan Edwards; Aesthetics and Morality (Ann Arbor, 1973), esp. pp. 104–105.

[6]True Virtue, Works, II, 262.

[7]See above, pp. 47–48.

[8]Works, I, 16.

[9]Religious Affections, Works, III, 108, 171.

[10]Alan Heimert in Religion and the American Mind exaggerates the role of evangelical activism in Edwards's theology and in the process creates an overdrawn portrait of the social and political implications of Edwards's thought. As Delattre notes, Heimert's chapter on "The Beauty and Good Tendency of Union" shows an understanding of the place of aesthetics in Edwards's theology, "but he overstates his case for the location of that divine beauty in human community" (Beauty and Sensibility, pp. 10–11).

[11]Edwards's dissertation was in part intended to refute Hutcheson's An Inquiry into the Original of Our Ideas of Beauty and Virtue (London, 1725). In his reply Edwards incorporated aspects of Hutcheson's ethical theory. See A. Oliver Aldridge, "Edwards and Hutcheson," The Harvard Theological Review, 44 (1951), 35–58; Clarence H. Faust and Thomas H. Johnson, Jonathan Edwards: Representative Selections (1935; rpt. New York, 1962), pp. lxxxv–xciii; and Conrad Cherry, The Theology of Jonathan Edwards: A Reappraisal (Garden City, N.Y., 1966), pp. 185–191.

[12]Conrad Wright, *The Beginnings of Unitarianism in America* (Boston, 1955), ch. 6. On the "common-sense" philosophy see Gladys Bryson, *Man and Society: The Scottish Inquiry of the Eighteenth Century* (Princeton, 1945), pp. 1–28; Douglas Sloan, *The Scottish Enlightenment and the American College Ideal* (New York, 1971), esp. chs. 3, 4; May, *The Enlightenment in America*, pp. 341–358; and Sydney Ahlstrom, "The Scottish Philosophy and American Theology," *Church History*, 24 (1955), 257–272.

[13]*A Vindication of the Power, Obligation and Encouragement of the Unregenerate to attend the means of Grace against the Exceptions of the Rev. Samuel Hopkins* . . . (Boston, 1772), p. 63.

[14]On these eighteenth-century self-love theorists see Jacob Viner, *The Role of Providence in the Social Order* (Philadelphia, 1972), pp. 62–85; also see Wright, *The Beginnings of Unitarianism in America*, pp. 142–145.

[15]*True Virtue*, *Works*, II, 283, 299.

[16]Ibid., p. 299.

[17]Ibid.

[18]Ibid.

[19]Ibid.

[20]Ibid., p. 297.

[21]Ibid., p. 273.

[22]Ibid.

[23]Bushman, *Puritan to Yankee*, pp. 278–279. On clerical and lay use of the concept of self-love in economic and social theory at mid-century, see J. E. Crowley, *This Sheba, Self: The Conceptualization of Economic Life in Eighteenth-Century America* (Baltimore, 1974), pp. 72–73; also see J.G.A. Pocock, "Virtue and Commerce in the Eighteenth Century," *The Journal of Interdisciplinary History*, 3 (1972), 119–134, and Henry W. Sams, "Self-Love and the Doctrine of Work," *Journal of the History of Ideas*, 4 (1943), 320–332.

[24]Haroutunian, *Piety versus Moralism*, esp. pp. 83–84.

[25]*An Inquiry into the Nature of True Holiness* . . . (Newport, 1773), p. 16. Hopkins's phrase "including ourselves" was not an acceptance of self-love. According to him, a man should have a "regard" to himself only as part of Being in general, "so that all his own particular interest is subordinate to that of the whole" (*True Holiness*, p. 24).

[26]*True Virtue*, *Works*, II, 268–270. Also see Edwards's *Dissertation concerning the End for which God created the World*, *Works*, II, 191–257.

[27]*True Holiness*, p. 53. At times Edwards moved closer to Hopkins's position. See, for example, "Miscellany 3" in Townsend, ed., *The Philosophy of Jonathan Edwards*, p. 193.

[28]*True Holiness*, p. 45.

[29]Mayhew, *Two Sermons on the Nature, Extent and Perfection of Divine Goodness* (Boston, 1763), p. 77. See also Charles Chauncy, *The Benevolence of the Deity* . . . (Boston, 1784), and Wright, *The Beginnings of Unitarianism in America*, ch. 7.

[30]*Sin . . . an advantage to the Universe*, pp. 45, 52.

[31]Where Hopkins liberalized Calvinism he drew heavily on the work of Joseph Bellamy who in the 1750's and 1760's developed an interpretation of the benevolence of Deity and a liberal approach to the atonement. For a fuller

discussion of the theologically liberal side of the New Divinity — including Bellamy's contributions to the movement and Hopkins's views on the atonement — see Chapter Ten, below.

[32]*True Holiness*, p. 23.

[33]Ibid., p. 29.

[34]The *Dialogue* was printed in West, ed., *Sketches of the Life of Hopkins*. The quotation is found on p. 150.

[35]*Charity and Its Fruits* (New York, 1851), p. 229.

[36]Townsend, ed., *The Philosophy of Jonathan Edwards*, p. 204; also see Holbrook, *The Ethics of Jonathan Edwards*, esp. pp. 56 – 63, for an excellent discussion of the place of self-love in Edwards's ethical theory. For the seventeenth-century background of Edwards's position on the willingness to be damned, see Jones, *The Shattered Synthesis*, pp. 36 – 37.

[37]*Charity and Its Fruits*, p. 236.

[38]*True Holiness*, p. 70.

[39]On this and several other suggestive implications of Hopkins's interpretation of disinterested benevolence, see Oliver Wendell Elsbree, "Samuel Hopkins and His Doctrine of Disinterested Benevolence," *New England Quarterly*, 8 (1935), 534 – 550.

[40]Heimert detects such a trend towards activism in the thought of Edwards's followers: "Within Calvinist doctrine itself the 1750's witnessed something of a redefinition of Christian virtue making 'zeal' a more distinguishing affection than love. The changing emphasis reflected the shift in focus from the heart to the will implicit in the *Religious Affections*" (*Religion and the American Mind*, p. 311). Such a shift occurred somewhat later than Heimert believes, largely, as I have tried to show, as a result of Hopkinsianism.

[41]*True Holiness*, p. 41.

[42]See Crowley, *This Sheba, Self*, pp. 96 – 97, and Edward M. Cook, Jr., "Social Behavior and Changing Values in Dedham," *William and Mary Quarterly*, 28 (1970), 546 – 580.

[43]Kenneth A. Lockridge, "Social Change and the Meaning of the American Revolution," *Journal of Social History*, 6 (1973), 423 – 424; also see Greene, "Search for Identity," pp. 191 – 205, and Michael Zuckerman, *Peaceable Kingdoms: New England Towns in the Eighteenth Century* (New York, 1970). On the traditional New England social values see Stephen Foster, *Their Solitary Way: The Puritan Social Ethic in the First Century of Settlement in New England* (New Haven, 1971).

[44]Bushman, *Puritan to Yankee*, p. 272.

[45]On the use of the concept of self-love by both Old Lights and New Lights see, for example, Samuel Cooper, *A Sermon Preached in Boston, New England, before the Society for Encouraging Industry and Employing the Poor* (Boston, 1753), pp. 2 – 3, and Thomas Clap, *An Essay on the Nature and Foundation of Moral Virtue and Obligation . . .* (New Haven, 1765), pp. 13 – 17.

[46]*True Holiness*, p. 78. For an interesting debate over the concept of self-love between Hopkins and a prominent secular leader, see the correspondence in Andrew P. Peabody, ed., "Hopkinsianism," American Antiquarian Society, *Proceedings*, 5 (1888), 437 – 461.

[47]*True Holiness*, p. 70.

NOTES

⁴⁸Lois Banner, "Religious Benevolence as Social Control: A Critique of an Interpretation," *Journal of American History*, 60 (1973), 23−41. Banner depreciates the contribution of Hopkins to a theology of religious reform and stresses (p. 25) that the idea of disinterested benevolence was a "general inheritance from a number of eighteenth-century sources."
⁴⁹See Chapter Eleven, below.

CHAPTER EIGHT

¹The relationship between American Protestantism and the Revolution has received considerable attention in recent years, largely as the result of Alan Heimert's positive reassessment of the contribution of evangelicals to the rebellion. See *Religion and the American Mind*; also see, Gordon S. Wood, *The Creation of the American Republic, 1776−1787* (Chapel Hill, 1969), esp. pp. 114−118. For different views, critical of Heimert's conclusions, see Bernard Bailyn, "Religion and the Revolution: Three Biographical Studies," *Perspectives in American History*, 4 (1970), 83−169, and Nathan O. Hatch, *The Sacred Cause of Liberty: Republican Thought and the Millennium in Revolutionary New England* (New Haven, 1977), esp. ch. 2. *Church History*, 45 (1976) is devoted to an examination of religion and the Revolution. See especially the articles by Mark A. Noll and Douglas H. Sweet. See also Catherine L. Albanese, *Sons of the Fathers: The Civil Religion of the American Revolution* (Philadelphia, 1976). Finally, a provocative essay by Harry S. Stout transcends the old categories and promises to reestablish the debate on a new level; see "Religion, Communications, and the Ideological Origins of the American Revolution," *William and Mary Quarterly*, 34 (1977), 519−541.
²Hopkins to Joseph Bellamy, July 1, 1757, Bellamy Papers, Hartford Seminary Foundation; Park, *Memoir of Hopkins*, p. 114.
³Two recent essays briefly analyze Hopkins as an antislavery reformer. See David S. Lovejoy, "Samuel Hopkins: Religion, Slavery and the Revolution," *New England Quarterly*, 40 (1967), 227−243, and David E. Swift, "Samuel Hopkins: Calvinist Social Concern in Eighteenth-Century New England," *Journal of Presbyterian History*, 47 (1969), 31−54. Also see Bernard Bailyn, *The Ideological Origins of the American Revolution* (Cambridge, Mass., 1967), pp. 232−241, and David B. Davis, *The Problem of Slavery in the Age of Revolution, 1770−1823* (Ithaca, 1975), pp. 293−299.
⁴Lorenzo J. Greene, *The Negro in Colonial New England, 1620−1776* (1942; rpt. Port Washington, N. Y., 1966), pp. 25−33, 86−88; Morgan, *The Gentle Puritan*, p. 116.
⁵These are the words of the Quaker poet-abolitionist, John Greenleaf Whittier, writing in an essay on Hopkins published in 1847 and later reprinted in Whittier, *Works*, 7 vols. (New York, 1888−89), VI, 130−140. See also Harriet Beecher Stowe's highly dramatic description of Hopkins's early anti-slavery efforts in *The Minister's Wooing* (Boston, 1859), ch. 15, and Park's equally romantic analysis in his *Memoir of Hopkins*, p. 116.
⁶A list of the First Church's members around 1760 is in Stiles, *Literary Diary*, I, 44−48, and may be compared against the Rhode Island Census of 1774 to get a rough picture of the extent of slave holding among Hopkins's

parishioners. See the *Census of the Inhabitants of the Colony of Rhode Island and Providence Plantations [in] 1774*, arranged by John Bartlett (1858; rpt. Baltimore, 1969). Also see Hammett, "History of the Congregational Churches in Newport," p. 171.

[7]Ferm, *Jonathan Edwards, The Younger*, p. 94. Edwards later republished much of this material in *The Injustice and Impolicy of the Slave-Trade and of the Slavery of the Africans . . .* (Providence, 1792).

[8]*Liberty Described and Recommended . . .* (Hartford, 1775), pp. 9, 23.

[9]Donald L. Robinson, *Slavery in the Structure of American Politics, 1765–1820* (New York, 1971), pp. 78–79.

[10]*A Dialogue Concerning the Slavery of the Africans, Shewing It to be the Duty and Interest of the American States to Emancipate All Their African Slaves* (Norwich, Conn., 1776), p. iii.

[11]For a discussion of the politicization of evangelical Calvinism during the Revolution, see Heimert, *Religion and the American Mind*, ch. 4.

[12]*A Dialogue Concerning the Slavery of the Africans*, p. iii.

[13]Ibid., p. 37.

[14]Ibid.

[15]Ibid., p. 34.

[16]Ibid., p. 5.

[17]Ibid., p. 53; Perry Miller, "From Covenant to Revival," in James Ward Smith and A. Leland Jameson, eds., *The Shaping of American Religion* (Princeton, 1961), pp. 322–368; Heimert, *Religion and the American Mind*, ch. 8.

[18]Hopkins to Erskine, Dec. 27, 1774, Gratz MSS., Historical Society of Pennsylvania; see also Edmund S. Morgan, "The Puritan Ethic and the American Revolution," *William and Mary Quarterly*, 24 (1967), 3–43.

[19]*A Dialogue Concerning the Slavery of the Africans*, p. 52.

[20]Hopkins, *The Life and Character of Miss Susanna Anthony* (Worcester, 1796), p. 193.

[21]West, ed., *Sketches of the Life of Samuel Hopkins*, p. 77; Morgan, *The Gentle Puritan*, pp. 278–279.

[22]Hopkins to Stiles, Nov. 10, 1779, Yale MSS., Sterling Memorial Library; West, ed., *Sketches of the Life of Samuel Hopkins*, p. 78; Stiles, *Literary Diary*, II, 390; Hammett, "History of the Congregational Churches in Newport," pp. 156, 185.

[23]Hopkins to Stiles, Nov. 10, 1779, Yale MSS.; "Subscription Letter of 1782," First Congregational Church Papers, Newport Historical Society; Hammett, "History of the Congregational Churches in Newport," pp. 163–165.

[24]Hopkins to West, June 23, 1780, Gratz MSS., Historical Society of Pennsylvania. Stiles blamed solely the New Divinity for Hopkins's difficulties. See *Literary Diary*, II, 504.

[25]West, ed., *Sketches of the Life of Samuel Hopkins*, pp. 78–80; First Congregational Church Records, Feb. 1, 1782, and Dec. 11, 1784, Newport Historical Society; Patten, *Reminiscences of Samuel Hopkins*, p. 133; Hopkins to William Hyslop, Dec. 15, 1792, Washburn Papers, Massachusetts His-

torical Society; George Channing, *Early Recollections of Newport, R.I., from the year 1793 to 1811* (Boston, 1868), p. 132.

[26]See Robinson, *Slavery in the Structure of American Politics*, ch. 1; Davis, *The Problem of Slavery in the Age of Revolution*, ch. 7; and Winthrop D. Jordan, *White over Black: American Attitudes Toward the Negro, 1550–1812* (Chapel Hill, 1968), ch. 9.

[27]Elizabeth Donnan, "The New England Slave Trade after the Revolution," *New England Quarterly*, 3 (1930), 251–278.

[28]See, Mack Thompson, *Moses Brown: Reluctant Reformer* (Chapel Hill, 1962), pp. 177–181.

[29]Ibid., p. 182.

[30]Brown to Hopkins, March 3, 1784, Moses Brown Papers, Rhode Island Historical Society, Providence.

[31]Hopkins to Brown, Apr. 29, 1784, Moses Brown Papers. See Hopkins's glowing description of Moses in a letter to Levi Hart, Nov. 27, 1787, Gratz MSS., Historical Society of Pennsylvania.

[32]First Congregational Church Records, Jan. 30, March 5, 1784, Newport Historical Society.

[33]See Davis, *The Problem of Slavery in the Age of Revolution*, pp. 202–209.

[34]*Newport Mercury*, May 1784; Hopkins to Brown, Apr. 29, 1784, Moses Brown Papers, Rhode Island Historical Society.

[35]Hopkins to Moses Brown, March 16, 1785, Moses Brown Papers; Hopkins to Levi Hart, Feb. 10, 1786, and Jan. 22, 1787, Gratz MSS., Historical Society of Pennsylvania; Park, *Memoir of Hopkins*, p. 117.

[36]Brown to Hopkins, Jan. 20, 1786, Moses Brown Papers.

[37]Hopkins to Hart, Feb. 10, Apr. 11, 1786, and Nov. 27, 1787, Gratz MSS.

[38]Hopkins to Brown, Sept. 16, 1787, Moses Brown Papers.

[39]Ibid., Aug. 13, 1787.

[40]Ibid.

[41]The essay was reprinted under the title "The Slave Trade and Slavery" in *Timely Articles on Slavery by the Rev. Samuel Hopkins* (Boston, 1854), a collection of Hopkins's antislavery writings. I have used this edition.

[42]*Timely Articles on Slavery*, pp. 614–615.

[43]Ibid., pp. 615, 619, 620–621.

[44]Hopkins to Moses Brown, Jan. 5, Feb. 25, 1788, Moses Brown Papers, Rhode Island Historical Society.

[45]Hopkins to Levi Hart, Nov. 27, 1787, Gratz MSS., Historical Society of Pennsylvania.

[46]Hopkins to Hart, Jan. 29, 1788, New York Historical Society MSS., New York City.

[47]Hopkins to Moses Brown, Oct. 22, 1787, Moses Brown Papers.

[48]Hopkins to Hart, Jan. 29, 1788, New York Historical Society MSS. For similar clerical responses, see Hatch, *The Sacred Cause of Liberty*, ch. 3.

[49]Donnan, "The New England Slave Trade after the Revolution," p. 253; Thompson, *Moses Brown*, p. 102.

[50]Hopkins to Hart, Nov. 27, 1787, and Sept. 8, 1788, Gratz MSS.,

Historical Society of Pennsylvania; Hopkins to Brown, Jan. 5, Sept. 24, 1788, Moses Brown Papers.

[51]Thompson, *Moses Brown*, pp. 194– 195.

[52]Hopkins to William Rogers, Sept. 22, 1788, Pennsylvania Abolition Society Papers, Historical Society of Pennsylvania; Eben Hazard to Hopkins, Dec. 10, 1788, Yale MSS.

[53]Hopkins to Brown, March 16, 1788, Moses Brown Papers.

[54]Hopkins to Brown, March 7, Aug. 17, 1789, Moses Brown Papers. In March the Pennsylvania Abolition Society wrote to Hopkins seeking information on the formation of the Providence Society and enclosed for his use the plan of an abolition society recently formed in Washington County, Pennsylvania. See the Pennsylvania Abolition Society to Hopkins, March 9, 1789, Pennsylvania Abolition Society Papers.

[55]Hopkins to Moses Brown, March 30, 1789, Moses Brown Papers; Thompson, *Moses Brown*, pp. 196– 200.

[56]Hopkins to Brown, Aug. 17, Nov. 18, 1789, Moses Brown Papers.

[57]Wilkins Updike, to E. A. Park, no date, Yale MSS. See also William Ellery Channing's similar youthful impressions recalled in a letter to E. A. Park, Feb. 14, 1840, ibid.; George Channing, *Early Recollections of Newport*, pp. 87– 89; and Patten, *Reminiscences of Samuel Hopkins*, pp. 117– 125.

CHAPTER NINE

[1]"A Sermon Delivered at the Tabernacle in Salem, Feb. 6, 1812, on the Occasion of the Ordination of the . . . Missionaries to the Heathen in Asia . . .," in R. Pierce Beaver, *Pioneers in Missions: The Early Missionary Ordination Sermons, Charges and Institutions* (Grand Rapids, 1966), p. 258. On Hopkins's theological influence on missions, see Oliver W. Elsbree, *The Rise of the Missionary Spirit in America, 1790–1815* (Williamsport, Pa., 1928); Wolfange E. Lowe, "The First American Foreign Missionaries: 'The Students,' 1810– 1829: An Inquiry into their Theological Motives" (Ph.D. diss., Brown University, 1962); and R. Pierce Beaver, "Missionary Motivation through Three Centuries," in Jerald C. Brauer, ed., *Reinterpretation in American Church History* (Chicago, 1970), pp. 122– 126. For a recent attempt to place the foreign missionary movement among Congregationalists in a social context, see John A. Andrew III, *Rebuilding the Christian Commonwealth: New England Congregationalists and Foreign Missions, 1800–1830* (Lexington, Ky., 1976).

[2][Samuel Hopkins], "A Narrative of the rise & progress of a proposal and attempt to send the gospel to Guinea, by educating, and sending two negroes there to attempt to christianize their brethren," Gratz MSS., pp. 1– 2. This document in Hopkins's handwriting offers a year by year account of the African mission to 1784 and is hereafter referred to as "A Narrative of the attempt to christianize Guinea." On Quamine and Yamma, see also Stiles, *Literary Diary*, I, 364– 366.

[3]*Literary Diary*, I, 366.

[4]The circular was printed and distributed in 1773 and reprinted, along

with a second circular, in Samuel Hopkins and Ezra Stiles, *To the Public* (Newport, 1776), pp. 1 – 3.

[5]*Literary Diary*, I, 364.

[6]"A Narrative of the attempt to christianize Guinea," p. 3.

[7]Hopkins and Stiles, *To the Public*, pp. 1 – 3; "A Narrative of the attempt to christianize Guinea," p. 3.

[8]Stiles, *Literary Diary*, I, 414.

[9]"A Narrative of the attempt to christianize Guinea," p. 8; Hopkins to Levi Hart, Feb. 7, 1774, in Park, *Memoir of Hopkins*, pp. 132 – 133.

[10]Hopkins to Joseph Bellamy, June 6, 1774, and to John Erskine, Dec. 28, 1774, Gratz MSS., Historical Society of Pennsylvania; "A Narrative of the attempt to christianize Guinea," p. 12.

[11]Quaque to Hopkins, May 19, 1773, and Hopkins to Quaque, Dec. 10, 1773, Gratz MSS., Historical Society of Pennsylvania.

[12]Wheatley to Hopkins, May 6, 1774, Boston Public Library MSS. See also Wheatley to Hopkins, Feb. 9, 1774, in Benjamin Quarles, "Documents: A Phillis Wheatley Letter," *Journal of Negro History*, 33 (1948), 464.

[13]Witherspoon to Hopkins, Feb. 27, 1775, Misc. MSS., New York Public Library; "A Narrative of the attempt to christianize Guinea," p. 9.

[14]Hopkins and Stiles, *To the Public*, pp. 4 – 8. One of the new missionary candidates was Salmar Nubia, a member of Stiles's church. Hopkins also considered sending the missionaries to the South, instead of to Africa, to educate and convert blacks whom he apparently assumed would be freed during the Revolution. See Hopkins to Roger Sherman, Oct. 8, 1776, Boston Public Library MSS.

[15]Hopkins, *A Discourse Upon the Slave Trade and the Slavery of the Africans* (Providence, 1793), pp. 18 – 19.

[16]"A Narrative of the attempt to christianize Guinea," p. 15.

[17]Ibid.

[18]Hopkins to Brown, Apr. 29, 1784, Moses Brown Papers, Rhode Island Historical Society.

[19]Quoted in Thompson, *Moses Brown*, pp. 185 – 186.

[20]Hopkins to Brown, March 7, 1787, Moses Brown Papers; William Thornton to the African Union Society of Newport, Rhode Island, March 6, 1787, in William H. Robinson, ed. *Proceedings of the Free African Union Society and the African Benevolent Society, Newport, Rhode Island* (Providence, R.I., 1976), p. 17. On the state of Africa colonization in the late 1780's see Floyd J. Miller, *The Search for a Black Nationality: Black Emigration and Colonization, 1787 – 1863* (Urbana, Ill., 1975), ch. 1.

[21]Hopkins probably first learned of the sailing of the colony from William Thornton. See Hopkins to Moses Brown, March 7, 1787, Moses Brown Papers. On the colony, see John Petersen, *Province of Freedom: A History of Sierra Leone, 1787 – 1870* (Evanston, Ill., 1969).

[22]Hopkins to Erskine, Jan. 14, 1789, Yale MSS., Sterling Memorial Library.

[23]Ibid. The Newport blacks were members of the African Union Society, a local self-help organization that was seriously interested in African colonization. For the Society's activities and its attempts in cooperation with Hopkins

and others to send blacks back to Africa, see Robinson, ed., *Proceedings of the Free African Union Society and the African Benevolent Society*, pp. 16–39.

[24]Hopkins to Sharp, Jan. 16, 1789, Yale MSS., Sterling Memorial Library. In 1789 Sharp published "An Account of a FREE SETTLEMENT OF NEGROES, now Forming at Sierra-Leone in Africa," *Columbian Magazine*, 3 (1789), 234–240.

[25]Hopkins to Sharp, Jan. 16, 1789, Yale MSS.

[26]Sharp to Hopkins, July 25, 1789, in Park, *Memoir of Hopkins*, pp. 142–143. Also see William Thornton to Hopkins, Sept. 29, 1790, in Robinson, ed., *Proceedings of the Free African Union Society and the Benevolent Society*, pp. 32–34. For an analysis of the poor conditions within the settlement at the time, see Petersen, *Province of Freedom*, pp. 26–27.

[27]Hopkins to Hart, June 10, 1791, Gratz MSS., Historical Society of Pennsylvania.

[28]Ibid.; Hopkins to Hart, Aug. 31, 1791, July 29, Aug. 31, 1793, Gratz MSS.

[29]*A Discourse upon the Slave Trade and the Slavery of the Africans*, pp. 6, 11–13.

[30]Ibid., pp. 11, 14, 18–19.

[31]Ibid., appendix.

[32]Ibid.; see also Hopkins to Levi Hart, July 29, 1793, Gratz MSS., Historical Society of Pennsylvania.

[33]See Leonard I. Sweet, *Black Images of America, 1784–1870* (New York, 1976), ch. 3. See also Miller, *The Search for a Black Nationality*, ch. 1.

[34]Hopkins to Hart, June 9, 1795, Gratz MSS.

[35]Macaulay to Hopkins, March 19, 1795, Yale MSS.; Robinson, ed., *Proceedings of the Free African Union and the African Benevolent Society*, pp. 43–46; Miller, *The Search for a Black Nationality*, pp. 14–20.

[36]Macaulay to Hopkins, Oct. 20, 1796, in Park, *Memoir of Hopkins*, pp. 151–153; Miller, *The Search for a Black Nationality*, p. 19.

[37]Park, *Memoir of Hopkins*, p. 156; Miller, *The Search for a Black Nationality*, p. 20.

[38]Quoted in Park, *Memoir of Hopkins*, p. 156.

[39]See J. Earl Thompson, Jr., "Abolitionism and Theological Education at Andover," *New England Quarterly*, 47 (1974), 238–261.

[40]Leonard Bacon, et al., *Contributions to the Ecclesiastical History of Connecticut* (New Haven, 1861), pp. 165–166. Most of the missionaries appointed by the Connecticut General Association prior to the establishment of the Society were New Divinity men. See Charles R. Keller, *The Second Great Awakening in Connecticut* (New Haven, 1942), pp. 72–73.

[41]Quoted in Park, *Memoir of Hopkins*, p. 64; see also *The Diary of William Bentley*, II, 317; and Wright, *The Beginnings of Unitarianism*, pp. 266–267. On the New Divinity association of ministers in eastern Massachusetts, see Dexter, ed., *Extracts from the Itineraries and Other Miscellanies of Ezra Stiles*, p. 402.

[42]See Hopkins, *Memoir of Mrs. Sarah Osborn*, pp. 78–79.

[43]*Connecticut Evangelical Magazine*, 5 (1806), 393–397.

[44]Macaulay to Hopkins, Oct. 20, 1796, in Park, *Memoir of Hopkins*, pp. 151 – 152.

[45]Hopkins to Fuller, Oct. 15, 1799, in ibid., p. 236.

CHAPTER TEN

[1]West, ed., *Sketches of the Life of Hopkins*, pp. 80 – 81.

[2]Ibid., p. 81.

[3]See, for example, Hopkins to Levi Hart, June 23, 1786, Gratz MSS., Historical Society of Pennsylvania; also see Park, *Memoir of Hopkins*, p. 240.

[4]West, ed., *Sketches of the Life of Hopkins*, p. 84; Park, *Memoir of Hopkins*, pp. 240 – 245.

[5]Two vols. (Boston, 1793).

[6]*A Genetic History of New England Theology* (Chicago, 1907), pp. 162, 185.

[7]See Lowrie, *The Shape of the Puritan Mind*, chs. 1 – 2.

[8]Foster, *A Genetic History of New England Theology*, p. 185. While recognizing the importance of the *System of Doctrines*, Foster often oversimplifies or inaccurately presents aspects of Hopkins's theology. For example, Foster states that "in the theory of virtue Hopkins had nothing to change in the teachings of Edwards, except to introduce the incorrect idea that all sin is selfishness" (p. 167).

[9]West, ed., *Sketches of the Life of Hopkins*, p. 101.

[10]Ibid.; Hopkins to Levi Hart, Aug. 30, Oct. 20, 1791; May 10, Aug. 9, Oct. 3, 1792; Jan. 26, 1793, Gratz MSS.

[11]*System of Doctrines*, p. iv.

[12]Ibid.; *A Treatise on the Millennium*, p. 58.

[13]Edwards, "Miscellaneous Observations on Important Doctrines," *Works*, I, 564 – 642. For an old but still useful history of the doctrine of the atonement in New England theology, see Edwards A. Park, *The Atonement: Discourses and Treatises* . . . (Boston, 1859); see also Haroutunian, *Piety versus Moralism*, pp. 157 – 161.

[14]See above, pp. 117 – 118.

[15]*True Religion Delineated* (1750), *Works*, I, 341 – 342.

[16]"An Essay on the Nature and Glory of the Gospel of Jesus Christ" (1762), *Works*, II, 381.

[17]*True Religion Delineated*, p. 292. Edwards wrote the preface to this work praising Bellamy's efforts. This suggests that Edwards's thought was moving in a similar direction to Bellamy's — a conclusion which does have some supporting evidence — or that Bellamy's views were not fully developed enough for Edwards to take exception to them. See the discussion in Park, *The Atonement*, p. xlvii, and Anderson, "Joseph Bellamy," p. 746.

[18]"The Millennium," *Works*, I, 512.

[19]Wright, *The Beginnings of Unitarianism*, pp. 219 – 220.

[20]Quoted in ibid., p. 191.

[21]Ibid., pp. 189 – 196.

[22]*An Inquiry Concerning the Future State of those who die in their sins* . . . (Newport, 1783), pp. 167 – 168.

[23]*System of Doctrines*, I, 322, 365, II, 165.

[24]See William G. McLoughlin, ed., *The American Evangelicals, 1800–1900* (New York, 1968), pp. 4–5. For a different assessment of the impact of the moral government theory, see Haroutunian, *Piety versus Moralism*, pp. 174–175.

[25]However, Hopkins did not include his controversial willingness to be damned doctrine in the *System*. He contemplated including it in a second edition. Jonathan Edwards, Jr., recommended against this. See his letter to Hopkins, Oct. 29, 1793, Yale MSS.

[26]Ibid.

[27]Clarence C. Goen, "Jonathan Edwards: A New Departure in Eschatology," *Church History*, 28 (1959), 25–40; Heimert, *Religion and the American Mind*, ch. 2.

[28]*Works*, I, 293–516; also see "Some Thoughts on the Revival of Religion in New England" (1740), *Works*, III, 310–316.

[29]*Humble Attempt*, ibid., III, 500.

[30]James W. Davidson, *The Logic of Millennial Thought [in] Eighteenth-Century New England* (New Haven, 1977), ch. 4, esp. p. 138.

[31]Ibid., pp. 131–141.

[32]Edwards to William McCulloch, March 5, 1744, quoted in ibid., p. 156.

[33]*Humble Attempt*, p. 482.

[34]Davidson, *The Logic of Millennial Thought*, p. 151. See also, Nathan O. Hatch, *The Sacred Cause of Liberty: Republican Thought and the Millennium in Revolutionary New England* (New Haven, 1977), p. 33; and Stephen J. Stein, "Cotton Mather and Jonathan Edwards on the Number of the Beast: Eighteenth-Century Speculations about Antichrist," American Antiquarian Society, *Proceedings*, 134 (1975), 293–315.

[35]Hopkins to Hart, May 1792, Gratz MSS. On similar clerical pessimism and its relationship to the millennialism of the 1790's, see Hatch, *The Sacred Cause of Liberty*, pp. 146–156.

[36]*A Treatise on the Millennium*, pp. 6, 146.

[37]Ibid., p. 10.

[38]Ibid., pp. 95, 145.

[39]Ibid., pp. 145, 152.

[40]Ibid., p. 152.

[41]*Humble Attempt*, pp. 446–447; see also Ernest Lee Tuveson, *Redeemer Nation: The Idea of America's Millennial Role* (Chicago, 1968), p. 59, and Davidson, *The Logic of Millennial Thought*, pp. 216–218.

[42]*A Treatise on the Millennium*, p. 71.

[43]Ibid., pp. 59, 71, 76.

[44]Ibid., pp. 56, 69, 71.

[45]William Ellery Channing, *Works*, 6 vols. (Boston, 1841), IV, 353.

[46]See Davidson, *The Logic of Millennial Thought*, p. 179.

[47]See an *Outline of the Course of Study in the Department of Christian Theology [at Andover Seminary]* (Andover, 1822), and Henry K. Rowe, *History of Andover Theological Seminary* (Newton, Mass., 1933), pp. 15–18.

[48]West to Hopkins, Sept. 19, 1797, in Park, *Memoir of Nathanael Em-*

mons, p. 213; see also Thomas Dwight to Theodore Sedgwick, March 9, 1796, Sedgwick Papers, Massachusetts Historical Society; and Barbara Cross, ed., *The Autobiography of Lyman Beecher*, 2 vols. (Cambridge, Mass., 1961), I, 44–45.

[49]Hopkins to Levi Hart, July 29, 1793, and June 9, 1794, Gratz MSS.

[50]Nathanael Emmons, *Hopkinsian Calvinism* (1811; rpt. Providence, 1858), p. 4.

CHAPTER ELEVEN

[1]See, for example, Sidney E. Mead, *Nathaniel William Taylor, 1786–1858: A Connecticut Liberal* (Chicago, 1942), esp. p. 96, and the work of Mead's student, Stephen E. Berk, *Calvinism versus Democracy: Timothy Dwight and the Origins of American Evangelical Orthodoxy* (Hamden, Conn., 1974), ch. 4.; also see Donald Meyer, "The Dissolution of Calvinism," in Arthur M. Schlesinger, Jr., and Morton White, eds., *Paths of American Thought* (Boston, 1963), pp. 77–80.

[2]Hopkins, *Life of Edwards*, pp. 53–54. On the Edwardsian approach to preaching see also Heimert, *Religion and the American Mind*, pp. 221–234.

[3]Harry S. Stout, "Religion, Communications, and the Ideological Origins of the American Revolution," *William and Mary Quarterly*, 34 (1977), 526–527.

[4]"Miscellaneous Observations on Preaching," Undated MSS., Andover-Newton Theological School Library. Edwards the younger did note that New Divinity men were "apt to run into an argumentative & what is commonly called a metaphysical way of preaching" (ibid.). However, he was not referring to the practice of reading abstruse sermons in the pulpit. A "metaphysical way of preaching" appears to have been a loose term that was used by both evangelical Baptists and rational Old Lights. Unlettered Baptist ministers used the term to characterize preaching that did not seem sufficiently emotional to them. On the other hand, Old Lights, who sought to avoid doctrinal controversies, used the term to discredit any discussion of polemical divinity in the pulpit. In any case, Edwards the younger, like other prominent New Divinity men, advocated a mode of preaching that rejected emotional excesses (a *"fancy way of preaching,"* he wrote) *and* metaphysical analyses in the pulpit (ibid.).

[5]Levi Hart, *The Christian Minister . . .* (Norwich, 1771), pp. 11–12.

[6]Emmons quoted in Park, *Memoir of Nathanael Emmons*, p. 277. Emmons's "homiletic principles" which were written "to aid young ministers" are reprinted in ibid., pp. 273–279. Emmons employed and advocated a non-metaphysical, essentially extemporaneous preaching style. On Bellamy's advice to students, see Anderson, "Joseph Bellamy," pp. 394–396.

[7]*A Complete History of Connecticut*, II, 124–125.

[8]Sprague, *Annals of the American Pulpit*, I, 410. On Bellamy's reputation as a preacher see also Anderson, "Joseph Bellamy," pp. 195–202, and Heimert, *Religion and the American Mind*, p. 234.

[9]Robbins to Bellamy, June 19, 1780, Bellamy Papers, Hartford Seminary Foundation. On the revival in surrounding towns see Stiles, *Literary*

Diary, II, 508, and James Manning, President of Rhode Island College (later Brown University), to Gardner Thurston, March 6, 1788, Brown University MSS., John Hay Library.

[10]Samuel Hopkins to Levi Hart, Sept. 8, 1788, Gratz MSS., Historical Society of Pennsylvania; Park, *Memoir of Emmons*, pp. 352–357.

[11]West to Joseph Bellamy, July 16, 1782, Congregational Historical Society MSS., Boston; Samuel Hopkins to West, Oct. 4, 1799, Hopkins Papers, Andover-Newton Theological School.

[12]Sprague, *Annals of the American Pulpit*, I, 553. West's neighbor, Jacob Catlin of New Marlborough, was also a successful New Divinity revivalist. See *The Connecticut Evangelical Magazine*, 2 (Dec. 1801), 224–226.

[13]Sprague, *Annals of the American Pulpit*, I, 34–39.

[14]On the Colebrook revival see Ferm, *Jonathan Edwards the Younger*, p. 151. On the Somers revival see *The Connecticut Evangelical Magazine*, 1 (1800), 19–21. The first issues of this monthly journal convincingly document New Divinity evangelical successes. See 1 (1800–1801), 27–30, 131–136, 217–233, 265–268, 311–314, 341–347. Keller, *The Second Great Awakening in Connecticut*, is helpful in charting the local revivals in Connecticut; see esp. ch. 3.

[15]Hopkins to Ryland, Oct. 17, 1799, Hopkins Papers, Andover-Newton Theological School.

[16]West, ed., *Sketches of the Life of Hopkins*, p. 124.

[17]See, for example, Morgan, "The American Revolution Considered as an Intellectual Movement," p. 20.

[18]Ibid., pp. 91–92; Park, *Memoir of Hopkins*, pp. 38–39.

[19]Hopkins, *Life of Edwards*, p. 55.

[20]West, ed., *Sketches of the Life of Hopkins*, p. 91. On Hopkins's preaching without notes see, for example, his *Journal*, July 5, 10, 1743, Williams College MSS., and Nov. 3, 24, and Dec. 1, 1754, Hopkins Papers, Andover-Newton Theological School.

[21]West, ed., *Sketches of the Life of Hopkins*, p. 91. Examples of Hopkins's sermon notes are in the Hopkins Papers at Andover-Newton Theological School and in the Sterling Memorial Library at Yale University.

[22]*Journal*, July 22, 1744, Williams MSS.

[23]West, ed., *Sketches of the Life of Hopkins*, p. 88.

[24]Channing to E. A. Park, Feb. 14, 1840, Yale MSS. See also George Channing, *Recollections of Newport*, pp. 87–88, and Patten, *Reminiscences of Hopkins*, pp. 132–133.

[25]West, ed., *Sketches of the Life of Hopkins*, p. 124. The absence of a revival in Hopkins's Newport church during the Second Great Awakening was not solely a consequence of his poor preaching. In the first place, his society was composed mostly of older people who were far less likely to experience conversion in a revival than younger people, particularly young adults. Secondly, for some reason the fires of the Awakening seemed to leap over a good part of Rhode Island and not simply the First Church of Newport (see Hopkins to Stephen West, Apr. 24, 1798, New York Public Library MSS., and Hopkins to West, Oct. 4, 1799, Hopkins Papers, Andover-Newton Theological School). Even a young, dynamic assistant pastor, who was appointed

to aid Hopkins after his health declined in 1799, failed to stimulate a religious awakening in the First Church.

[26]These figures are taken from Stiles, *Literary Diary*, III, 463–464. See also Keller, *The Second Great Awakening in Connecticut*, pp. 36–37, 50–52.

[27]Stiles, *Literary Diary*, III, 247, 463–464.

[28]Ibid., 465.

[29]Ibid., II, 508; see also Wright, *The Beginnings of Unitarianism*, p. 254.

[30]*The Diary of William Bentley*, I, 161.

[31]Ibid., III, 364. On Bentley's assessment of the popularity of Hopkinsianism see also above, p. 5.

[32]*Literary Diary*, III, 364.

[33]West, ed., *Sketches of the Life of Hopkins*, pp. 102–103.

[34]Hopkins to Ryland, Oct. 17, 1799, Hopkins Papers, Andover-Newton Theological School.

[35]Leonard Bacon et al., *Contributions to the Ecclesiastical History of Connecticut* (New Haven, 1861), p. 240. At least two ministerial associations, those in New Haven and Windham counties, split into pro- and anti-New Divinity factions. (See ibid., p. 323, and Eleanor Larned, *History of Windham County, Connecticut* [2 vols., Worcester, 1874, 1880], II, 391–392.)

[36]The most influential statement of this view has been made by Sidney Mead in *Nathaniel William Taylor*. See also Berk, *Calvinism versus Democracy*, and Lois Banner, "Religious Benevolence as Social Control: A Critique of an Interpretation," *Journal of American History*, 60 (1973), 25–41.

[37]I have discussed this problem in "Samuel Hopkins and the New Divinity," esp. pp. 588–589. See also Kenneth A. Lockridge, "Social Change and the Meaning of the American Revolution," *Journal of Social History*, 6 (1973), 423–424, and William G. McLoughlin's discussion of Awakenings as cultural revitalization movements in *Revivals, Awakenings, and Reform: An Essay on Religion and Social Change in America* (Chicago, 1978), pp. 106–122.

[38]"Connecticut Moral Society," *The Connecticut Evangelical Magazine*, 15 (1815), 80, 225–229, 257–264; Richard D. Birdsall, "The Second Great Awakening and the New England Social Order," *Church History*, 39 (1970), 360–362; Douglas H. Sweet, "Church Vitality and the American Revolution: Historiographical Consensus and Thoughts towards a New Perspective," *Church History*, 45 (1976), 341–357.

[39]Quoted in Birdsall, "The Second Great Awakening and the New England Social Order," p. 354.

[40]*The Connecticut Evangelical Magazine*, 1 (1800), 26. For similar observations of the hyper-Calvinist emphasis of local revivals, see, for example, ibid., pp. 135–136, and 6 (1805), 66; also see Birdsall, "The Second Great Awakening and the New England Social Order," pp. 353–354.

[41]Morgan, "The American Revolution Considered as an Intellectual Movement," p. 20.

[42]Stiles. *Literary Diary*, III, 505–506n.

[43]Ibid., II, 508.

[44]See "Early Theological Education," in Bacon et al., *Contributions to the Ecclesiastical History of Connecticut*, pp. 296–297.

[45]Calhoun, *Professional Lives in America*, pp. 157–166; Lois W. Ban-

ner, "Religion and Reform in the Early Republic: The Role of Youth," *American Quarterly*, 22 (1971), 677–695; also see above, pp. 12–13, 85–86.

[46]Quoted in Park, *Memoir of Emmons*, p. 231.

[47]Quoted in Keller, *The Second Great Awakening in Connecticut*, p. 124.

[48]Ibid., pp. 124–125.

[49]*The Constitution and Associate Statutes of the Theological Seminary in Andover* (Andover, 1817), p. 10; Henry Rowe, *History of Andover Theological Seminary* (Newton, Mass., 1933), pp. 25, 29.

[50]Rowe, *History of Andover Theological Seminary*, pp. 29–30. The quotation may be found on p. 30.

[51]David F. Allmendinger, "The Strangeness of the American Education Society: Indigent Students and the New Charity, 1815–1840," *History of Education Quarterly*, 11 (1971), 3–22; Allmendinger, *Paupers and Students*, chs. 1–5; Keller, *The Second Great Awakening in Connecticut*, pp. 126–127; Natalie Ann Taylor, "Raising a Learned Ministry: the American Education Society, 1815–1860" (Ed.D. diss., Teachers College, Columbia Univ., 1971); Scott, *From Office to Profession*, ch. 4.

[52]See above, pp. 11–15.

[53]Quoted in Calhoun, *Professional Lives in America*, p. 111; see also Banner, "Religion and Reform in the Early Republic," 684.

[54]Like these two societies, other reform agencies of the benevolent empire evolved from local and state organizations in New England (see Birdsall, "The Second Great Awakening and the New England Social Order," 360). New Divinity men were involved in these societies from the beginning (see Keller, *The Second Great Awakening in Connecticut*).

[55]*The Hopkinsian Magazine*, which was published for several years beginning in 1824.

[56]West, ed., *Sketches of the Life of Hopkins*, p. 105.

[57]Hopkins to John Ryland, Oct. 17, 1799, Hopkins Papers, Andover-Newton Theological School; Channing, *Recollections of Newport*, pp. 91–92; Park, *Memoir of Hopkins*, p. 252.

[58]West, ed., *Sketches of the Life of Hopkins*, pp. xx–xxi.

EPILOGUE

[1]On the origins and development of Taylorism, see Mead, *Nathaniel Taylor*, and Berk, *Calvinism versus Democracy*.

[2]The Arminianized Calvinism of New England evangelicals like Taylor and Beecher was related to and influenced by the work of Charles Grandison Finney, whose evangelicalism clearly reflects many of the values of Jacksonian Democracy. See William G. McLoughlin, "Charles Grandison Finney," in David Brion Davis, ed., *Ante-Bellum Reform* (New York, 1967), pp. 97–107.

[3]Whittier, *Works*, VI, 144; see also above, pp. 126–127.

[4]*The Minister's Wooing*, p. 8; see also William Ellery Channing to E. A. Park, Feb. 14, 1840, Yale MSS., and Park, *Memoir of Hopkins*, p. 116. For a brief, recent assessment of the influence of Hopkins and the New Divinity on nineteenth-century reform, see Davis, *The Problem of Slavery in the Age of Revolution*, p. 296.

APPENDIX:
New Divinity Men

THE following list of New Divinity men includes full-fledged Hopkinsians and other ministers who might be called semi-Hopkinsians. The latter group is comprised of New Divinity men who admired and respected Hopkins and who, in varying degrees, were influenced by his theology but who did not accept certain Hopkinsian language or doctrinal emphases. Many New Divinity men in this group closely followed the thought of Joseph Bellamy. It is not always easy to distinguish followers of Hopkins from followers of Bellamy. There were not sharp theological divisions within the New Divinity movement. In the first place, Hopkins and Bellamy worked together closely and were in substantial theological agreement. Secondly, Hopkins's *System of Doctrines* synthesized the work of Bellamy and other New Divinity theologians and further blurred theological distinctions within the movement. By the late eighteenth century, the members of the New Divinity movement were either full-fledged or semi-Hopkinsians. Charles Backus of Somers, Connecticut, was representative of this last group. Backus studied theology with Levi Hart, the Hopkinsian minister of Preston, Connecticut. As one of his own divinity students noted, Backus "read with interest the writings of Dr. Hopkins, and thought highly of his 'System of Divinity.' But he did not adopt all the points of doctrine contained in that System, nor did he think all those which he did adopt were set forth by that writer in the best manner" (Sprague, *Annals of the American Pulpit*, II, 65).

Austin, Punderson, 1743 – 1773; born, New Haven, Conn.; Yale 1762;

theological teacher, Joseph Bellamy; temporary minister to several churches.

Austin, Samuel, 1760– 1830; born, New Haven, Conn.; Yale, 1783; theological teacher, Jonathan Edwards, Jr.; settled, New Haven, 1786; dismissed, 1789; settled, Worcester, 1790; resigned, 1815; President of the University of Vermont, 1815– 1821; resigned, 1821; settled, Newport, R. I., 1821– 1825.

Avery, David, 1746– 1817; born, Norwich, Conn.; Yale, 1769; theological teacher, Eleazar Wheelock; settled, Gageborough, Vt., 1773; resigned 1777; Army Chaplain, 1777– 1780; settled, Wrentham, Mass., 1786; dismissed, 1794; served vacant churches in Conn., Mass., and Vt., 1796– 1817.

Backus, Azel, 1765– 1817; born, Norwich, Conn.; Yale, 1787; theological teacher, Charles Backus; settled, Bethlehem, Conn., 1791; resigned, 1812; President of Hamilton College, 1812– 1817.

Backus, Charles, 1749– 1803; born, Norwich, Conn.; Yale, 1769; theological teacher, Levi Hart; settled, Somers, Conn., 1774– 1803.

Bacon, John, 1745– 1820; born, Canterbury, Conn.; College of New Jersey, 1765; theological teacher unknown; settled, Boston, 1769; dismissed, 1775; left the ministry and settled in Berkshire County.

Baldwin, Ebenezer, 1745– 1776; born, Norwich, Conn.; Yale, 1763; tutor and graduate divinity student, Yale, 1766– 1770; settled, Danbury, Conn., 1770– 1776.

Barker, Joseph, 1751– 1815; born, Branford, Conn.; Yale, 1771; theological teacher, unknown; settled, Middleborough, Mass., 1781– 1815.

Bellamy, Joseph, 1719– 1790; born, New Cheshire, Conn.; Yale, 1735; theological teacher, Jonathan Edwards; settled, Bethlehem, Conn., 1740– 1790.

Benedict, Abner, 1740– 1818; born, North Salem, N.Y.; Yale, 1769; theological teacher, Joseph Bellamy; settled, Middlefield, Conn., 1771; dismissed, 1786; settled, New Lebanon Springs, N.Y., 1786; dismissed, 1791; served various churches in N.Y., Conn., and N. J., 1792– 1818.

Benedict, Joel, 1745– 1816; born, Westchester, N.Y.; College of New Jersey, 1765; theological teacher, Joseph Bellamy; settled, Newent, Conn., 1771; dismissed, 1782; settled, Plainfield, Conn., 1784– 1816.

Bradford, Ebenezer, 1746– 1801; born, Canterbury, Conn.; College of New Jersey, 1773; theological teacher, Joseph Bellamy; settled, Rowley, Mass., 1782– 1801.

Catlin, Jacob, 1758– 1826; born, Harwinton, Conn.; Yale, 1784;

theological teacher, Stephen West; settled, New Marlborough, Mass., 1787—1826.

Chapman, Jedediah, 1741—1813; born, East Haddam, Conn.; Yale, 1762; theological teacher, Joseph Bellamy; settled, Orange, N. J., 1766; resigned 1800; became a missionary; settled, Geneva, N.Y., 1800—1813.

Day, Jeremiah, 1737—1806; born, Colchester, Conn.; Yale, 1756; theological teacher, Joseph Bellamy; settled, Washington, Conn., 1769—1806.

Edwards, Jonathan, Jr., 1745—1801; born, Northampton, Mass.; College of New Jersey, 1765; theological teachers, Samuel Hopkins and Joseph Bellamy; settled, New Haven, Conn., 1769; dismissed 1795; settled, Colebrook, Conn., 1796; resigned, 1799; President of Union College, 1799—1801.

Emmons, Nathanael, 1745—1840; born East Haddam, Conn.; Yale, 1767; theological teacher, John Smalley; settled, Franklin, Mass., 1769—1840.

Everett, Noble, 1747—1819; born, Bethlehem, Conn.; Yale, 1775; theological teacher, Joseph Bellamy; settled, Wareham, Mass., 1782—1819.

Fitch, Ebenezer, 1756—1833; born, Norwich, Conn., but raised in Canterbury, Conn.; Yale, 1777; tutor, Yale, 1780—1785; tutor and graduate divinity student, Yale, 1786—1791; Preceptor and President, Williams College, 1791—1815; resigned, 1815; settled, West Bloomfield, N.Y., 1815; resigned, 1827, because of ill health.

Fowler, Abraham, 1745—1815; born, Lebanon, Conn.; Yale, 1775; theological teacher, Eleazar Wheelock; settled, Waterbury, Conn., 1785; dismissed, 1799; settled, Litchfield, Conn., 1807; dismissed, 1813; settled, Prospect, Conn., 1815.

Gillett, Alexander, 1749—1826; born, East Granby, Conn.; Yale, 1770; theological teacher, unknown; settled, Farmingbury, Conn., 1773; dismissed, 1791; settled, Torrington, Conn., 1792—1826.

Goldsmith, Benjamin, 1736—1810; born, Southold, L.I.; Yale, 1760; theological teacher, unknown; settled, Riverbend, L.I., 1764—1810.

Hart, Levi, 1736—1808; born, Southington, Conn.; Yale, 1760; theological teacher, Joseph Bellamy; settled, Preston, Conn., 1762—1808.

Hawley, Gideon, 1727—1807; born, Stratford, Conn.; Yale, 1749; theological teachers, Jonathan Edwards and Joseph Bellamy; missionary to the Six Nations, 1754; settled, Mashpee, Mass., 1755—1807.

Hopkins, Daniel, 1734– 1814; born, Waterbury, Conn.; Yale, 1758; theological teacher, Samuel Hopkins; settled, Salem, Mass., 1775– 1814.

Judson, Adoniram, 1750– 1826; born, Woodbury, Conn.; Yale, 1775; theological teacher, Joseph Bellamy; settled, Malden, Mass., 1787; dismissed 1791; settled, Wenham, Mass., 1792; dismissed 1799; settled, Plymouth, Mass., 1802; dismissed, 1817; became a Baptist minister, serving several churches in eastern Mass., 1818– 1826.

Judson, Ephraim, 1737– 1813; born, Woodbury, Conn.; Yale, 1763; theological teacher, Joseph Bellamy; settled, Norwich, Conn., 1791; dismissed, 1778; settled, Taunton, Mass., 1780; dismissed, 1791; settled, Sheffield, Mass., 1791– 1813.

Kinne, Aaron, 1744– 1824; born, Lisbon, Conn.; Yale, 1765; theological teacher, Eleazar Wheelock; settled, Groton, Conn.; 1769; dismissed, 1798; preached in various vacant pulpits in Mass. and Conn., 1800– 1824.

LeBaron, Lemuel, 1747– 1836; born, Plymouth, Mass.; Yale, 1768; theological teacher, Daniel Brinsmade; settled, Rochester, Mass., 1772– 1836.

Lewis, Amzi, 1746– 1819; born, Waterbury, Conn.; Yale, 1768; theological teacher, unknown; settled, Goshen, N.Y., 1772; dismissed, 1787; taught school and preached in North Salem, N.Y., 1787– 1795; settled, Stamford, Conn., 1795– 1819.

Mills, Samuel, 1743– 1833; born, Kent, Conn.; Yale, 1764; theological teacher, Joel Bordwell; settled, Torringford, Conn., 1769– 1833.

Niles, Samuel, 1743– 1814; born, Braintree, Mass.; College of New Jersey, 1769; theological teacher, Joseph Bellamy; settled, Abington, Mass., 1771– 1814.

Olcott, Allen, 1746– 1806; born, East Hartford, Conn.; Yale, 1768; theological teacher, unknown; settled, Farmington, Conn., 1787; dismissed, 1791; supplied vacant pulpits in Conn., 1791– 1806.

Parish, Elijah, 1762– 1825; born, Lebanon, Conn.; Dartmouth, 1785; theological teacher, Ephraim Judson; settled, Byfield, Mass., 1787– 1825.

Perry, David, 1746– 1817; born, Stratford, Conn.; Yale, 1772; theological teacher, Mark Leavenworth; settled, Harwinton, Conn., 1774; dismissed, 1783; settled, Richmond, Mass., 1784– 1817.

Perry, Joshua, 1745– 1812; born, Stratford, Conn.; Yale, 1775; theological teacher, unknown; settled, Hamden, Conn., 1783; dismissed, 1790; became a farmer in Bristol, Conn.

Robbins, Ammi, 1740– 1813; born, Branford, Conn.; Yale, 1760;

theological teacher, Joseph Bellamy; settled, Norfolk, Conn., 1761–1813.

Robbins, Chandler, 1738–1799; born, Branford, Conn.; Yale, 1756; theological teacher, Joseph Bellamy; settled, Plymouth, Mass., 1759–1799.

Robinson, William, 1754–1825; born, Lebanon, Conn.; Yale, 1773; graduate divinity student, Yale; settled, Southington, Conn., 1778–1821.

Sanford, David, 1737–1810; born, New Milford, Conn.; Yale, 1755; theological teacher, Joseph Bellamy; settled, Medway, Mass., 1773–1810.

Searle, John, 1721–1787; born, Northampton, Mass.; family moved to Simsbury, Conn.; Yale, 1745; theological teacher, Jonathan Edwards; settled, Sharon, Conn., 1749; dismissed, 1754; settled, Stoneham, Mass., 1759; resigned, 1776; settled, Royalton, Vt., 1783–1787.

Smalley, John, 1738–1808; born, Lebanon, Conn.; Yale, 1756; theological teacher, Joseph Bellamy; settled, New Britain, Conn., 1758–1808.

Smith, Cotton Mather, 1731–1807; born, Suffield, Mass.; Yale, 1751; theological teacher, Timothy Woodbridge; settled, Sharon, Conn., 1755–1807.

Spring, Samuel, 1746–1819; born, Northbridge, Mass.; College of New Jersey, 1771; theological teachers, Joseph Bellamy, Samuel Hopkins, and Stephen West; settled, Newburyport, Mass., 1777–1819.

Strong, Cyprian, 1743–1811; born, Farmington, Conn.; Yale, 1763; theological teacher, unknown; settled, Chatham, Conn., 1767–1811.

Strong, Jonathan, 1764–1814; born, Bolton, Conn.; Dartmouth, 1786; theological teacher, Ephraim Judson; settled, Randolph, Mass., 1789–1814.

Strong, Nathan, 1748–1816; born, Coventry, Conn.; Yale, 1769; graduate divinity student, Yale; settled, Hartford, Conn., 1774–1816.

Swift, Job, 1743–1804; born, Sandwich, Mass.; raised in Kent, Conn.; Yale, 1765; theological teacher, Joseph Bellamy; settled, Richmond, Mass., 1767; dismissed, 1774; settled, Dutchess County, N.Y., 1775; dismissed, 1783; settled, Bennington, Vt., 1786; dismissed, 1801; settled, Addison, N.Y., 1801–1804.

Swift, Seth, 1749–1807; born, Kent, Conn.; Yale, 1774; theological teachers, Joseph Bellamy and Stephen West; settled, Williamstown, Mass., 1779–1807.

Trumbull, Benjamin, 1735– 1820; born, Hebron, Conn.; Yale, 1759; theological teacher, Eleazar Wheelock; settled, North Haven, Conn., 1760– 1820.

Tullar, David, 1748– 1839; born Simsbury, Conn.; Yale, 1774; theological teacher, Joseph Bellamy; settled, Windsor, Vt., 1779; dismissed, 1784; settled, Milford, Conn., 1784; dismissed, 1802; settled, Rowley, Mass., 1803; dismissed, 1810; missionary, western New York, 1811– 1823; settled in Linebrook, Mass., 1823– 1830; retired, 1830– 1839.

Tullar, Martin, 1753– 1813; born, Simsbury, Conn.; Yale, 1777; theological teacher, unknown; settled, Derby, Conn., 1783; dismissed, 1793; settled, Royalton, Vt., 1793– 1813.

Weld, Ezra, 1736– 1816; born, Pomfret, Conn.; Yale, 1759; theological teacher, unknown; settled, Braintree, Mass., 1762– 1816.

West, Stephen, 1735– 1818; born, Tolland, Conn.; Yale, 1755; theological teacher, Timothy Woodbridge; settled, Stockbridge, Mass., 1759– 1818.

Woodbridge, Ephraim, 1746– 1776; born, Groton, Conn.; Yale, 1765; theological teacher, unknown; settled, Norwich, Conn., 1769– 1776.

BIBLIOGRAPHICAL NOTE

THE correspondence and papers of Samuel Hopkins are scattered in a dozen-and-a-half libraries, mostly in the northeast. The largest collection is at the Historical Society of Pennsylvania in Philadelphia. It consists mainly of correspondence but also includes other manuscript material relating to Hopkins's career as an antislavery reformer. The Samuel Hopkins Papers at Andover-Newton Theological School contain additional correspondence as well as Hopkins's diary for the years 1754–1760 and other manuscripts. Another extant portion of Hopkins's diary is in the Williams College Library. There are small but important collections of Hopkins's manuscripts, mostly correspondence, in the libraries of Yale University, the Hartford Seminary Foundation, the Massachusetts Historical Society, the Boston Public Library, the Congregational Historical Society, the Rhode Island Historical Society, and the Newport Historical Society. Other letters, usually only two or three in number, are located at several institutions ranging from the Presbyterian Historical Society in Philadelphia to Dartmouth College.

The papers of other New Divinity men were important in this study. The large collection of Joseph Bellamy Papers at the Hartford Seminary Foundation was by far the most useful. The papers of Jonathan Edwards, Jr., at Yale and Andover-Newton Theological School are invaluable for an understanding of the New Divinity movement. Also helpful are the papers of Gideon Hawley at the Massachusetts Historical Society and the diary of Levi Hart at the Connecticut Historical Society.

The numerous publications of Hopkins and the other major New Divinity theologians are readily available in the *Early Amer-*

ican Imprints, 1639 – 1800 microprint collection of the American Antiquarian Society. Collected editions of the works of Hopkins, the two Edwardses, Bellamy, and Nathanael Emmons were published in the first half of the nineteenth century. One published primary source that deserves special mention is Hopkins's autobiography, *Sketches of the Life of Samuel Hopkins . . .*, edited by Stephen West (Hartford, 1805). Not only is this work valuable as an autobiography, but it contains passages from lost parts of Hopkins's diary and the theological work in which Hopkins explained his willingness-to-be-damned doctrine. *Sketches of the Life of Hopkins* gives an insider's view of the New Divinity movement, and the *Literary Diary of Ezra Stiles, D. D., LL.D.*, 3 vols. (New York, 1961) and the *Diary of William Bentley, D. D.: Pastor of the East Church, Salem, Massachusetts*, 4 vols. (Salem, 1905 – 1914) give outsiders's views.

Hopkins has been the subject of two nineteenth-century works and two modern, unpublished studies. John Ferguson's *Memoir of Rev. Samuel Hopkins, D. D.* (Boston, 1830) is a brief, laudatory summary of Hopkins's life written for the purpose of Christian edification. Edwards A. Park, *Memoir of the Life and Character of Samuel Hopkins, D. D.* (Boston, 1852) is a far more significant work. Park, Professor of Theology at Andover Seminary, was an admirer of Hopkins, and he wrote the *Memoir* as an introduction to a collected edition of the theologian's works published in 1852. Park's *Memoir* is a conventional nineteenth-century biography. The author's admiration for his subject is evident throughout the work. Park manages to cover Hopkins's life by stringing together a large number of lengthy quotations from published and unpublished sources. Still, Park's work remains more useful than the modern studies of Hopkins. Dick L. Van Halsema, "Samuel Hopkins: New England Calvinist" (Th.D. diss., Union Theological Seminary, 1956) and Hugh H. Knapp, "Samuel Hopkins and the New Divinity" (Ph.D. diss., University of Wisconsin, 1971) are expositions of Hopkins's theology that are often uncritical and that fail to move our knowledge and understanding of the New Divinity beyond the conventional wisdom in the secondary literature on the subject.

Any discussion of that secondary literature must begin with Frank H. Foster's *A Genetic History of New England Theology* (Chicago, 1907). Foster produced the first comprehensive history of New England theology from the First Great Awakening to the middle of the nineteenth century. In places he presents oversimplified or incorrect interpretations of the thought of individual theologians. For example, he claims that Hopkins's definition of true virtue was identical with Edwards's. Nevertheless, Foster's work remains useful.

A more influential study that established much of the framework for the standard interpretation of the New Divinity movement is Joseph Haroutunian, *Piety versus Moralism: The Passing of the New England Theology* (New York, 1932). Writing from a neo-orthodox perspective that was highly favorable to the theology of Jonathan Edwards, Haroutunian sharply criticized the New Divinity men for moralizing Edwardsianism. He accused the New Divinity men of lacking both Edwards's piety and acumen. Pushing his simplistic piety-to-moralism thesis through a vast amount of material from the middle of the eighteenth century to the middle of the nineteenth, Haroutunian produced a distorted interpretation of the theology of Hopkins and other New Divinity men.

The basic problem with Haroutunian's work was pointed out by Sidney E. Mead in *Nathaniel William Taylor, 1786–1858: A Connecticut Liberal* (Chicago, 1942). Mead noted that Haroutunian established Edwardsianism as being synonymous with Calvinism. Haroutunian then went on to select only those New Divinity alterations of Edwardsianism which proved his point that Edwards's followers were responsible for transforming Calvinist piety into American moralism. In spite of such criticism, Haroutunian's work had a major influence on subsequent assessments of the New Divinity.

Mead, while sharply critical of Haroutunian's methodology and conclusions, had little positive to say about the New Divinity men. Viewing "the New England theology" as it was contrasted with the moderate, mid-nineteenth-century evangelical Calvinism of Nathaniel Taylor, Mead argued that the New Divinity men retreated from social reality and evangelicalism and became dry scholastics. Thus, where Haroutunian criticized the New Divinity movement from a neo-orthodox perspective, Mead criticized it from the perspective of the moderate Calvinism of Taylor and the eighteenth-century Old Lights, whose thought, Mead argued, Taylor sought to reassert and extend. In particular, Mead stressed, the metaphysical bent of the New Divinity men severed their movement from the dynamic piety of the First Great Awakening, necessitating the common sense evangelical Calvinism of Taylor and Lyman Beecher who emerge from the pages of Mead's book as the clerical "engineers" of the Second Great Awakening. Mead's view of New England theology between the First and Second Great Awakenings has been restated recently by one of his students. Stephen E. Berk, *Calvinism versus Democracy: Timothy Dwight and the Origins of American Evangelical Orthodoxy* (Hamden, Conn., 1974) describes Dwight, the teacher of Taylor, as a third moderate Calvinist theological engineer of the Second Great Awakening.

Most modern assessments of the New Divinity have relied heavily on the interpretations of Haroutunian and/or Mead. See the analyses of the New Divinity in the following works, for example: Douglas J. Elwood, *The Philosophical Theology of Jonathan Edwards* (New York, 1960); Edmund S. Morgan, *The Gentle Puritan: A Life of Ezra Stiles, 1729–1795* (New Haven, 1962); Morgan, "The American Revolution Considered as an Intellectual Movement," and Donald Meyer, "The Dissolution of Calvinism," in Arthur M. Schlesinger, Jr., and Morton White, eds., *Paths of American Thought* (Boston, 1963); and Cedric Cowing, *The Great Awakening and the American Revolution: Colonial Thought in the Eighteenth Century* (Chicago, 1971).

There have been a few exceptions to the Haroutunian-Mead interpretations of the New Divinity. Both Edwin S. Gaustad, *The Great Awakening in New England* (New York, 1957), and Sydney E. Ahlstrom, "Theology in America," in James Ward Smith and A. Leland Jamison, eds., *The Shaping of American Religion* (Princeton, 1961) offer balanced evaluations of the New Divinity. Richard D. Birdsall, "Ezra Stiles versus the New Divinity Men," *American Quarterly*, 18 (1965), 248–258, questioned the standard view of the New Divinity and made several suggestions for a new approach. Joseph A. Conforti, "Samuel Hopkins and the New Divinity: Theology, Ethics, and Social Reform in Eighteenth-Century New England," *William and Mary Quarterly*, 34 (1977), 572–589, discusses the historiography of the New Divinity and, building upon the work of Birdsall, outlines a conceptual framework for reassessing the movement. For a recent theological analysis of the movement, see William K. Breitenbach, "The New Divinity and the Era of Moral Accountability" (Ph.D. diss., Yale University, 1978).

INDEX